**Bridging Formal and Conceptual Semantics
Selected papers of BRIDGE-14**

Kata Balogh & Wiebke Petersen (eds.)

d|u|p

Hana Filip, Peter Indefrey, Laura Kallmeyer,
Sebastian Löbner, Gerhard Schurz & Robert D. Van Valin, Jr. (eds.)

Studies in Language and Cognition

4

Table of Contents

Preface
Kata Balogh & Wiebke Petersen 9

Live Meanings
Paul Dekker 13

Kinds, descriptions of kinds, concepts, and distributions
Louise McNally 39

Dependencies, semantic constraints and conceptual closeness in a dynamic frame theory
Ralf Naumann 63

What Cost Naturalism?
Martin Stokhof & Michiel van Lambalgen 91

Measuring out the relation between formal and conceptual semantics
Tillmann Pross & Antje Roßdeutscher 121

Representing the Lexicon:
Identifying Meaning in Use via Overspecification
Henk Zeevat, Scott Grimm, Lotte Hogeweg, Sander Lestrade & E. Allyn Smith 153

Russian predicates selecting remarkable clauses:
Corpus-based approach and Gricean Perspective
Natalia Zevakhina & Alex Dainiak 187

Preface

Kata Balogh & Wiebke Petersen

This long-awaited volume on bridging Formal and Conceptual Semantics is the final result of the successful BRIDGE Workshop held in Düsseldorf in 2014. The workshop gathered a number of distinguished researchers from formal semantics and conceptual semantics. We aimed to bring semanticists from two different "fashions" together and initiate a deeper conversation and collaboration between them instead of separating the two sides as competing views. The workshop provided a platform to further discuss parallelisms on specific semantic issues on the one hand and on the other hand to confront opposed claims from the two different perspectives. This volume contains a selected number of high-quality papers presented at the workshop featuring various approaches to meaning from linguistics, logic and philosophy of language.

In LIVE MEANINGS Paul Dekker argues for a collaboration between cognitive and model-theoretic theories regarding 'meaning'. As he claims, 'meanings' – if they exist – are context or theory dependent artifacts, and the oppositions of the two aforementioned disciplines lead back to their "unrealistic preconception" and misunderstanding of the nature of 'meaning'. The paper presents a theory-independent understanding of 'meaning' as part of a public conceptual space. While characterizing the various aspects of this conceptual space, different, previously antagonistic theories of 'meaning' are rather complementing each other.

The central focus of KINDS, DESCRIPTIONS OF KINDS, CONCEPTS AND DISTRIBUTIONS by Lousie McNally is the semantics of nominals. She presents an analysis connecting the distributional semantic representation with classical referential semantics in order to overcome the limitations of previous semantic approaches to kinds and common nouns. The starting point of her discussion is the two-fold view on the semantics of common nouns: claimed to denote kinds according to one view, and to denote descriptions of kinds according to others. An opposition that appears in cognitive semantics approaches. McNally argues that kinds are bridging referential and conceptual approaches and makes a substantial step towards an analysis of this bridge.

Ralf Naumann in DEPENDENCIES, SEMANTICS CONSTRAINTS AND CONCEPTUAL CLOSENESS IN A DYNAMIC FRAME THEORY proposes a bridge between dynamic semantic frameworks and cognitive semantics. He proposes an analysis for the characterization of semantic relations between lexical items – a topic, he claims to be missing in formal semantic theories. Naumann's approach introduced here is based on Frame Theory extended with formal methods from Dependency Logic and belief theories.

In their paper, WHAT COST NATURALISM?, Martin Stokhof and Michiel van Lambalgen investigate a crucial question from the perspective of the philosophy of science. The core issue of their paper is the nature of linguistics in the broader context of (natural) sciences. They discuss notions like structural explanation, which provided the basis of earlier discussions between different linguistic theories. In their paper, Stokhof and van Lambalgen discuss various examples that illustrate the differences of views in philosophy of science.

In MEASURING OUT THE RELATION BETWEEN FORMAL AND CONCEPTUAL SEMANTICS, Tillmann Pross and Antje Roßdeutscher propose an analysis that can bridge the gap between formal and conceptual semantics, which they claim exists due to the different principles that derive sentence meaning (formal semantics / compositionally) and word meaning (lexical / conceptual semantics). They propose a logical form based framework, in which the above meanings are derived by the same principles. As an illustration of their framework, they provide an analysis of German spatial denominal prefix- and particle verbs.

The joint paper, REPRESENTING LEXICON: IDENTIFYING MEANING IN USE VIE OVERSPECIFICATION, by Henk Zeevat, Scott Grimm, Lotte Hogeweg, Sander Lestrade and E. Allyn Smith investigates the format of a formal account of the lexicon that should contain for each lexical items as many senses as possible. Their primary goal is to

Preface

solve the problem of how to predict the meaning of a lexical item in use. Their proposed approach is based on lexical decomposition with a distinctive way of overspecification in meaning, which is reduced the meaning in use in combination with the given context.

Natalia Zevakhina and Alex Dainiak, in RUSSIAN PREDICATES SELECTING REMARKABLE CLAUSES: CORPUS-BASED APPROACH AND GRICEAN PERSPECTIVE, present a study on Russian predicates that select exclamatives, or in their terms 'remarkable clauses'. They discuss the distributional properties of such predicates from different perspectives. Based on cross-linguistic evidence, they argue for four conceptual classes of predicates that take exclamatives, and provide an explanation of the data in terms of the Gricean maxims.

Acknowledgements

First of all, we would like to thank all of our reviewers both in the period of the workshop submissions and the review process of the selected papers. We also thank all the participants of the workshop for the inspiring talks and the lively discussions. We would like to express our special gratitude to Friedhelm Sowa for his support and advice in editing the volume, to our publisher Düsseldorf University Press, to Marie-Luise Fischer for helping organizing the workshop and to the DFG CRC 991 for supporting us financially.

Live Meanings

Paul Dekker[*]

A notion of 'Live Meanings' serves to relativize the ambitions of formal semantics and to strictly maintain a principle of compositionality; this enables one to enjoy, not deny, findings of the contextualists—as well as those of cognitive or conceptual semanticists. The paper can be taken to argue for a cohabitation of the distinguished disciplines.

1 Introduction

An age old incompatibility is felt between those who advocate the philosophical analysis of language versus those who plead for a logical one, and between those who favour or practice cognitive versus those who adopt model-theoretic theories of meaning. The controversies appear in various guises, in the philosophy of language, in linguistics, and in the cognitive sciences, and show up in debates under the headings of contextualism and compositionality, and in debates on the benefits and misfits of cognitive or conceptual, and truth-conditional semantics.

It seems to me that the antagonies can be traced back to an unrealistic preconception of meaning, and, paired to it, a misapprehension of the results obtained in the area of formal semantics. The preconception and misapprehension are shared by opponents as well as proponents of formal semantics. The basic, and I think mistaken, or wrongly appreciated, idea is that there are such things as meanings, and that semantics consists in the intellectual endeavour of finding out what they are and studying them. In his overview of "Theories of Meaning" in the Stanford Encyclopedia of Philosophy, Jeff Speaks recently formulated the task of

---

[*] I would like to thank an anonymous reviewer, Peter Bosch, Martin Stokhof, Ken Turner and Seyed Mohammad Yarandi for inspiring comments and discussion.

the philosopher of language interested in semantics as follows: "her job is [to] say what different sorts of meanings expressions of a given language have, and which expressions have which meanings" (Speaks 2010/4). Martin Stokhof speaks of an 'Availability Assumption', "which holds that meanings are available independently of their being expressed, in a natural language or in a formal language. Only on that assumption does it make sense to (...) use one expression as a formal representation of the meaning of another. And especially the latter is the daily work of the formal semanticist" (Stokhof 2013, p. 210). Actually, I don't think these are proper qualifications of the findings of formal semanticists, even if these are endorsed by those themselves.

I believe it does not make any real sense to talk, out of the blue, of "the meaning of an expression", or believe in the existence of such things, without any very specific context or theory appended—almost obligatorily a context or theory that defines the term 'meaning'. (More radically, perhaps, I also do not believe in the existence of categories of expressions, of sentences, or names, without such qualification, but this matter goes beyond the purposes of the present paper.) Yet, like I said, such a conception of meaning is endorsed by proponents as well as opponents of the formal semantic enterprise. François Recanati speaks of "context-independent meanings of our words" which can be "contextualized" and "modulated" (Recanati 2004, p. 131); Jerry Fodor starts an argument against formal semantics by "taking for granted that either sentences mean what they do because they express the thoughts that they do, or vice versa (whatever, exactly, vice versa comes to here.)" (Fodor 2001, p. 2); William Croft presents the "pairing of a complex grammatical structure with its meaning" as a basic form and the fundamental principle behind construction grammar (Croft 2010, p. 463).

Without the intention to oppose or ridicule, colloquial or academic, discourse about meanings, these discourses can be taken to involve profoundly contextual and abstract theoretical uses of the term 'meaning'. But what are meanings, if they do not exist? Figuratively speaking I would like to put it thus. One can, at any moment, make any arbitrary distinction —cut the pie this way or another— and then we have what is on the one side of the distinction, and what is on the other. The two then are possible meanings, without any assumed characteristics other than that of being distinct from one another. In practice, but also in theory, we continuously make, and mask, such kinds of distinctions, and the very practice of doing so is embedded in a publicly conceptualized environment, partly governed by conventional and intentional principles. Aligning with (Quine 1948) and (Wittgenstein 1953), we may recognize human verbal, or linguistic, behavior as meaningful, without thereby postulating a realm of meanings, by conceiving of it as embedded in such practices.

Typically, verbal, or linguistic, practices have all kinds of structural characteristics which semanticists (and linguists, psychologists and philosophers in general) may want to lay bare, even though unavoidably abstractly and sketchily. If need be, we can distinguish various dimensions of meaningfulness, e.g., a realistic or representational one, a cognitive or conceptual one, or a social and practical one. Various, theoretically possible, notions of meaning may emerge once one focuses on one of these dimensions of meaning, and fixes or ignores others. Certain types of expressions, or items recognized as of certain types of expressions, then can be taken to stand for certain categories of beings, thus rendering beings so-characterized as the possible meanings of expressions so-typed; or certain conventional or functional categories of linguistic items, or items thus identified, can be associated with types of cognitive or social acts. Whatever the typologies are, they may each induce their own ontology, and help to uncover or state relatively systematic distinctions and generalizations that appear significant along that dimension of meaning. Notice, however, that nowhere in the statement or observation of such general characterizations need it be assumed that purported 'meanings' are, or are like, 'real' meanings. A good reason being that, I think, it is highly inappropriate to speak of 'real meanings' in the first place. One may best think of these 'meanings', so-called, as mere artefacts of theories that help one lay bare structural meaningful aspects of the use of natural language.

In the next section I will discuss how this reserved attitude towards meaning bears on contextualist insights, and more in particular on the conclusions that can be drawn from them. These insights will be taken to motivate an arguably intuitive understanding of the principle of compositionality—a principle one can take to be Iphigenia's heart and the Achilles' heel of formal semantics. This moderate, here called 'live', understanding of the principle initiates a fresh look at a series of cases which seem to escape a rigid understanding of the principle. These cases can or have been taken to support contextualist arguments against compositionality. As we will see, however, they, instead, can be taken to favour the principle upon its proper, live, understanding; consequently, they can be seen to speak in favour of formal semantics more in general. The picture that results from these considerations finally provides an outlook on the semantic landscape as cohabitated by various, preferably collaborative, disciplines.

2 Contextualism and Compositionality

The formal study of meaning in natural language is seriously devoted to the Fregean principle of compositionality. This principle can be found at work in Frege's writings (e.g., Frege 1892), and although it is not stated as such by Gottlob Frege himself, it can be formulated as follows. "The meaning of an expression is a function of the meanings of its parts and their mode of composition." (The Principle of Compositionality, PoC.) The intuitive idea should be familiar. If an expression is syntactically built up in a certain way from meaningful constituent expressions, then the meaning of the whole can be taken to depend on, be defined by, the meanings of these constituent expressions. (And, it needs to be added, by the interpretation of the specific way in which these constituent expressions have been combined into the whole.) This principle, in this or one other formulation, shows up in the vast body of 20th century work on logic, language and computation. (For a solid, general overview, see Janssen 1997, Partee 2004.) The principle allows for a formal explanation of the fact that finite language users may be able to create, use and understand a possibly infinite number of expressions so as to express a possibly infinite number of meanings.

The principle can be conceived of, with reason, the heart and heel of formal semantics. The heart, because it portrays interpretation as a most rudimentary and principled formal mapping between two recursive structures, as a homomorphism of a given syntactic algebra to an algebra of meanings, independently specified (Montague 1974, Janssen 1986). The heel, precisely because it has to assume this algebra of meanings, and, because, given its rigid formal specification, it does not seem to allow for modulations in this mapping. An old but fairly common conception of a so-called 'minimalist' formal semantics does allow for pragmatic modifications of semantic meanings, but only after these are compositionally assigned to analyzed syntactic structures (Borg 2004, Cappelen & Lepore 2005).

As I said at the start of this paper, I do not believe in a realm of independently existing meanings, and it is at this point that the compositionality principle can be questioned, and revaluated, as we will see. The principle has been challenged in the first place, from a 'contextualist' angle. A natural challenge to the principle springs from the observation that meaning is generally determined by parameters of interpretation, other than those provided by syntactic clues, parameters which can probably not better be characterized than 'contextual'. (Hence, the label 'contextualism'.) In the philosophy of language it is generally observed, often following the lead of the later Wittgenstein (Wittgenstein 1953), that the context of the use of language plays a pervasive role in its interpretation, and this to such an extent that it hardly deserves the effort any longer to try and systematically characterize meanings of natural language expressions without paying due attention to these contextual aspects.

The contextual impact on meaning and interpretation has been subsumed under various labels. To name a few, there is pragmatic enrichment, argument saturation, domain restriction, predicate loosening, semantic coercion, deferred reference, and what have you. Generalizing somewhat crudely, one may bring them all under the label of 'modulations' of meaning (Recanati 2004). It can be attested that the various types of modulation indeed affect all acknowledged types of semantic phenomena, reference, predication, quantification, and other semantic constructions alike. It will not do to repeat all the contextualist examples that have been presented, as they are many and they are also probably fairly well-known.

François Recanati adequately summarizes the general findings, and Emma Borg resumes what seems to be a common conclusion:

> Contextualism holds that what is said depends on the context of utterance. The evidence in favor of contextualism is provided by indefinitely many examples in which the same sentence, which does not seem to be ambiguous, is used in different contexts to say different things (Recanati 1994, p. 164). According to these philosophers, sentences can never express complete propositions independent of context, however explicit speakers try to be. In other words, content is always under-determined by the linguistic material (Recanati 2006, p. 23). Contextualism ascribes to modulation a form of necessity which makes it ineliminable. *Without contextual modulation, no proposition could be expressed*—that is the gist of contextualism (Recanati 2005, p. 179–80).

> These days, the natural descendent of the formal approach, known as minimalism, has been consigned to the margins: not everyone rejects minimalism, but lots of people do. Minimalism is rejected in favour of contextualism: roughly, the idea that pragmatic effects are endemic throughout truth-evaluable semantic content (Borg 2007, p. 339).

There are few indeed that contest the contextualist's observations, but there are also those who do not consider these findings a threat for the formal semanticist. (E.g., Herman Cappelen and Ernest Lepore, Emma Borg, Peter Pagin and Jeff Pelletier, and Peter Lasersohn.) More particularly, Pagin and Pelletier 2007 and Lasersohn 2012 have shown the contextualist observations to be consistent with a compositional rendering of the syntax-semantics interface. The first develop a classical compositional architecture of interpretation which provides room for the outcomes of pragmatic modulations within the composition of meaning. They propose a compositional syntax/semantics architecture which allows, for any analyzed sentence, modulation of every constituent of its construction-tree and of the corresponding meaning-tree. Such an architecture suits the theoretical goals very well, but also, I think, does not reach to the heart of the matter, which is where the principle of compositionality is both valuable and vulnerable. Pagin and Pelletier still build on a fixed semantic algebra, start off from given meanings of atomic constituent expressions, and then allow for virtually any assignment of meanings of compound constructions on the basis of no matter what meanings of their constituent expressions. Now I do agree that in principle *any expression, however constructed*, can be assigned *any meaning*. (Who could possibly be in charge of excluding any such meaning assignment?) But in a formal logical space of postulated set-theoretical meanings, a systematic interpretation procedure which is so open may strike one as vacuous.

Lasersohn sketches a compositional assignment of contents which also takes contextual, 'radical pragmatic', effects on the interpretation of constituent expressions to heart. His proposal relates to specific occasions of use, and employs, e.g., what certain parts of a sentence are "used to talk about" in a given context, and allows these to enter into a compositional meaning assignment. Lasersohn himself is deliberately pretty open about what goes under the heading of "what you are talking about" and mentions, e.g., speaker's reference and semantic reference, and "perhaps other kinds of "talking about" ". As we will see, Lasersohn's proposal is actually very close in spirit to the one I am about to propose, but I hope to formulate mine in both a more radical and a more principled manner.

To the extent that it makes sense to talk about meanings in the first place, I think the meaning of an expression cannot but simply be whatever meaning it has on its occasion of use. Let us label this the 'live meaning' of the expression on its occasion of use. A live meaning can, indeed, be *anything*, but it should obviously be tied to such an occasion of use, and be live and determined there. Notice that this notion does not deny, or threaten, or even empty, the principle of compositionality, as essentially also Lasersohn observed. For, the meaning of a compound expression, on its occasion of use, can be taken to be determined by whatever are the meanings of its constituent expressions, on that occasion of use. We can capture these observations by slightly reformulating the principle of compositionality as follows.

Live Principle of Compositionality (LPoC) *The* live *meaning of a compound expression is a function of the* live *meanings of its parts and their* live *mode of composition.*

I claim that this formulation of the principle preserves its original intent, in keeping with how it can be meant to apply. Let me elaborate somewhat on the present statement of the principle, in particular on the adjective 'live' employed here.

First, if one chooses to read the adjective as 'real,' the principle as stated is just an emphatic statement of the original principle. Thus understood, assuming real meanings and real composition of meaning, the live principle of compositionality states what formal semanticists and logicians have been working with for years. Second, the live meaning of an expression when used on a certain occasion may serve to distinguish it from the live meaning of that expression when used on another occasion. (Obviously, this raises the question of how one can identify the two uses as uses of one and the same expression. As indicated above, this is a very serious question, but not one I will go into in this paper.) This, as a matter of fact, is where the contextualist findings fit in.

If one assumes or believes that expressions are associated with meanings independent of their use —ideally, so-called 'literal' meanings— still one needs to acknowledge that the very same expression can be used in a whole variety of different ways, with different meanings associated. The point here is that upon the LPoC it is the 'deviant', or better, 'instant', meaning of the expression on that occasion of use, that contributes to the meaning of the whole in which that expression occurs as a constituent. Otherwise, I take it, there would be no sense in saying that the expression had occurred with a non-literal meaning. This seems to be fairly obvious. If, on the other hand, one does not believe in such things as literal meanings, then, I believe, the live meanings of expressions are the only things that are left to talk about, if, that is, one wants to make some sense of the talk of 'the meanings of expressions' at all.

This brings me to the third point, the question, of course, what these live meanings are? The 'live meanings' of expressions are here understood to be their actual interpretations in their specific contexts of use. They are what the interlocutors, and a suitably informed observer, can agree upon as to what the expressions mean, in those contexts of use, and they are assumed to be public, and determinate, in the context, in principle. (The contexts, as well, are supposed to provide the background relative to which they are determinate.) If any of this fails, if assumptions are not warranted, or not intended, or if possible interpretations don't make sense, then one might judge there is no live interpretation, or another suitable one has to be constructed. The point is that if, or once, such interpretations remain unquestioned, they *are* determinate (enough) to enter, indeed, into the compositions of (live) meanings. Obviously, this leaves no need nor room for further contextualist qualifications, because upon the present picture the meanings we are dealing with, and which enter the composition process, are contextually completely saturated.

In the next section I will discuss some cases in which one can imagine such construction of meanings at work. (These are fabricated cases, but not fabricated for the present purposes.) Contextualists, or at least some of them, have taken such examples to motivate contextualism, cast doubt on the principle of compositionality and, thus, disqualify a formal semantic approach to meaning. But actually, as I will argue, quite a few, if not all, examples are understood best precisely in terms of the principle of compositionality, upon its live understanding, and thus supply support for compositionality, and, by implication, for formal semantics.

3   The Performance of Meaning

Upon the live understanding of the principle of compositionality, the building blocks in the composition of live meaning on a certain occasion of use are the live meanings of the participating constituent expressions—not any other meanings that these constituent expressions may have on other occasions. This may look like a trivial observation, but actually it is not, as it goes against the ways in which the principle of compositionality has been assumed to apply in the analysis of natural language. Our discussion of the following five cases is meant to show that, not only live meanings are actively 'present' on the relevant occasions of use, but also that 'past' meanings are not. The cases, together with a few others, are discussed somewhat more extensively in (Dekker 2014). [Whatever are 'past meanings' is left to the reader. She may think of them as 'literal meanings' —if she can make sense of that term— once these have been superseded by live interpretations; or, otherwise, as just whatever other live meaning the relevant expressions have been associated with before their present use. Choosing the latter option would of course come close to agreeing with the conception of interpretation advocated in this paper.]

Case 1 (The Jones's) [The first case arises in a reaction from Saul Kripke on an ambiguity that Keith Donnellan seems to have propagated.]

> Two people see Smith in the distance and mistake him for Jones. They have a brief colloquy:
>
> (1) "What is Jones doing?"
>   "Raking the leaves."
>
> "Jones," in the common language of both, is a name of Jones; it *never* names Smith. Yet, in some sense, on this occasion, clearly both participants in the dialogue have referred to Smith, and the second participant has said something true about the man he referred to if and only if Smith was raking the leaves (whether or not Jones was). In the example above, Jones, the man named by the name, is the semantic referent. Smith is the speaker's referent, the correct answer to the question, "To whom were you referring?" (Kripke 1979, p. 14/15)

Kripke acts in this case as a suitably informed observer, and we can imagine him intruding into the colloquy saying:

(2) That is true, but he is not Jones.

He would, thus, indicate, that he picked up an understanding of (1) as being about Smith, refer back to him with his own use of the pronoun 'he', and re-establish the past, 'official', interpretation of 'Jones' by reusing the name 'Jones'. Alternatively, assuming that the real Jones is as a matter of fact not raking the leaves, Kripke might have interjected with:

(3) That is false, he is not Jones.

What would be false, then, is that Jones is raking the leaves, so the statement that gets corrected is not that Smith is raking the leaves, which is obvious, but the statement that Jones is raking the leaves. With (3) Kripke would thus show that he actually construes (1) as about Jones, at the same time realizing, of course, that the interlocutors are discussing Smith. This is apparent from his use of the pronoun 'he' in (3), which demonstratively refers to the guy who is raking the leaves, Smith.

Upon this understanding, Kripke might as well have pointed out, slightly wittily:

(4) That is false, *he* is not *him*.

If replying thus, 'he' would again have been used as a demonstrative referring to Smith, actually present, and the pronoun 'him' could be conceived to be coreferential with the term 'Jones' used by the first speaker, and according to Kripke's own picture of the common language. So there is an amalgam of referents here: the person actually present, Smith, who figures as the so-called speaker's referent, and Jones himself, which can be supposed to be called by his name.

Interestingly, it appears to be very difficult, if not impossible, to construe (1) as a true statement—about Smith, that is— while at the same taking 'Jones' to involve Jones.

(5) ?True, but he is not him.

The confirmation indicates that Kripke construes (1) as being about Smith, which then is his live understanding of 'Jones', and somehow he cannot then pick up on this as involving the real Jones, in order to select him, Jones, as a referent for the second pronoun 'him' in (5). I take it that a reply with (5) indeed sounds quite bizarre. This is to say, I take it, that 'Jones' may have a semantic referent, and a speaker's referent, which can be distinct, but when the two are different, only one meaning can be live.

Case 2 (The Ham Sandwiches) [This is also a famous case, brought to us by Geoffrey Nunberg.]

For example, a restaurant waiter going off duty might remind his replacement:

(6) The ham sandwich is sitting at table 20.

(Nunberg 1979, p. 149)

It is clear to most of us that the restaurant waiter, by uttering (6), refers to a person, not a ham sandwich, so that in our terms the live meaning of 'the ham sandwich' is someone who, e.g., orders, or has been served, a ham sandwich; it is not the ham sandwich. Thus, later in the scenario, one can imagine the waiter, still there, to follow up with, for instance, (7):

(7) The ham sandwich wants to pay. He is in a hurry.

Once the phrase 'the ham sandwich' is understood thus, as referring to a person, it seems awkward to suppose that it still is about ham sandwiches. A statement like the following therefore appears to be too overly underspecified.

(8) ?The ham sandwich wants to pay for it.

Of course, the pronoun 'it' can, as always, be used to point at anything that makes sense, for instance, at whatever was *served* to him, or at whatever was *done* to him. I do not, however, succeed in taking it to refer to—that is what it would be—the ham sandwich by means of which the waiter just focused the hearer's attention to the person who ordered it.

The replacement in the restaurant might of course be unfamiliar with the deferred use of 'ham sandwich' in (7). After asking (9), it can thus be illuminating if the waiter replies with (10):

(9) *Who* wants to pay?
(10) The ham sandwich. The ham sandwich is the person who ordered the ham sandwich.

It seems pretty unilluminating, on the other hand, if (9) were countered by (11):

(11) The ham sandwich. The ham sandwich is the person who ordered it.

Upon hearing (11) the replacement probably wonders 'the person who ordered *what*?' He may be able to figure out, upon reflection, that it should be the person who ordered the *ham sandwich*. But *this* ham sandwich [digestible] is not as lively present as the ham sandwich [person] referred to by means of 'the ham sandwich' in (7).

Nunberg later observes that it may not so much be the whole (referential) noun phrase that gets a 'deferred meaning', or whose live meaning is at stake, but, rather, the (predicative) noun. "(…) there are a number of reasons for concluding that the transfer here takes place on the common noun meaning–that is, that this is a case of meaning transfer, rather than reference transfer. (…) the transfer actually takes place at the level of the common noun, which contributes only a property of persons (…)" (Nunberg 1995, p. 115–6). If the restaurant's replacement appears to be familiar with the indicated use, he might also wonder about (7) and reply with (12):

(7) The ham sandwich wants to pay. He is in a hurry.
(12) There are three of them. Which one wants to pay?

It, then, seems perfectly appropriate to answer his question with (13), but a reply with (14) appears to be pretty odd again.

(13) The one that stumbled in the toilet.
(14) ?The one that fell on the floor in the kitchen.

Apparently, in the cases above the noun 'ham sandwich' is interpreted as a predicate applying to persons, not digestibles. And it is the first, not the second, interpretation that is most likely alive. And the one that is live is present, and the other one is not.

Case 3 (The Philosophers) [The third case is as a matter of fact a whole array of cases.] Consider the following sentence.

(15) Few philosophers are linguists.

It seems to be common opinion in the semantics literature that quantified structures of the form $DET(A, B)$—where DET is a determiner phrase, and A a nominal or set denoting expression, and B a verbal one— presuppose a domain of A's and contribute discourse referents A's who are B, and possibly A's who are not B. There is also quite some consensus that quantified noun phrases generally serve to quantify over contextually restricted domains of quantification, and, of course, that nouns like 'philosophers' can be used to classify philosophers in various ways: as professional philosophers, as persons displaying a certain kind of philosophical behavior, persons otherwise distinguished as philosopher-like, etc.

Independent of any analysis of presupposition, contextually restricted quantification, and discourse reference, one thing seems to be entirely clear. If the term 'philosopher' is used to characterize or distinguish individuals in one of these ways, relative to some contextually given domain of quantification, then the presupposition is that there is a domain of philosophers classified precisely that way in that domain of quantification; also, if a discourse referent is introduced for the philosophers who are linguists, then this discourse referent involves all those who classify as philosophers in the way in which the term 'philosopher' was understood, or intended in the first place, and in the contextually given domain of quantification. (And, likewise, for them being 'linguists' in the way in which few of them were said to be linguists.)

Actually, it seems very hard to explain how this could not be the case. Let me give it a try. No sense can be made of an, almost inconceivable, use of (15), according to which few of a contextually salient group of philosophically behaving children practice linguistics, while it presupposes a domain of professional philosophers, and sets up a discourse referent for a world-wide group of professional philosophers and linguists. Like I said, it is very difficult to explain what I think is excluded, which is that a statement made by (15), its presupposition, and its discourse anaphoric potential, relate to different possible interpretations of the term. Upon any sensible

Live Meanings

understanding of a use of (15) only one interpretation is the live one, although many other interpretations are possible, yet these are claimed to simply be not present. Not alternative ones, not even, literal ones—if any.

The very point is perhaps illustrated more concisely by the following two examples. Everybody, except maybe certain formal semanticists, can make sense of (16).

(16) You have philosophers and philosophers.

Two uses of one and the same term easily invoke—here invite—a different live interpretation. One use of it doesn't do so, or so it seems. At least I am unable to state what (16) can be taken to say, by using (17):

(17) ?You have philosophers and them (they themselves).

If a live, 'secondary', interpretation of the first use of 'philosophers' in (16) were derivative on a 'primary', 'literary', meaning of the term, then one should be able to say what (16) says by using (17). But, like I said, I do not succeed in making this work.

Case 4 (The Presidential Elections) [This case involves a factual state of affairs.]

> In 1969, January 20-th, Richard Nixon succeeded Lyndon B. Johnson as the president of the United States, so that after eight years of Democratic rule (with John F. Kennedy and Johnson), an eight year period of Republican rule started (with Nixon and Gerald Ford).

One could have described this situation, correctly, if one had uttered, in 1969:

> (18) For the last eight years the president was a Democrat and the next eight years he will be a Republican.

Example (18) could have been used, in 1969, to state something true, if the noun phrase 'the president' was rendered, or read, as whoever has been residing in the Oval Office over a certain stretch of time. On this reading it would merely serve to sum up the outcomes of the presidential elections over some sixteen years. Alternatively, example (18) could have been rendered as being about the actual president, in 1969, Johnson. On this reading it would state that Johnson had been Democrat the past eight years, and, surprisingly, and falsely I assume, would have turned out Republican the next eight years.

Theoretically one might want to try and use (18) to state that we had had 8 years of Democratic rule, and that Johnson now will be Republican the next 8 years, for the president [whoever it was] was democratic the last 8 years, and the president [the actual one now] will be republican the next 8 years. Formally there is no problem in stating such an interpretation. However, it is an extremely unlikely—many will say impossible—way of construing an understanding of 'the president' in example (18).

It is assumed that the pronoun 'he' in the second sentence of example (18) picks up the president from the first sentence, and it should intuitively do so under the interpretation that 'the president' had there—i.e., its live meaning. Thus, if 'the president' would have been read as Johnson, then so would 'he', and if 'the president' would have been read as whoever, in any of these sixteen years, had won and would win the elections, then so would 'he' be read. A 'mixed' interpretation which would enable the interpretation of the phrase 'the president' to work out referential on its use relative to the coming eight years, while it applied in an attributive way relative to the previous eight years, does not appear to be a viable live interpretation at all—it has no chance of survival.

Case 5 (The Brothers Karamazov) [The last case involves the writing and reading of *The Brothers Karamazov*.]

> Although Dostoyevsky began his first notes for *The Brothers Karamazov* in April 1878, he had written several unfinished works years earlier. Dostoyevsky spent nearly two years writing *The Brothers Karamazov*, which was published as a serial in The Russian Messenger and completed in November 1880.
> (http://en.wikipedia.org/wiki/The_Brothers_Karamazov)

One may conclude:

(19) Dostoyevsky began *The Brothers Karamazov* in 1878. He finished it in 1880.

As a matter of fact, I got a copy of *The Brothers Karamazov* from my grandmother early in the winter of 1977, and I read it over the Christmas break. It is true to say that:

(20) I began the book by the end of 1977, and finished it ten days later.

Books are written, published, read, started, and completed. As can be seen from the examples (19) and (20), the noun phrase '*The Brothers Karamazov*' can be used to denote the event of writing the book, which Dostoyevsky started in 1878, and an event of reading it, which I for instance completed in 1978. Interestingly, it cannot be used to denote both events at the same time. It appears to be particularly odd to conclude, from (19) and (20) that.

(21) ?Dostoyevsky began *The Brothers Karamazov* in 1878. I finished it in 1978.

Live Meanings

What I read is what Dostoyevsky wrote, *The Brothers Karamazov*. So what he began in 1878 is what I finished in 1978. Or not? What he began was writing *The Brothers Karamazov*, and what I finished was reading it, so not the writing of it. So what Dostoyevsky began in 1878 is not what I finished in 1978, and upon the most likely understanding of (19) and (20), it does not allow one to conclude to (21).

We see that once the book is 'coerced' into an event, it is the event, and no longer the book, that is present. Stated thus, this might actually be surprising. Not so, however, upon our formulation of what goes on. When the live interpretation of '*The Brothers Karamazov*' is an event, it is not a book, and this is a very trivial observation, of course.

These five cases are meant to illustrate, not so much the fact (taken as obvious) that the interpretation of constituent expressions of compound constructions can be heavily context dependent, but that these live interpretations contribute to, or determine, the (live) meanings of the whole of these expressions. As a matter of fact, once we drop the assumption that meanings are non-contextually givens, and allow live meanings to enter the interpretative architecture, one can clearly see the principle of compositionality at work in our actual understanding of natural language. The findings of the present section are, thus, in complete agreement with Lasersohn's conclusion: "(...) far from being problematic for compositionality, contextual variation in interpretation is precisely what *rescues* the claim that interpretation is compositionally assigned from apparent counterexamples" (Lasersohn 2012, p. 188).

In the statement of the LPoC mention was made also of the 'live mode of composition' and I want to conclude this section with some tentative reflections on this.

Linguists and philosophers with a proper interest in language alike share an interest in so-called "structural ambiguities", apparently or potentially present in almost every natural language sentence. The phenomenon of a structural ambiguity can be tuned down, in the present terminology, to the possibility of having one, rather than another, live mode of composition of a given utterance. We intend and interpret a string like, e.g., "old men and women", as if it were constructed by first modifying the noun "men" by the adjective "old", and then conjoining the result with the noun "women", or, alternatively, as if it were obtained by modifying the conjunction of the two nouns by the adjective. The string itself, however, is appropriately characterized as consisting of three linearly ordered words, and does not itself display any structure. It is a matter of theoretical idealisation (mythification, or metaphor, if one wants), when we speak of the string of three words having two or more readings, out of which we pick one. Instead, there is only one, *according to the rules currently in charge*. Not the string, but its occurrence, is associated with an analysis, and then the LPoC tends to dictate only one analysis, reading, interpretation.

Analogous observations, and more subtle distinctions, can be made regarding the ways in which nouns and noun phrases are combined in possessive constructions such as "Michelle's portrait", "Derek's omelet", "Tony's roots", "the back of the car", "the construction of the city" and "the start of the play". Given the many various ways in which nouns can be, thus, taken to be combined, it appears hard, even unrealistic, to imagine a grammar handing out the theoretical combinatory possibilities, from which a context should help us pick one. Instead, we assume a felicitous use of such combinations to yield the proper one, which, if not contextually questioned, decides on the interpretation, or meaning of the whole. If the ensuing conceptual construction, or the associated truth conditions, conflict with other indicators in the context, then, apparently, we have misconstrued the complex. Such, however, would not mean that the grammar has failed.

Proper, live, compositions also seem to be required when we employ or face noun-noun compounds, such as "book shelf", "bicycle pump", "kitchen knife", "university hospital" and "machine learning". Here, even more, we face a theoretical wealth of combinatory possibilities, while on their regular, that is unproblematic, occurrences, we only use one. There is of course the obvious, decontextualized question, "which one–or which of the ones?" And, again, the only, theoretically uninformative, but correct, answer is "the right one".

The possible modes of composition, and the distinctions that can be made among them, are theoretically intriguing, but they are mentioned here only to point out what the live principle of compositionality apparently implies: that we employ modes of composition *according to the rules assumed currently in charge*, that is, 'live'. Again, if one chooses to assume, or live by, one rigid, stipulative, grammar, the live principle of compositionality only dictates compositions of (live) meanings according to *the* rules of grammar, as it is usually taken to dictate. Allowing, more flexibly, for, theoretically unconstrained, but contextually induced modes of composition, it seems we can naturally accommodate the heterogeneity of natural language generation and interpretation. I will not go into the implications of this

4 Context and Conceptual Space

I take it that the principle of compositionality can be maintained with regard to any contextualist findings, and possibly contrary to some contextualist conclusions. It may have occurred to the reader that the preceding discussion has been stated in all kinds of semantic terms, like meanings, interpretations, speaker's reference, presupposition, coercion, etc. Obviously, the principle of compositionality, also on its 'live' formulation or understanding, does invoke the concept of (live) meanings of constituent expressions, and refers to or quantifies over them. The discussion, however, should not be taken to build on a given category of meanings, as repudiated by Quine and ourselves. "I remain free to maintain that the fact that a given linguistic utterance is meaningful (or *significant*, as I prefer to say so as not to invite hypostasis of meanings as entities) is an ultimate and irreducible matter of fact; or, I may undertake to analyze it in terms directly of what people do in the presence of the linguistic utterance in question and other utterances similar to it" (Quine 1948, p. 30-1). All semantic vocabulary is intended to reflect our intuitive and everyday understanding of 'significant' verbal behavior. All we suppose is that, relative to the envisaged contexts, the semantically relevant distinctions can be made, intelligible to us, here, and to the envisaged participants.

It must be submitted that indeed, if one wants to give a formal characterization of observations of the kind indicated above, which after all constitutes an aim of the formal semantic enterprise, this implies that such relevant distinctions get formalized, too. If different occurrences of one and the same term are associated with different live meanings, they have to be formally distinguished. Such is expedient in order to keep the compositional architecture formally transparent, but it does delegate quite some work to the mapping from concrete utterances to 'logical forms', however understood. E.g., an utterance, sensibly interpreted, of 'All philosophers are philosophers' will presumably have to be mapped to something like the formally transparent '$\forall x(Px \rightarrow P'x)$'. We can, however, leave the required mappings to the formal linguists, and to those who seek to apply the formal semantic insights and results. Such is not our main concern here though.

More relevant to the present discussion is the observation, directly taken from the contextualists, that live meanings are determined in a context of use. We have to be careful when using the term 'determined' here though. I emphatically want to abstain from the idea that this involves the existence of meanings, which get subsequently 'determined' ('specified', ...) in a context of use. I think that on any successful or unproblematic occasion of use, these so-called meanings are there, completely, and as determinate as required and defined by the context. The idea is that, in principle, we can all engage in an assessment of the relevant distinctions, in the context, and of the relevant distinctions imported by a specific utterance in that context. The only formal, or philosophical, requirement is that these distinctions are *public*.

Such a context can be conceived of as a public space, publicly accessible, and we evaluate (interpret, ...) utterances as acts in such a space. This may seem like a vacuous truism, but it does, or should, help in qualifying the semantic abstractions made from those contexts. At the end of the day, the 'live meanings' that we talk about are eventually *not* the instantiations of (suitable) abstractions, but the abstractions are artefacts of a theory modeling interesting, structural, features of specific acts in the first place meaningfully performed in a public space. One ought to just realize that all of the discussion in the preceding section—and probably all sensible work discussed under the heading of semantics, only makes sense if the reader interprets or assesses it against the background of any context of use—most often an imaginary one, but at least an (imagined) publicly accessible context of use.

It may be noticed that there is nothing that prevents us from thinking of this public space as a conceptual space. On the contrary: much discussion in linguistics and semantics *is* apparently conceptual. After all, there does not seem to be any ground for anyone to make a fundamental or categorical distinction between the real and the conceptual, or, better, between things that we know only really, but not conceptually, and those that are by their nature only conceptual, but not real. But then it is only a small step to recognize that the public space where we locate live meanings, can be very much of the kinds proposed in various systems of conceptual or cognitive semantics. Mental spaces, frames, conceptual space, discourse representation structures if one wants, can all be taken to present their own ways of formulating or modeling cognitively significant aspects of the very same public space.

That a public space is considered a conceptual space may not come as a surprise to many. That the kind of conceptual space we are interested in here is public, may also need no argument, but it may have to be emphasized. Mental spaces, frames, their constituents, conceptual categories, prototypes, semantic features and relations, are postulated in a public, theoretical, language, and described as generally accessible and publicly available objects, sets, or other constructs with a consensual status in the various theories. They are general coin and a common good.

> I propose that frames provide the fundamental representation of knowledge in human cognition. I assume that frames represent all types of categories, including categories for animates, objects, locations, physical events, mental events, and so forth (Barsalou 1992, p. 21/9). Mental spaces are very partial assemblies constructed as we think and talk for purposes of local understanding (Fauconnier 2010, p. 351). [T]he notion of a construction (…) is a uniform model for the representation of all grammatical knowledge—syntax, morphology, and lexicon (Croft 2010, p. 463). An expression's content consists in a set of cognitive *domains*. (…) These are not themselves concepts but irreducible realms of experience within which conception can emerge (Langacker 2010, p. 98).

Such public conceptions may of course serve as a challenge, but only rarely picked up, it seems.

> Prima facie, this appears to be an enigma for the cognitive approach to semantics: meanings are things that are *common* to the language users. (…) The idea is that the conceptual structures of different individuals will become *attuned* to each other, otherwise linguistic communication will break down. Thus, for practical purposes, cognitive linguists often write as if every (adult) speaker of a language is enodowed with the same conceptual structure (Gärdenfors 2000, p. 155).

It seems that proceeding on that, practical, assumption, and assuming that linguistic communication factually does not break down, we do well in declaring conceptual space public. Gärdenfors' conception of conceptual spaces is presented as an attempt to make sense, after all, of the cognitive structures as purely individual cognitive structures. "One advantage, in contrast to cognitive semantics, is that we need not assume that the interlocutors share identical mental spaces" (Warglien & Gärdenfors 2013, p. 2189). This paper indeed provides a mathematically sophisticated and scientifically motivated explanation of how purely individual conceptual spaces can be seen at work. Yet, the authors do also acknowledge that "[w]hat makes communication possible is the capacity to establish similarity-preserving mappings between the conceptual spaces of the participants" (Warglien & Gärdenfors 2013, p. 2181). It seems that this capacity of preserving similarity is still presented, also here, as a necessary or constitutive condition of communication.

We have by now reached an interesting point in our contemplations. Starting from supposed contextual and conceptual worries about formal semantics, formal semantic reflection on a notion of meaning has led to a notion of context, which is a public space, suitably conceived of as a conceptual space—not orthogonal to, but actually and inherently inviting contextual and conceptual exploration. We may then, once again, reflect on the question what it is that we are doing in (formal) semantics? Well, what are we doing with significant verbal behavior? We are inhabiting logical space, or more adequately in the present context, meaning space. As indicated above, such a meaning space can be charted along various dimensions.

Charting the realist or representational dimension of meaning, we observe truth-conditional structure, which has been tracked and still is mapped out extensively in the work carried out under the heading of truth conditional semantics.

> What formal semantics delivers is a systematic account of broadly 'referential' aspects of meaning. [Under 'referential' we include all those aspects that are analysed in terms of a determinate relationship between expressions and extra-linguistic reality (...).] As such that is an essential ingredient of an overall account, since in certain circumstances, as part of certain practices, these are the relevant features that our use of language turns around. (...) From this perspective, then, formal semantics is one methodology that deals with one particular aspect of the heterogeneous phenomenon of meaning. Its contribution to our understanding consists of systematic, conceptual reconstructions of certain aspects of meaning at the idealised level of competence (Stokhof 2013, p. 229).

It has also proven more than worthwhile, of course, to chart the cognitive or conceptual dimension of meaning, the results and insights from which are also very impressive indeed. There is this vast body of work on cognitive grammar and semantics, frames, mental spaces and conceptual spaces. Cf., e.g., (Barsalou 1992, Croft & Cruse 2004, Fauconnier 2010, Gärdenfors 2000, Lakoff 1987, Langacker 2010). One can of course also track the social, normative, dimension of meaning, which, however, has not been mapped out elaborately yet in formal systems. The main point of all this is that uncovering structure in one dimension of meaning should not need one to exclude any of the others. Of course, I am inclined to add. The insights from the various strands of work can be, and better be, brought together as far as is feasible. Warglien and Gärdenfors 2013 provides for an eminent bridge.

Traditional formal semanticists may be worried about the present 'surrenderings' to the contextualist and conceptualist challenges, but this would be unseemly. The assignment of meanings to constituent expressions, and to composite wholes, is not taken to be arbitrary, and the impact of the LPoC itself is built on that assumption. The live meaning of a compound is determined by means of the live meanings of its constituents, and such an argument rests on the assumption that one can make sense of such live meanings of such constituents in the first place. Moreover, the simple idea that, in the interpretation of natural language anything *might* go, but *doesn't* go in practice, can be put to work in an assessment of proposals for things that *don't* go, but, for as far as the LPoC suggests, *might* have worked out well after all. An example of this can already be distilled from a case discussed above.

In my discussion of the case of the Karamazovs, I qualified example (21) with a '?', yet, in passing I denied the claim that what Dostoyevsky began in 1878 is what I finished in 1978. Indeed example (21) should not be deemed *infelicitous*, but probably *false*, upon the live interpretation suggested by the description of the case. But this assumes a reading of the example as possibly true, but actually false. False, if, for instance, we can conceive what Dostoyevsky started and what I finished as the onset and completion of one big event. Thus, a literary critic, who thinks very highly of himself, may think of the whole *The Brothers Karamazov* as one big hoax that he is now concluding by writing the ultimate, killing, review of it—after which nobody is supposed to ever want to read it any more. How unlikely this is, it is not impossible, and if the critic were to state something to that effect using (21), one could very well argue that he said something *false* —not *infelicitous*— if one finds out that the discussion about the book still continues. Proper, maybe unlikely, live interpretations of certain constituents may thus render examples which seem to be infelicitous on a first encounter to be felicitous after all.

The case just discussed nicely illustrates a more general, methodological, moral. It is good and customary practice in semantics to investigate certain structural phenomena, by opposing completely unproblematic samples of language with slight variants deemed unacceptable, infelicitous, or 'marked'. It is solid practice to next propose a semantic explanation of the difference, for instance, by blaming the presence or absence of a particular semantic feature or characteristic. The concept of live meanings can be called upon to test such explanations. For, a most obvious test of the proposed explanation would consist in setting up a case in which the constituents held responsible for the infelicity in the original examples, are read as having, or lacking, the responsible semantic property. If the proposed explanation runs well, the infelicity disappears in such a case.

Interference Principle *If (the absence of) a semantic property π of an expression X is to explain the fact that X does not felicitously figure in configuration $^*\phi(X)$, then in a context in which the live meaning of X fails (has) π, it should, all else being equal, render X felicitous in $^{\checkmark}\phi(X)$ again.*

As a matter of fact, such a test can be and has been applied successfully in specific semantic discussions. (See Dekker 2014 for some more discussion.) If such an interference test is performed, a sceptic might be inclined to see it serve as the disconfirmation of a proposed hypothesis, and the whole test could be considered to ridicule formal semantics. But such a move would be very wrong indeed. As a matter of fact the test may serve to possibly confirm the hypothesis proposed, by, instead, providing the proverbial 'exception that proves the rule.'

Notice that the whole conception of an interference test makes sense only when one allows for a notion of live meanings. For if expressions are assumed to have one literal or linguistic meaning only, then infelicity would be systematic, and ought to be exception free. It may be clear, from the position adopted in this paper, and from the contextualist findings, that such a rigid notion of interpretation had better be given up. Otherwise, as a matter of fact, the principle offers a recipe to disconfirm *any* semantic hypothesis, rigidly, understood. And that really *is* a threat for traditional formal semantics.

5 Conclusion

I hope I have demonstrated in this paper that a modestly realist, not (yet) theoretically infected, conception of meaning enables one to conceive of meaning as featuring in a public conceptual space. The various (realist, cognitive, social, ...) dimensions of the space can be conceived to be structurally characterized by diverging, possibly orthogonal, theoretical disciplines devoted to that exercise—disciplines which are nonetheless consistent and ideally complementing each other.

References

Barsalou, Lawrence W. 1992. Frames, concepts, and conceptual fields. In Adrienne Lehrer & Eva Feder Kittay (eds.). *Frames, fields, and contrasts.* 21–74. Hillsdale, NJ: Lawrence Erlbaum Associates.

Borg, Emma. 2004. *Minimal semantics.* Oxford: Clarendon Press.

Borg, Emma. 2007. Minimalism versus contextualism in semantics. In Gerhard Preyer & Georg Peter (eds.). *Context-sensitivity and semantic minimalism.* 339–360. Oxford: Oxford University Press.

Cappelen, Herman & Ernie Lepore. 2005. *Insensitive semantics.* Oxford: Blackwell.

Croft, William. 2010. Construction Grammar. In Dirk Geeraerts & Hubert Cuykens (eds.). *The Oxford Handbook of Cognitive Linguistics.* 463–508. Oxford: Oxford University Press.

Croft, William & D. Alan Cruse. 2004. *Cognitive linguistics.* Cambridge: Cambridge University Press.

Dekker, Paul. 2014. The live principle of compositionality. In Daniel Gutzmann, Jan Köpping & Cécile Meier (eds.). *Approaches to meaning: Composition, values, and interpretation.* 45–84. Leiden: Brill.

Fauconnier, Gilles. 2010. Mental spaces. In Dirk Geeraerts & Hubert Cuykens (eds.). *The Oxford Handbook of Cognitive Linguistics.* 351–376. Oxford: Oxford University Press.

Fodor, Jerry A. 2001. Language, thought and compositionality. *Mind and Language* 16. 1–15.

Frege, Gottlob. 1892. Über Sinn und Bedeutung. *Zeitschrift für Philosophie und philosophische Kritik* NF 100. 25–50.

Gärdenfors, Peter. 2000. *Conceptual spaces: The geometry of thought.* Cambridge, MA: MIT Press.

Janssen, Theo M. V. 1986. *Foundations and application of Montague grammar* CWI Tract 19. Amsterdam: Centre for Mathematics and Computer Science.

Janssen, Theo M. V. 1997. Compositionality. In Johan van Benthem & Alice ter Meulen (eds.). *Handbook of logic and language.* 417–473. Amsterdam: Elsevier.

Kripke, Saul. 1979. Speaker's reference and semantic reference. In Peter A. French, Theodore E. Uehling & Howard K. Wettstein (eds.). *Contemporary perspectives in the philosophy of language.* 6–27. Minneapolis: University of Minnesota Press.

Lakoff, George. 1987. *Women, fire, and dangerous things: What categories reveal about the mind.* Chicago: Chicago University Press.

Langacker, Ronald W. 2010. Cognitive grammar. In Bernd Heine & Heiko Narrog (eds.). *The Oxford handbook of linguistic analysis.* 87–109. Oxford: Oxford University Press.

Lasersohn, Peter. 2012. Contextualism and compositionality. *Linguistics and Philosophy* 35(2). 171–189.

Montague, Richard. 1974. Universal grammar. In Richmond Thomason (ed.). *Formal philosophy. Selected papers of Richard Montague.* 222–46. New Haven: Yale University Press. Originally published in 1970. *Theoria* 36. 373–98.

Nunberg, Geoffrey. 1979. The non-uniqueness of semantic solutions: Polysemy. *Linguistics and Philosophy* 3. 143–184.

Nunberg, Geoffrey. 1995. Transfers of meaning. *Journal of Semantics* 12. 109–132.

Pagin, Peter & Francis Jeffry Pelletier. 2007. Content, context, and composition. In Gerhard Preyer & Georg Peter (eds.). *Context-sensitivity and semantic minimalism.* 25–62. Oxford: Oxford University Press.

Partee, Barbara H. 2004. *Compositionality in formal semantics.* Oxford: Blackwell.

Quine, W. V. 1948. On what there is. *Review of Metaphysics* 2. pp. 21–38.

Recanati, François. 1994. Contextualism and anti-contextualism in the philosophy of language. In S. L. Tsohatzidis (ed.). *Foundations of speech act theory: Philosophical and linguistic perspectives.* 156–66. London and New York: Routledge.

Recanati, François. 2004. *Literal meaning.* Cambridge: Cambridge University Press.

Recanati, François. 2005. Literalism and contextualism: Some varieties. In Gerhard Preyer & Georg Peter (eds.). *Contextualism in philosophy: Knowledge, meaning, and truth.* 171–196. Oxford: Oxford University Press.

Recanati, François. 2006. Crazy minimalism. *Mind and Language* 21(1). 21–30.

Speaks, Jeff. 2010/4. Theories of meaning. In Edward N. Zalta (ed.). *The Stanford encyclopedia of philosophy.* Stanford: http://plato.stanford.edu/.

Stokhof, Martin. 2013. Formal semantics and Wittgenstein: An alternative? *The Monist* 96(2). 205–231.

Warglien, Massimo & Peter Gärdenfors. 2013. Semantics, conceptual spaces, and the meeting of minds. *Synthese* 190. 2165–2193.

Wittgenstein, Ludwig. 1953. *Philosophische Untersuchungen/Philosophical investigations.* Oxford: Blackwell.

Author

Paul Dekker
University of Amsterdam
ILLC/Department of Philosophy
p.j.e.dekker@uva.nl

Kinds, descriptions of kinds, concepts, and distributions

Louise McNally[*]

Within referential approaches to meaning, Carlson's (1977) notion of kind as an entity has played an influential role not only in the analysis of generic sentences, but also in the analysis of common noun semantics within so-called "layered" approaches to the syntax and semantics of nominals (e.g. Zamparelli 2000). Within the latter approaches, two competing views of the role of kinds in the semantics of nominals have developed, neither of which is entirely satisfactory. In this paper I argue that by modeling the semantics of common nouns using distributional semantic representations and connecting them in a very specific way to an otherwise standard referential semantics, we overcome the limitations of these kind-based accounts of the semantics of common nouns while preserving their insights. Insofar as distributional representations have been proposed as ersatz conceptual representations (Lenci 2008b), the analysis also exemplifies a concrete proposal about how conceptual and referential approaches to meaning might be integrated.

1 Introduction

Carlson (1977) defended the hypothesis that natural language ontology includes not only "ordinary" (token) object-level entities such as people or artefacts but also kind-level entities, which are of the same semantic type but of a different

---

[*] I am grateful to the members of the FLoSS virtual reading group and the participants in the 2013 Daghstuhl Seminar on Computational Models of Meaning in Context, especially Gemma Boleda, Marco Baroni, Katrin Erk and Roberto Zamparelli, for helping me learn about and develop my thinking on distributional semantics. I would also like to thank an anonymous reviewer for very helpful comments on an earlier version of this paper. This work has been supported by Spanish Ministry of Innovation and Science grants FFI2010-15006, FFI2010-09464, FFI2013-41301, grant 2014SGR698 from the Catalan government, and an ICREA Academia award.

sort.¹ He argued that bare plurals in English (as in (1a)), as well as some uses of definite singulars, (as in (1b)) are rigid designators that denote kind-level entities. In other words, they could be thought of as proper names for kinds.

(1) a. Snakes are reptiles.
    b. The snake is a reptile.

This hypothesis led to significant advances in the study of genericity, and though the specifics of Carlson's account of reference to kinds have subsequently been the subject of much debate (see e.g. Carlson & Pelletier 1995; Mari et al. 2013), kinds themselves have persisted in natural language ontology and have been used in the analysis of other semantic phenomena that do not involve genericity, notably in the internal semantics of nominals (e.g. Zamparelli 2000, Chierchia 1998, McNally & Boleda 2004, Déprez 2005, Espinal 2010).² Within this latter line of research, which will be our primary focus in this paper, all analyses start from the basic idea developed in Zamparelli 2000 that nominal expressions have a "layered" structure, as will be described in section 2, and that kinds are somehow involved in the semantics of the innermost or deepest layer. However, they divide into two main groups based on the way in which kinds are appealed to in the syntax-semantics interface: One line of analysis posits that common nouns denote kinds themselves (i.e. a subsort of entity), while the other argues that they denote descriptions of kinds (i.e. sets of (sub)kinds in an extensional set-theoretical semantics).

While this work as a whole has yielded considerable insights into natural language data, the modeling of kinds as atomic entities is rather uninformative, telling us little about what a kind actually is. Krifka (1995) suggests that kinds correspond to sortal concepts but says little about what these are. Müller-Reichau (2011), p. 46, suggests that kinds are reifications of concepts, where he understands a concept as "information in the mind that allows us to discriminate entities of [one] kind from entities of other kinds" (citing Löbner 2002:20) or "accumulated knowledge about a type of thing in the world" (citing Barsalou 2000). Note that the

---

[1] Carlson's ontology also included a third sort of entity, so-called stages of individuals, but these will not be relevant in the following discussion and I will say no more about them here. Hereafter I use the term "token entity" to refer to Carlson's object-level entities, but I retain Carlson's use of the marker o (mnemonic for "object-level") as a subscript to distinguish variables over token-level entities from variables over kind-level entities.

[2] I use the term 'nominal' as the most general label for expressions whose main descriptive content is provided by a noun. More specific terms such as NP (noun phrase) and DP (determiner phrase) will be used when relevant.

formal distinction between kinds and descriptions of kinds thus has a counterpart in the cognitively oriented literature. Both Löbner and Barsalou consider concepts and kinds as distinct: Concepts are the descriptive basis for kinds (which Löbner equates with categories, and which we might assume to be equivalent to Barslou's "type" in the quote above). However, this distinction is arguably not exactly the same one that Müller-Reichau makes: intuitively, the reification of a concept is not the same thing as a category, a point to which I return below.

Kinds thus serve as a bridge to connect referential and cognitive or conceptual approaches to meaning, and the goal of this paper is to take a very modest step onto this bridge. I will do so by proposing a way to resolve the debate about what exactly common nouns denote by appealing to recent developments in so-called distributional semantics (see Turney & Pantel 2010 and references in Section 3). This appeal is in line with recent work that seeks to use distributional representations as ersatz conceptual representations (see e.g. the papers in Lenci 2008b). The specific features of these representations and the method I sketch for connecting them to a relatively standard referential semantic analysis will overcome the limitations of previous analyses of common nouns in layered approaches to the syntax of nominals. More generally, the analysis also constitutes a concrete proposal for combining insights from referential and conceptual approaches to meaning that, while still very preliminary, I hope will promote further synergies between the two traditions.

The paper is structured as follows. In section 2, I briefly review the two main uses of kinds within nominals. Section 3 provides a brief introduction to distributional semantic representations. Finally, in section 4 I develop the idea that such representations could serve as models of common noun denotations and, very briefly, I discuss the implications for kind reference.

2 Carlsonian kinds and determiner phrase semantics

As mentioned in the introduction, Carlson's (1977) ontology included kind-level and token-level entities as primitives. He related these kinds and tokens via a realization relation, **R**: If a token entity x_o realizes a kind y_k, then $\mathbf{R}(x_o, y_k)$. By hypothesis, all token-level entities are realizations of some kind-level entity.

Carlson took common nouns to denote sets of what he called individual-level entities (the union of kind- and token-level entities, as opposed to stage-level entities), and used plurality (in the case of English bare plurals) to convert this set-type denotation into a kind-referring expression. For example, *snake* was assigned a logical translation that can be represented as in (2a), and *snakes*, as in (2b). This latter translation says that *snakes* denotes that kind-level entity all of whose token instances are snakes (see Carlson 1977:145ff,[3] non-essential details modified from the original; x_i is a variable over the union of kinds and tokens).

(2) a. snake: $\lambda x_i[\mathbf{snake}(x_i)]$
 b. snakes: $\iota x_k[\forall z_o \Box[\mathbf{R}(z_o, x_k) \rightarrow \mathbf{snake}(z_o)]$

The reader is referred to Carlson's work for the details of how this basic proposal was incorporated into a broader analysis of English.

Carlsonian kinds were given a different application in Zamparelli 2000. Zamparelli argued that full determiner phrases (DPs) have a 3-layered structure consisting of a kind phrase (KIP), a predicative determiner phrase (PDP), and a strong determiner phrase (SDP). The goal was to account for a complex array of facts involving the relation between the internal syntax and semantics of nominals and their external syntax and semantics, such as the fact that certain kinds of apparent "determiner stacking" (e.g. *the*/*every*/demonstratives + numeral) are possible. (3) provides an example of a Zamparelli-style syntactic analysis for the DP *that one child*.

(3) [SDP that [PDP one [KIP child]]]

We will not go into the details of Zamparelli's analysis of the SDP and PDP here. What is relevant for our purposes is his claim that all common nouns project into nominals as kind phrases and "denote individual 'kinds of objects' in the domain." (2000: ex. (436)). He then used the type-shifting operations **KO** and **KSK** to convert the kind phrase into an expression that denotes a set of token entities or subkinds, respectively (see (4) and Zamparelli 2000: ex. (461)-(462), where **KIP** stands for the logical translation of the kind phrase; other irrelevant details modified from Zamparelli's original).

(4) a. $\mathbf{KO}(\mathbf{KIP}) : \lambda x_o[\mathbf{R}(x_o, \mathbf{KIP})]$
 b. $\mathbf{KSK}(\mathbf{KIP}) : \lambda x_k \forall z \Box[\mathbf{R}(z, x_k) \rightarrow \mathbf{R}(z, \mathbf{KIP})]$

---

[3] Page numbers correspond to the version of this work published in 1980.

Kinds, descriptions of kinds, concepts, and distributions

The output of these operations can then be the input to a higher determiner, as in (5a) and (5b), respectively: *two books* in (5a) is understood as referring to two token books (which could be of the same (sub)kind), while *two wines* in (5b) necessarily refers to two different subkinds of wine.

(5) a. Max read two books.
    b. Max produces two wines.

Curiously, Carlson's and Zamparelli's analyses of common nouns are essentially inverses of each other. Carlson takes common nouns to be fundamentally descriptions or predicates and uses syntax to convert them into referring expressions. Zamparelli takes them to be fundamentally referring expressions and uses syntax to convert them into descriptions or predicates.

One phenomenon that might be thought to distinguish between these two analyses is modification. McNally & Boleda 2004 argued that relational adjectives such as *legal* in (6a), in contrast to other adjectives, such as *clever* in (6b), denote descriptions of kinds, rather than of token entities.

(6) a. a legal adviser
    b. a clever adviser

On this analysis, *legal* and similar adjectives serve to restrict kind descriptions, thus forming subkind descriptions, which are later converted to descriptions of token entities that can be further restricted with token-entity modifiers such as *clever*. Though McNally and Boleda did not use the layered DP structure, their proposal can easily be adapted to the layered analysis, as shown in (7). The noun denotes a set of (sub)kinds (including not only the maximally general adviser kind but also legal advisers, political advisers, economic advisers, etc.), represented as in (7a). The relational adjective also denotes a set of kinds, those that stand in some relation to the law: for example, (legal) system, (legal) document, (legal) issue, as in (7b).[4] These combine at the KIP level (7c), and the result can serve as the input to a variant of the **KO** type-shifter (call it **KO′**) that, instead of taking kinds, takes

---

[4] McNally and Boleda treated the adjective as a first order property that combined with the noun intersectively via an *ad hoc* composition rule; here I treat it as a second order property for the sake of simplicity. The difference is not crucial.

descriptions of kinds and saturates the kind variable (7d,e).[5] The resulting property of tokens can combine (e.g. via predicate conjunction) with other token modifiers, such as *clever*, to yield descriptions such as *clever legal adviser*; see (7f,g).

(7) a. adviser: $\lambda x_k[\mathbf{adviser}(x_k)]$
  b. legal: $\lambda P_k \lambda x_k[P_k(x_k) \wedge \mathbf{legal}(x_k)]$
  c. [KIP legal adviser]: $\lambda x_k[\mathbf{adviser}(x_k) \wedge \mathbf{legal}(x_k)]$
  d. **KO'**: $\lambda P_k \lambda x_o[\mathbf{R}(x_o, y_{k_i}) \wedge P_k(y_{k_i})]$
  e. **KO'**([KIP legal adviser]):
     $\lambda x_o[\mathbf{R}(x_o, y_{k_i}) \wedge \lambda x_k[\mathbf{adviser}(x_k) \wedge \mathbf{legal}(x_k)](y_{k_i})]$
     $= \lambda x_o[\mathbf{R}(x_o, y_{k_i}) \wedge \mathbf{adviser}(y_{k_i}) \wedge \mathbf{legal}(y_{k_i})]$
  f. clever: $\lambda P_o \lambda x_o[P_o(x_o) \wedge \mathbf{clever}(x_o)]$
  g. clever legal adviser:
     $\lambda x_o[\mathbf{R}(x_o, y_{k_i}) \wedge \mathbf{adviser}(y_{k_i}) \wedge \mathbf{legal}(y_{k_i}) \wedge \mathbf{clever}(x_o)]$

Note that once the type-shifter **KO'** applies, we no longer have a property of kinds; rather, we have a property of token entities. This entails that any kind-level modifiers will have to combine with the noun *before* the type-shifter. The layered structure also guarantees that any token entity modifiers will have to apply *after* the type-shifter. These constraints, as McNally and Boleda observed, lead to a natural account of the fact that relational adjectives must appear closer to the noun than other sorts of adjectives, as shown in (8):

(8) a. a clever legal adviser
  b. ??a legal clever adviser

Now let us return to the main issue, which is the distinction between treating the contents of KIP as a kind-level entity vs. a description of such entities. Neither analysis is completely satisfactory. Treating nouns as kind-denoting leaves the mechanics of modification involving relational adjectives and related phenomena[6] imperfectly explained. On this hypothesis, the contents of KIP denotes an entity, which is then fed into the **KO** or **KSK** type shifter to yield a property that can

---

[5] This is done here indexically, following McNally and Boleda. However, it could be done by other means, such as existential closure. Another variant on this analysis involves using the functional projection Number for the purpose effected here by **KO**; see Espinal 2010, Arsenijević et al. 2014 for details of this latter alternative.
[6] See e.g. Espinal 2010 for additional examples.

eventually combine with a determiner. Let's assume, following McNally and Boleda, that the adjective in (6a) denotes a property of kinds, and let's represent the kind denoted by *adviser* as **a**. If we combine the adjective and the entity-denoting noun directly, the result is a proposition:

(9) **legal(a)**

A proposition is not the right sort of semantic object to feed the rest of the semantic composition of the DP.

Alternatively, we could first apply the type shifter **KSK** to the kind denoted by adviser:

(10) $\mathbf{KSK(a)} : \lambda x_k \forall z \Box [\mathbf{R}(z, x_k) \to \mathbf{R}(z, \mathbf{a})]$

However, this output denotes a set of kinds, not a kind, and therefore cannot serve as input to the **KO** type shifter for purposes of creating a description of token entities. While we could of course posit both **KO** and a counterpart **KO'** like that used in the alternative analysis in (7), a perfect parallelism between the derivation of *clever adviser* and *clever legal adviser* is lost. In the former case, only **KO** would apply to generate a description that could combine with *clever*; in the latter, first **KSK** and then **KO'** would apply. Not only is this inelegant: crucially, it fails to capture the fact there is no evidence that *adviser* and *legal adviser* are of distinct semantic types.

The analysis of common nouns as properties of kinds fares better on this point, insofar as it maintains a parallelism between the semantics of *adviser* and *legal adviser*. However, it has a couple of weaknesses. First, it forces the introduction of a kind variable as an ordered argument of the noun whose existence is motivated exclusively by the need to mediate modification (see McNally 2006 for more on this point). If, as (7g) suggests, the phrase *clever legal adviser* introduces a variable y_{k_i} referring to the legal adviser kind, we might expect that variable to license discourse anaphora systematically. However, such reference is not systematically felicitous, as shown in (11), in which it is very difficult to interpret they as picking out legal advisers in general (as opposed to clever legal advisers).

(11) The banker avoided jail thanks to **clever legal advisers. They** are usually worth the investment.

While there could be a variety of explanations for this fact, it is hardly a merit of the analysis in (7g).

A second weakness of both this analysis and Zamparelli's, as noted in the introduction, is that this appeal to kinds and kind descriptions implicitly acknowledges that not all descriptive content within the DP is fulfilling the same function: kind-level modifiers serve to create subkind descriptions – complex concepts, in Löbner's sense of concept mentioned above – while token-level modifiers simply provide additional description of the referent(s) of the DP. Our understanding of the former function is not particularly aided by a characterization grounded in a fundamentally referential semantics of the sort that Carlson used, and indeed Löbner (loc. cit.) suggests that common nouns pick out concepts. However, if indeed the layered approach is justified, it suggests that, conversely, not all descriptive material with the DP serves to form complex concepts, and therefore we do not necessarily want to abandon a referential approach to meaning entirely.

As a concrete proposal for bringing something of the spirit of conceptual semantics into a referential framework, with the specific goal of being able to model the composition of subkind descriptions in a more interesting way than is possible using standard formal semantic tools, I will appeal to distributional semantics.[7] After presenting a brief introduction to the crucial features of distributional semantics in the next section, I will then suggest a method for integrating it into the layered analysis of DPs.

3 A brief introduction to distributional semantics

Distributional semantic models vary in detail, but the sorts of models that will concern us all represent expression meanings as vectors or matrices based on co-occurrence distributions in a corpus. For example, in the study described in Boleda et al. 2013, to represent a noun, we automatically compiled the number of occurrences of that noun with each of the 10000 most frequent content words in our corpus (chosen from nouns, verbs, adjectives and adverbs), within a same-sentence window. Using these criteria, in the representation of *dog*, the count for the verb *bark*, would include the instance of bark in (12a), but not that in (12b).

---

[7] The terms *Latent Semantic Analysis* and *vector-space semantics* are also used for essentially this sort of approach. See Landauer & Dumais 1997 for an early discussion of the psychological interest of these representations; see Turney & Pantel 2010 and Baroni et al. 2014 for overviews of more recent developments in distributional semantics and additional background.

Kinds, descriptions of kinds, concepts, and distributions

(12) a. The dog barked.
    b. We saw the dog. It barked.

Distributional models vary in the number and kinds of expressions that are included in the vector representation, as well as in the nature and size of the window.[8] In the simplest models the co-occurrence counts follow a "bag-of-words" approach and do not take into account grammatical information: for example, in the representation of *dog*, the count for the verb *bark* would include both the co-occurrence found in the sentence *the dog barked at the child* and in *the child barked at the dog*. More sophisticated analyses (e.g. Erk & Padó 2008, Baroni & Lenci 2009) take the grammatical relations between words into account.[9]

Table 1 offers a toy example of what distributional representations might look like for the words *dog, cat, car,* and *ink*. From a simple inspection of this example it is easy to see how distributional representations roughly approximate concepts. High co-occurrence values for a given word in a vector indicate strong associations; low values indicate little or no association. Thus, the information in Table 1 suggests that there is a comparatively strong relation between dogs and fur (and cats and fur), but no relation between cars or ink and fur. Note that these representations differ sharply from logical semantic representations insofar as these associations need not be entailed. For instance, nothing in the lexical entailments for *dog*, as these are normally understood by formal semanticists, would directly include anything about chasing or running, but the distributional representation indicates some sort of relation between dogs and both running and chasing.

	fur	bark	purr	run	chase	pen
dog	53	22	0	16	29	0
cat	44	2	40	15	45	0
car	0	4	10	10	30	0
ink	0	0	0	10	0	33

Table 1: Toy distributional representations for *dog, cat, car,* and *ink*

---

[8] The question of how best to set such parameters is far from trivial, but fortunately it is not crucial to the point being made in this paper. I therefore will not explore it further here.
[9] Note also that typically, the information in these vectors is compressed by additional mathematical operations such as Singular Value Decomposition or Nonnegative Matrix Factorization. These details will not concern us here.

Crucial for our purposes is the fact that distributional representations for words can be combined to make distributional representations for phrases (see Mitchell & Lapata 2010, Baroni & Zamparelli 2010, Garrette et al. 2011, Coecke et al. 2011, Clarke 2012, Copestake & Herbelot 2012, Socher et al. 2012, Lewis & Steedman 2013, Grefenstette 2013, Baroni et al. 2014 and references cited in these works for various proposals and general discussion). Even more interestingly, there is a very lively debate over whether it is preferable to rely exclusively on distributional representations for modeling sentence meaning, or whether distributional semantics might be better used in combination with logical semantics, and limited to modeling only some parts of sentence semantics. One of the roots of this debate is the fact that distributional models work well for what we might loosely refer to as "content words" and short phrases made up of them, but fare rather poorly with "function" words such as determiners, auxiliary verbs, or conjunctions – that is, those expressions that referential semantic approaches handle well. These and other considerations will lead us to use a combination of distributional and formal modeling in the next section.

Before moving on, however, let me briefly illustrate semantic composition with distributional representations so that the potential for improvement over the analyses presented in the previous section becomes apparent. One finds significant variation not only in the operations used to combine vector, for words but also in other parameters, such as whether specific values in the operations should be weighted. Here we will limit ourselves to using the simplest method, namely vector addition, to illustrate. Table 2 presents a toy model of how the vectors for two words can be added to yield a vector representation for a phrase.

	bright	irritated	burn	stop	warn	apple
red	99	20	40	98	29	15
flag	19	2	1	50	45	0
skin	6	90	79	8	2	15
red flag	118	22	41	148	74	15
red skin	105	119	119	106	31	30

Table 2: Semantic composition modeled by vector addition

What can be observed is that when two words share high values for a given co-occurrence item in the vector (e.g. *stop* in the case of *red* and *flag*), the association

Kinds, descriptions of kinds, concepts, and distributions

between that item and the resulting phrase is proportionally strengthened – for example, the association between *stop* and *red flag* is stronger than that for *stop* and *red*. Conversely, when two words share low values for some item, the corresponding value for the resulting phrase is proportionally weakened. When the values on an item for individual words go in opposite directions (e.g. *bright* for *red* and *skin*), the value for the result lies somewhere in between.

The quality of distributional representations as models of meaning can be evaluated in at least two different ways. First, since vector representations fundamentally encode similarity relations, one can measure the similarity between words or phrases as determined by the model against human judgments of similarity. One specific measure of similarity is the cosine between the vector for a word or phrase of interest and that of some target: a cosine of 0 indicates orthogonality, i.e. high dissimilarity; the higher the cosine, the greater the similarity. Another measure is the quality of the so-called nearest neighbors of a vector for an expression matched against human judgments. The nearest neighbors of a vector v are those vectors with the largest cosine values with respect to v. Thus, vectors that are nearest neighbors are very similar, and we would expect the expressions they represent to be judged as very similar by humans. Table 3 offers an example (larger numbers of neighbors than just 3 could of course also be evaluated). Note that nearest neighbors need not be of the same grammatical category; it is also relevant to consider not only the quality of the nearest neighbors but also their density, that is, their absolute distance from the vector of interest and from each other.

historical map	important route
topographical	important transport
atlas	important road
historical material	major road

Table 3: The 3 nearest neighbors of the corpus-derived distributional vectors of two ANs (from Baroni and Zamparelli 2010), cited in Table 4 of Baroni et al. 2014.

A second way to evaluate the quality of distributional representations is to test them on a specific task, such as the analogical reasoning tasks given on the SAT exam (see Turney & Pantel 2010 for examples). The fact that machines using distributional representations are currently able to perform at levels comparable to humans on such tasks suggests that the representations are at least in some sense a meaningful model of human semantic knowledge.

Distributional representations for words, as well as operations such as vector addition for combining them, have a number of interesting features for the modeling of certain aspects of semantic composition in natural language that are not shared by logical models. Perhaps the most important one is that they are relatively successful at handling the resolution of polysemy and co-composition-type phenomena (Pustejovsky 1995), particularly for small phrases and generic contents (Boleda et al. 2013, McNally & Boleda to appear). They also offer the possibility of modeling metaphor (e.g. Kintsch 2000, Lemaire & Bianco 2003, Utsumi 2006). The fact that distributional representations can be constructed using exactly the same method for both words and phrases in a sense blurs the line between word and phrase, suggesting an interesting avenue for exploring the origins and nature of idiomatic expressions. Finally, as noted above, these representations make no sharp distinction between "linguistic meaning" and world knowledge; depending on one's view of meaning, this is a bug or a feature. In addition to these theoretically relevant properties, they have the practical advantage of being very easy to build automatically for very large lexicons.

However, distributional models also have limitations beyond their poor handling of function words mentioned above. First, it is not obvious how to model phenomena grounded in reference and discourse dynamics, such as anaphora or information structure. Second, at present distributional models say little or nothing about how to capture mid-level semantic generalizations of the sort that are embodied in approaches that posit semantic features for causation, change, agentivity, etc. Third, it is not obvious how these models can account for most patterns of entailment and logical inference, particularly those based on the behavior of logical connectives such as conjunction, disjunction, or negation. For a review of all of these issues, see Baroni et al. 2014. Finally, there is some question as to the adequacy of distributional representations as models for language acquisition (Lenci 2008a, Copestake & Herbelot 2012, though see also Landauer & Dumais 1997). Though these limitations are daunting, distributional models are an active area of research and efforts are under way to overcome them or, as will be done here, to find an optimal division of labor between distributional and formal modeling (see Kamp et al. 2013 and references cited therein).

Kinds, descriptions of kinds, concepts, and distributions

4 Distributional representations as alternatives to kinds and kind descriptions

With this brief introduction to distributional semantics in hand, let us return to the focus of the paper, namely, if we accept the layered DP hypothesis, how do we analyze the noun at the heart of the DP so as to avoid the weaknesses both of the kind-as-entity and the kind-description accounts? Recall the problems: If kinds are treated as entities, it is not obvious how to handle modification processes that produce expressions picking out subkinds. On the other hand, if we treat nouns as kind descriptions we end up introducing a variable into the syntax, corresponding to the kind that is described, whose existence is not otherwise motivated. Moreover, on both accounts, the notions of kind and kind description are rather poor.

Let us suppose that we treat common nouns as denoting distributional representations (or sometimes I will use simply *distributions* for short).[10] In other words, we use distributional representations instead of Carlsonian kinds or kind-descriptions, the intuitions being 1) that the distributional representation serves as a convenient way of modeling a concept and 2) kinds have been used, for better or for worse, as the referential semantics counterpart to concepts (more on this latter point below). Distributions will be represented in the logical translations by constants with an arrow over them, as in (13a), to distinguish them from constants that refer to ordinary entities; following Espinal 2010, I will refer to the lowest layer of the nominal where nouns are inserted as NP, rather than KIP. I will use Number as the functional projection that contributes the type shifter **KO′**, which creates properties of token entities, as in (13b), where the definition of the type shifter and the realization relation **R** are revised to select for distributions rather than kinds (i.e., dr is the variable over distributions). The **R** relation holds between an entity and a distribution (understood here as standing in for a concept) just in case the entity in question is taken as an instance or exemplar of that concept. If we combine a simple noun such as *adviser* with **KO′**, the result is a predicate of token entities, as in (13c).

(13) a. [$_{NP}$ adviser]: $\overrightarrow{\textbf{adviser}}$
 b. [$_{Num}$ **KO′**]: $\lambda dr \lambda x_o [\textbf{R}(x_o, dr)]$
 c. [$_{NumP}$ **KO′**[$_{NP}$ adviser]]: $\lambda x_o [\textbf{R}(x_o, \overrightarrow{\textbf{adviser}})]$

---

[10] The expression "denotes a...representation" should not raise any concern, insofar as these representations are mathematical objects and not translations of natural language into some other representational language that then needs to be interpreted.

Let us further assume a parallel analysis for adjectives. We have seen that (McNally & Boleda 2004) argued that adjectives, like nouns, must be able to denote properties of kinds, in addition, in most cases, to being able to denote properties of token entities. We can therefore hypothesize that adjectives also denote distributional representations and can be converted into properties of token entities in combination with functional structure in the morphosyntax. This functional structure will be different from that which is relevant for nouns (e.g. Number, as suggested in footnote 5), insofar as adjectives typically do not have the same function in language as do nouns. For example, one candidate might be Agr(eement) (see e.g. Cinque 2005), and indeed this is what I will assume here for the sake of illustration.

I will also assume a second difference between adjectives and nouns. Instead of introducing the realization relation **R**, I take the adjective's functional structure to introduce a bearer relation (represented in (14) as **Bear**) between the distributional representation and the individuals to which it is ascribed, as illustrated in the logical translation in (14) for the adjective *clever*. I take the bearer relation to be distinct from the realization relation insofar as when an individual stands in the former relation to some concept, that concept will be manifest in that individual without serving as a criterion for identifying the individual; when an individual stands in the latter relation to some concept, that concept can be said to be both manifest in the individual and to serve as a criterion for indentity.[11]

(14) a. [$_{AP}$ clever]: $\overrightarrow{\textbf{clever}}$
 b. Agr: $\lambda dr \lambda x_o [\textbf{Bear}(x_o, dr)]$
 c. [$_{AgrP}$ Agr [$_{AP}$ clever]]: $\lambda x_o[\textbf{Bear}(x_o, \overrightarrow{\textbf{clever}})]$

---

[11] On this view, adjectives and nouns, as represented in the lexicon, differ only in the sorts of concepts that they represent. We might therefore expect an expression like *clever* to be able to combine with functional structure like Number to make a description that serves to identify individuals. Indeed, this sort of thing is possible, as illustrated in English examples in (i) from Glass (2014) and the Dutch ones in (ii) from McNally & de Swart (2015), though its nature and productivity vary from language to language.

(i) a. In Tacloban, **the dead** are being taken to a mass grave in a public cemetery.
 b. "progress" always seems to go in one direction — toward **the dead** and **the dull**.

(ii) a. Hoe leer je   een kind dat het niet met **een vreemde** mee mag gaan?
   how teach you a child that it not with a   strange   with may go
   'How do you teach a child not to leave with a stranger?'
 b. Ze   moeten wennen aan **al het nieuwe, al het vreemde** dat dit land hen biedt.
   they must get-used to all the new   all the strange that this land them offers
   'They must get used to everything new, everything strange that this land offers them.'

See McNally & de Swart 2015 and references cited there for more general discussion of the syntax and semantics of such constructions.

Kinds, descriptions of kinds, concepts, and distributions

With these elements in hand, we can now develop an analysis of modification at the NP level that distinguishes it from modification above NP and that overcomes the problems faced by the analyses in section 2. We now have as the basic denotation for nouns and adjectives saturated, concept- or kind-description-like objects for which interesting compositional rules, such as the vector addition illustrated in the previous section, are defined. We need only posit that semantic composition within the NP involves not functor-argument application or predicate conjunction, but rather vector addition (or whatever vector compositional method eventually proves to be most effective). The result of this operation will a new vector – that is, an object of the same semantic type as the noun. Specifically, we can revise the first step of the derivation (7) as in (15), where + stands for the composition operation that combines two distributional representations, e.g. vector addition.

(15) a. [$_{NP}$ adviser]: $\overrightarrow{\textbf{adviser}}$
 b. [$_{NP}$ legal]: $\overrightarrow{\textbf{legal}}$
 c. [$_{NP}$ legal adviser]: +($\overrightarrow{\textbf{legal}}, \overrightarrow{\textbf{adviser}}$)

We therefore maintain a uniform analysis of all expressions in the NP category, whether simple or complex, improving upon the kind analysis of common nouns. We also avoid any appeal to variables that do not have any motivation beyond mediating in semantic composition, thus improving upon the kind-description analysis.

Exactly like simple nouns, complex NPs such as that in (15c) can be turned into predicates of token entities via the **KO'** type shifter, as in (16a). At this point, an adjective phrase that has also been converted to a predicate of token entities as in (14) can be conjoined with it in the usual fashion used for modification in formal semantics. In this way, it is possible to derive an analysis of phrases like *clever legal adviser* that distinguishes two kinds of adjectival modification, as in (16b,c).

(16) a. [$_{NumP}$ **KO'**[$_{NP}$ legal adviser]]: $\lambda x_o[\textbf{R}(x_o, +(\overrightarrow{\textbf{legal}}, \overrightarrow{\textbf{adviser}}))]$
 b. [$_{AgrP}$ Agr [$_{AP}$ clever]]: $\lambda x_o[\textbf{Bear}(x_o, \overrightarrow{\textbf{clever}})]$
 c. [$_{NumP}$ [$_{AgrP}$ Agr [$_{AP}$ clever]] [$_{NumP}$ **KO'**[$_{NP}$ legal adviser]]]:
  $\lambda x_o[\textbf{R}(x_o, +(\overrightarrow{\textbf{legal}}, \overrightarrow{\textbf{adviser}})) \wedge \textbf{Bear}(x_o, \overrightarrow{\textbf{clever}})]$

The use of distributional representations to model common noun and adjective denotations has some additional advantages. I close this section by briefly mentioning three of these.

First, the use of these representations allows for the integration into formally-oriented semantic analysis of techniques for handling the problems of polysemy in modification and other phenomena involving the lexicon that are poorly handled by traditional formal semantic tools. This integration can improve the empirical coverage of existing formal semantic theories and yield models that are better suited to natural language processing.[12]

Second, distributional models arguably come closer to capturing the intuition that common nouns and adjectives name concepts, and thus establish a point of connection to conceptual approaches to meaning. Having a richer model of what words and phrases describe than that provided by kinds or descriptions of kinds brings formal semantics, with its emphasis on reference, closer to that sector of cognitive science that is concerned with conceptual representation. Indeed, conceptually oriented semantic theories have arguably attracted much more attention from cognitive scientists than have referential theories precisely because they focus specifically on the cognitive component of meaning; referential theories have largely failed in this respect.

On the other hand, conceptual and cognitive approaches to meaning representation (e.g. Frame Semantics, Fillmore & Baker 2010) have met resistance from formally-oriented semanticists both because of concerns about how to ground the representations and because of skepticism about implementability on a large scale. Though distributional models as described here are still highly inadequate as models of concepts, they can be augmented, e.g. by incorporating image information (see e.g. Andrews et al. 2014), and the ease with which they can be constructed and implemented makes them useful as a methodological tool. Mixed conceptual and referential approaches are also arguably less susceptible to concerns about grounding.

Finally, integrating distributional representations into a formal semantics via a specific hypothesis about the syntax/semantics interface allows us to return to and address in a clearer way an issue alluded to in the introduction. I noted that Müller-Reichau 2011 proposes that kinds are the reification of concepts, while the view of Barsalou 2000 and Löbner 2002 seems to be that kinds are categories of entities that are established based on conceptual information. If we now ask ourselves what kind terms such as *snakes* or *the snake* in (1), repeated in (17), denote, we can consider at least two explicit hypotheses.

---

[12] See especially Garrette et al. 2011, Copestake & Herbelot 2012, Lewis & Steedman 2013, Kamp et al. 2013, Erk 2016, and Baroni et al. 2014 for discussion and examples.

Kinds, descriptions of kinds, concepts, and distributions

(17) a. Snakes are reptiles.
  b. The snake is a reptile.

Following Müller-Reichau, a kind term should arguably have a representation such as the following, picking out the unique distributional representation – the concept – associated with *snake*.

(18) $\iota dr[dr = \overrightarrow{\textbf{snake}}]$

In other words, when we use *the snake* generically, we are referring to the snake concept, rather than to any class of individuals that it might serve to individuate. If we maintain the analysis of common nouns developed in the previous section, this would also be the predicted denotation for definite kind terms if we accept the syntactic analysis of them defended in Espinal 2010, where (based on independent considerations) such DPs are assigned a syntax in which Number does not intervene:

(19) [$_{DP}$ [$_{D'}$ the [$_{NP}$ snake]]

Interestingly, this is more explicit than the semantics that emerges from Espinal's proposal, which is based on the premise that common nouns denote descriptions of kinds. The representation for the semantics of (19) given her assumptions would thus be as in (20):

(20) $\iota x_k[\textbf{snake}(x_k)]$

Whether this is substantively equivalent to (19) of course depends on whether kinds are equivalent to concepts or not, an issue that the formal literature has done a notoriously poor job of addressing (see e.g. the discussion in Müller-Reichau 2011, Chapter 3). One advantage of the introduction of distributional representations is that it forces one to address precisely this issue.

On the other view, where concepts serve to support categorization of entities as belonging to one kind or another, the notion of kind or category is not the reification of a concept. As a result, whatever semantics we assign to the kind terms in (17), it should not be that in (19). For example, we might consider the sort of proposal advocated in Chierchia 1998, on which kinds are conceived of as "regularities that occur in nature...similar to individuals like you and me, but [whose] spatiotemporal manifestations are typically 'discontinuous'" (p. 348). Formally, Chierchia models kinds as "individual concepts of a certain sort: functions from worlds (or situations) into pluralities, the sum of all instances of the kind" (p. 349). Implemented in the system proposed here, a first attempt a such a semantics for *the snake* would look as follows:

(21) [$_{DP}$ [$_{D'}$ the [$_{NumP}$ snake]]: $\lambda w[\mathbf{max} x_o[\mathbf{R}_w(x_o, \overrightarrow{\mathbf{snake}})]]$

If we assume that x_o ranges over both singular (atomic) and plural (nonatomic) entities, the result is very close but not identical to what Chierchia proposes. Interestingly, he adds a slight refinement on which the sum identified by the equivalent of $\mathbf{max} x_o[\mathbf{R}(x_o, \overrightarrow{\mathbf{snake}})]$ is converted into an atomic group whose members are not accessible for compositional semantic purposes (Landman 1989a, 1989b). In other words, he essentially reifies the class of entities picked out by (21). However, on what morphological basis this additional reification is motivated is not clear.

Though this is not the place to decide what is, in fact, the best analysis of the different sorts of nominals that appear in generic sentences,[13] this brief discussion has allowed us to model two different possibilities in an explicit and easily distinguishable fashion. This is arguably an improvement over the previous situation, in which the use of the same formal object, namely kinds, both to model common noun denotations (whether directly, or indirectly via descriptions of kinds) as well as to model the denotations of DPs such as *the snake*, hampered the identification of relevant differences between different proposals. Given the semantics for common nouns advocated here, the analysis on which kind terms such as *the snake* refer to the concepts themselves, rather than to the class of entities identified by the concept, is derived more naturally from the syntactic structure. To the extent that this result might seem prima facie counterintuitive, the implications for the analysis of generic sentences as well as for so-called kind-referring predicates such as *to be extinct* are non-trivial.

---

[13] It should also be noted in passing that both Chierchia and Espinal suggest analyses for bare plurals in English that are distinct from the analyses they defend for general definite singulars; I set aside bare plurals because a proper treatment of them would take us too far afield.

5 Conclusion

The linguistic salience of something like Carlsonian kinds has been amply supported in the formal linguistics literature, as has the idea that DPs have a layered structure in which kinds or descriptions of them serve as the semantic core. I have argued here that distributional representations have potential to serve as models for the semantics of this lowest layer, with the advantage that there are explicit compositional mechanisms for combining them that make interesting and testable predictions, and that they avoid using otherwise unmotivated variables in the composition process. I have also very briefly sketched how these representations could be integrated into a more standard compositional semantic framework.

Though the paper has focused on layered DPs, it is possible to imagine extending the analysis advocated here to other linguistic categories. Within what Borer 2003 refers to as "exo-skeletal" approaches to morphosyntax, such as Distributed Morphology (Halle & Marantz 1993; see Borer 2003 for additional references to related work), the open-class lexicon consists of:

> ...sound-meaning pairs, where by meaning we refer to the appropriate notion of a concept, and where by sound we mean an appropriately abstract phonological representation. Following tradition, I will refer to that reservoir as the encyclopedia, and to items within it as encyclopedic items (EIs). Crucially, an EI is not associated with any formal grammatical information concerning category, argument structure, or word-formation. It is a category-less, argument-less concept, although its meaning might give rise to certain expectations for a felicitous context... (Borer 2003, p. 34)

These lexical items combine with other, possibly abstract, morphemes in the lexicon that contribute functional material (e.g. plural morphology, tense) that convert them into categorized expressions – full-fledged nouns or verbs, for example.

The similarities to the layered DP hypothesis are obvious, and in particular, the idea that these category-less encyclopedic items are paired with concepts looks very much like the idea we have developed in the previous section. We might therefore consider extending distributional representations to model the denotations of roots more generally. But that is a task for another paper.

References

Andrews, M., S. Frank & G. Vigliocco. 2014. Reconciling embodied and distributional accounts of meaning in language. *Topics in Cognitive Science* 6. 359–370.

Arsenijević, B., G. Boleda, B. Gehrke & L. McNally. 2014. Ethnic adjectives are proper adjectives. In R. Baglini, A. Baker, T. Grinsell, J. Keane & J. Thomas (eds.). *Proceedings of the 46th Annual Meeting of the Chicago Linguistic Society.* 17–30. Chicago, IL.

Baroni, M., R. Bernardi & R. Zamparelli. 2014. Frege in space. *Linguistic Issues in Language Technology* 9(6). 5–110.

Baroni, M. & A. Lenci. 2009. Concepts and properties in word spaces. *Italian Journal of Linguistics* 20. 55–88.

Baroni, M. & R. Zamparelli. 2010. Nouns are vectors, adjectives are matrices: Representing adjective-noun constructions in semantic space. In *Proceedings of EMNLP.* 1183–1193. Boston, MA.

Barsalou, L. W. 2000. Concepts: Structure. In A. Kazdin (ed.). *Encyclopedia of psychology.* Vol. 2. 245–248. Oxford: Oxford University Press.

Boleda, G., M. Baroni, N. T. Pham & L. McNally. 2013. Intensionality was only alleged: On adjective-noun composition in distributional semantics. In *Proceedings of IWCS 2013.* Potsdam.

Borer, H. 2003. Exo-skeletal vs. endo-skeletal explanations. In J. Moore & M. Polinsky (eds.). *The nature of explanation in linguistic theory.* 31–67. Standford, CA: CSLI Publications.

Carlson, G. N. 1977. *Reference to kinds in English.* PhD dissertation, University of Massachusetts at Amherst.

Carlson, G. N. & F. J. Pelletier (eds.). 1995. *The generic book.* Chicago, IL: University of Chicago Press.

Chierchia, G. 1998. Reference to kinds across languages. *Natural Language Semantics* 6. 339–405.

Cinque, G. 2005. Deriving Greenberg's Universal 20 and its exceptions. *Linguistic Inquiry* 36(3). 315–332.

Clarke, D. 2012. Challenges for distributional compositional semantics. *CoRR* abs/1207.2265. Online: http://arxiv.org/abs/1207.2265

Coecke, B., M. Sadrzadeh & S. Clark. 2011. Mathematical foundations for a compositional distributed model of meaning. *Linguistic Analysis* 36. 345–384.

Copestake, A. & A. Herbelot. 2012. Lexicalised compositionality. Ms.

Déprez, V. 2005. Morphological number, semantic number and bare nouns. *Lingua* 115. 957–883.

Erk, K. 2014. What do you know about an alligator when you know the company it keeps? *Semantics and Pragmatics* 9(17). 1–63.

Erk, K. & S. Padó. 2008. A structured vector space model for word meaning in context. In *Proceedings of the 2008 Conference of Empirical Methods in Natural Language Processing*. 897–906. Honolulu, HI.
Online: http://www.aclweb.org/anthology/D08-1094

Espinal, M. T. 2010. Bare nominals: Their structure and meaning. *Lingua* 120. 984–1009.

Fillmore, C. J. & C. F. Baker. 2010. A frames approach to semantic analysis. In B. Heine & H. Narrog (eds.), *Oxford handbook of linguistic analysis*. 791–816. Oxford: Oxford University Press.

Garrette, D., K. Erk & R. Mooney. 2011. Integrating logical representations with probabilistic information using Markov logic. In *Proceedings of IWCS 2011*. Oxford.

Glass, L. 2014. Deriving the two readings of English determiner+adjective. In U. Etxeberria, A. Fălăuş, A. Irurtzun & B. Leferman (eds.). *Proceedings of Sinn und Bedeutung 18*. 164–181. Online: http://semanticsarchive.net/sub2013/

Grefenstette, E. 2013. Towards a formal distributional semantics: Simulating logical calculi with tensors. In *Second Joint Conference on Lexical and Computational Semantics (*SEM). Vol. 1: Proceedings of the main conference and the shared task*. 1–10. Atlanta, GA.

Halle, M. & A. Marantz. 1993. Distributed morphology and the pieces of inflection. In K. Hale & S. J. Keyser (eds.). *The view from Building 20: Essays in linguistics in honor of Sylvain Bromberger*. 111–176. Cambridge, MA: MIT Press.

Kamp, H., A. Lenci & J. Pustejovsky. 2013. Computational models of language meaning in context. *Dagstuhl Reports* 3. 79–116.

Kintsch, W. 2000. Metaphor comprehension: A computational theory. *Psychonomic Bulletin and Review* 7. 257–266.

Krifka, M. 1995. Common nouns: A contrastive analysis of Chinese and English. In G. N. Carlson & F. J. Pelletier (eds.). *The generic book*. 398–411. Chicago: University of Chicago Press.

Landauer, T. & S. Dumais. 1997. A solution to Plato's problem: The latent semantic analysis theory of acquisition, induction, and representation of knowledge. *Psychological Review* 104(2). 211–240.

Landman, F. 1989a. Groups, I. *Linguistics and Philosophy* 12. 559–605.

Landman, F. 1989b. Groups, II. *Linguistics and Philosophy* 12. 723–744.

Lemaire, B. & M. Bianco. 2003. Contextual effects on metaphor comprehension: Experiment and simulation. In *Proceedings of the 5th International Conference on Cognitive Modeling (ICCM'2003)*. Bamberg.

Lenci, A. 2008a. Distributional approaches in linguistic and cognitive research. *Italian Journal of Linguistics* 20. 1–31.

Lenci, A. 2008b. From context to meaning: Distributional models of the lexicon in linguistics and cognitive science. Special issue of the *Italian Journal of Linguistics* 20.

Lewis, M. & M. Steedman. 2013. Combined distributional and logical semantics. *Transactions of the Association for Computational Linguistics* 1. 179–192.

Löbner, S. 2002. *Understanding semantics*. London: Arnold.

Mari, A., C. Beyssade & F. Del Prete (eds.). 2013. *Genericity*. Oxford: Oxford University Press.

McNally, L. 2006. Lexical representation and modification within the noun phrase. *Recherches Linguistiques de Vincennes* 34. 191–206.

McNally, L. & G. Boleda. 2004. Relational adjectives as properties of kinds. In O. Bonami & P. Cabredo Hofherr (eds.). *Empirical issues in syntax and semantics*. Vol. 5. 179–196. Online: http://www.cssp.cnrs.fr/eiss5

McNally, L. & G. Boleda. to appear. Conceptual vs. referential affordance in concept composition. In J. A. Hampton & Y. Winter (eds.). *Compositionality and concepts in linguistics and psychology*. Berlin: Springer.

McNally, L. & H. de Swart. 2015. Reference to and via properties: The view from Dutch. *Linguistics and Philosophy* (In press).

Mitchell, J. & M. Lapata. 2010. Composition in distributional models of semantics. *Cognitive Science* 34. 1388–1429.

Müller-Reichau, O. 2011. *Sorting the world: On the relevance of the kind-level/object-level distinction to referential semantics*. Frankfurt: Ontos Verlag.

Pustejovsky, J. 1995. *The generative lexicon*. Cambridge, MA: MIT Press.

Socher, R., B. Huval, C. D. Manning & A. Y. Ng. 2012. Semantic compositionality through recursive matrix-vector spaces. In *Proceedings of the Joint Meeting of the Conference on Empirical Methods in Natural Language Processing and the Conference on Computational Natural Language Learning (EMNLP-CONLL)*. Jeju Island, Korea: http://aclweb.org/anthology//D/D12/D12-1110.pdf

Turney, P. & P. Pantel. 2010. From frequency to meaning: Vector space models of semantics. *Journal of Artificial Intelligence Research* 37. 141–188.

Utsumi, A. 2006. Computational exploration of metaphor comprehension processes. In *Proceedings of CogSci 2006*. 2281–2286.

Zamparelli, R. 2000. *Layers in the determiner phrase*. New York: Garland Press.

Author

Louise McNally
Universitat Pompeu Fabra
louise.mcnally@upf.edu

Dependencies, semantic constraints and conceptual closeness in a dynamic frame theory

Ralf Naumann

A neglected, if not almost ignored topic in formal semantic theories of natural language are semantic (or meaning) relations between lexical items. Results from psycholinguistics and neuroscience, in particular based on the N400, provide ample evidence that such relations play indeed an important and prominent role during the (semantic) processing of sentences in the brain. For example, although neither *John squeezed an orange* nor *John squeezed an apple* contain a semantic anomaly, they are processed differently in the brain, because *orange* is more expected as the direct object of *squeeze* than *apple*. Similarly, *This melon sounds ripe* is acceptable whereas *This melon sounds oval* is not, although in both cases an adjective is used that is semantically not directly related to the sound dimension of a melon.

In this article we propose a dynamic and probabilistic extension of frame theory (Löbner 2014, Naumann 2013) in which data like the above can be analyzed. In order to capture both semantic relations and constraints (or expectancies), we use techniques from Dependence Logic (Väänänen 2007) and theories of belief revision and belief update (Spohn 1988, Goldszmidt & Pearl 1992, Boutilier 1998, Gärdenfors 1988). Using frames makes it possible to use a decompositional analysis: an object is related to a set of properties that can be changed by events. As a consequence, a lexical item like 'orange' can be taken as a table in a database or knowledge base consisting of attribute-value pairs. This way of interpreting lexical items makes it possible to apply the strategies from Dependence Logic and theories of belief revision and belief update mentioned above. In particular, it is possible (i) to define dependency relations between different properties of an object and (ii) to define quantitative plausiblity relations (κ-rankings) on a frame that determine how this frame is revised or updated with new information.

1 Introduction

According to many, if not most, current formal semantic theories, common nouns like 'orange' or 'paper' are basically analyzed as sets of objects. For example, 'orange' is first translated as the lambda-term $\lambda x.orange(x)$, which, in a second step, is interpreted as a subset of the domain, or, more precisely, as a function from this domain to the set of truth values (1a). Similarly, using an event-based approach, verbs like 'run' are interpreted as sets of events or the corresponding characteristic function (1b).

(1) a. $[[orange]]^\mathcal{M} = \lambda x \in D_{\langle e_{object}\rangle} f_{orange}(x) = 1$
    b. $[[run]]^\mathcal{M} = \lambda e \in D_{\langle e_{event}\rangle} f_{run}(e) = 1$

In recent years, such approaches to defining the semantics of basic lexical items like common nouns and verbs have been criticized from neuroscience. According to Baggio & Hagoort (2011), those theories are 'by design insensitive to differences between words of the same syntactic category denoting objects of the same type' (Baggio & Hagoort 2011, 1343). As a consequence, they are inappropriate as a theory of semantic processing in the brain. This criticism is based on empirical results from neurophysiological and neuroimaging phenomena like the N400[1], which is a component of event-related potentials (ERP's), whose amplitude is modulated by semantic complexity.

N400.

Consider the examples in (2) and (3).

(2) a. Jenny put the sweet in her mouth after the lesson.
    b. Jenny put the sweet in her pocket after the lesson.

(3) Every morning John makes himself a glass of freshly squeezed juice. He keeps his refrigerator stocked with (oranges/apples/carrots).

---

[1] For details on this component, see Baggio & Hagoort (2011).

Dependencies, semantic constraints and conceptual closeness in a dynamic frame theory

A formal semantic analysis of the sentences in (2) differs only in the sort of object assigned to the locative argument of the verb *put*: *mouth* versus *pocket*. Yet, when this sentence is uttered in a context where Jenny leaves the classroom after a lesson, Hagoort & Brown (1994) found a difference in the N400 between *mouth* and *pocket*, showing that there is a difference during processing in the brain that needs to be accounted for by formal semantic theories.

Sentences like (3) were used by Federmeier & Kutas (1999) in an ERP experiment also targeting the N400. The authors found an increasing N400 effect with the ordering 'oranges' < 'apples' < 'carrots'. According to one interpretation of the N400, this effect is closely related to predicting upcoming words in a sentence which is based on semantic relations between words in the memory component of the brain. For example, in (3) both 'apple' and 'carrot' trigger a larger N400 compared to 'orange' because the former are semantically less related to an event of squeezing a fruit than the latter (Kutas & Federmeier 2011). As an effect, the cost of semantically integrating 'apple' or 'carrot' in the given semantic context (say 'John squeezed') is higher than in the case of 'orange'. Thus, the N400 is an effect that is directly related to semantic relations between concepts expressed by words in the lexicon, in particular by relations between nominal and verbal concepts.

Stimulus subject perception verbs.
Perception-based verbs (henceforth PBVs) refer to sensory properties of objects like 'taste' or 'sound'. Correlated to each sense modality is a set of values that this property can take and which are specific to it. For example, for the property 'sight' appropriate values are 'square', 'oblong' and 'oval'. PBVs admit of a direct-sensory use in which a predicative complement is added. Semantically, this complement specifies an intra-dimensional value, i.e. an element of the set of values appropriate for the property expressed by the verb.

(4) This melon sounds muffled/tastes sweet/smells fruity.

In addition to the direct perception use, PBVs can be used inferentially. In this case the predicative complement does *not* determine a value of the scale corresponding to the modality expressed by the verb, but a value belonging to another modality.

(5) a. This melon sounds ripe/old/*oval.
    b. This melon looks oval/*muffled.

The examples in (5) show that the inferential use is not always admissible but depends on the types of sense modalities expressed by the verb and the predicative complement. Thus, similar to the examples of simple sentences, semantic processing of this use of PBVs involves semantic relations. In this case, these are relations between different properties of objects that can be changed by actions or events.

The *the* ... *the* construction.
The third and final construction involving semantic relations discussed in this article is the *the* ... *the*-construction.

(6) a. The older a stamp, the more expensive it is.
  b. The more alcohol you drink, the higher is your blood alcohol concentration.
  c. The more residents are affected, the sooner noise abatement measures will be implemented.

Similar to the inferential use of PBVs, this construction expresses a dependency relation between the values of two properties over time. The relation between the values of the two properties need not be strict, as shown by the following example: 'The older a stamp, the more likely it is that it gets more expensive'.

What is common to all the examples discussed in this section are the following points: (i) there is an explicit or implicit reference to properties of objects or events. Events of squeezing are semantically more related to objects of sort 'orange' than to, say, objects of sort 'carrots'; this reference is explicit in the case of the inferential use of PBVs and the *the* ... *the* construction. It is always implicit in the case of verbs, at least if they are formally analyzed as given in (1b). (ii) this reference to properties of objects and events is not used in isolation but rather in the context of a semantic relation between various properties. So what is at stake are semantic relations and, even more importantly, the degree to which those properties are semantically related to each other. This latter aspect will be called *semantic closeness* between properties (or between the concepts related to those properties) and (iii) since all example involve non-stative verbs like 'squeeze', or analogous constructions like 'getting older', which denote events that bring about changes with respect to objects, one also has to consider semantic relations between properties *over time* when the values of these properties are changed by actions or events.

2 Outline of the theory

According to Baggio and Hagoort (2011:1342), formal semantic theories which describe how words belonging to different syntactic categories or denoting different sorts of objects combine to more complex units are 'by design insensitive to differences between words of the same syntactic category denoting objects of the same type'. The authors put the blame for this 'insensitivity' on the fact that such theories focus on truth conditions, i.e. how language relates to the world, and not on considering natural language as a psychological phenomenon. What is required, instead, is to provide a theory of semantic processing that is both combinatoric and able to track usage-based semantic expectations of the kind involved in the data from section 1. It is important to note that this criticism not only applies to static formal semantic theories in which the notion of truth conditions is taken as central but equally to dynamic variants of formal semantics if the dynamic component is restricted to account for inter-sentential anaphoric relations, which are analyzed in terms of discourse referents or pegs. Consider (3) again. The dynamic aspect of the update operation triggered by the direct object (say 'an orange') is independent of the particular sort of object, but only depends on the context change potential of the existential quantifier associated with the translation of 'a' in the formal language since this constituent introduces a new discourse referent. By contrast, the head noun receives a completely static interpretation. It is analyzed as a test. The sortal information provided by the common noun is used to eliminate all possibilities in which the object assigned to the discourse referent fails to satisfy this condition. As a result, there is no further difference between, say, 'an orange' and 'an apple' at this level of information.

What is completely missing from this view of information encapsulated both in static and dynamic approaches to meaning in natural language is the aspect that (declarative) sentences describe situations in the world. Such a description can either concern the fact that some property of an object holds (or fails to hold) or that an event (action) occurs which changes some property of an object. One area in which this type of information is dealt with are theories of belief revision and belief update. Belief revision is usually taken as dealing with incorporating new information about a static, unchanging world. By contrast, belief update is about incorporating information about changes in the world that are triggered by actions or events. New information about a static world is incorporated into a ranked belief set (often called an epistemic state). As a consequence, the way such an epistemic state is changed not only depends on the formulas that currently form the belief set (or knowledge base) of an agent but also on the way those formulas (or the possible worlds used to interpreted those formulas) are ranked. Such information cannot be inferred if the meaning is restricted to sortal information, say it is an orange or a running, and if the dynamics only captures discourse information.

The conclusion that we draw from this failure of current formal semantic theories is that semantic processing cannot solely be based on (i) truth-conditional content and (ii) discourse information in form of information about anaphoric relations which leads to the notion of a context change potential in terms of discourse referents or pegs and (iii) (possibly) world knowledge and context information. In addition, there are at least three further types of information: (i) information about the semantic closeness between nominal and verbal concepts, which expresses degrees of expectancy or plausibility between these two types of concepts. This type of information corresponds to ranking functions in theories of belief revision and belief update; (ii) dependency relations between the values of two properties of an object which can be expressed in Dependence Logic and (iii) information about the way such dependencies are related over time if the values of the corresponding properties are changed by events. Such information requires the use of various ranking functions that not only consider static semantic relations but also the way of how such relations can be defined in the context in which not only a static world but a world in which events bring about changes is taken into consideration (belief update).[2]

Consider the following example. When processing a common noun like 'orange', a language user only gets sortal information: it is an object of sort 'orange' belonging to a particular subset of the universe (or the domain of the model). This kind of information is exactly what is usually captured in an (extensional, type-theoretic) truth-conditional semantics and which is formalized by the meaning or satisfaction clauses in (1). This aspect of meaning will be called the *proper* or *lexical* meaning of a common noun or an intransitive verb. Thus, as in model-theoretic semantics, the *lexical* meaning of common nouns and verbs is defined in terms of only sortal information and (possibly) its arity.

---

[2] Another way of looking at the difference between current dynamic approaches and our approach is the following: whereas the former defines the dynamics with respect to words belonging to closed word classes like determiners ('a' or 'some') or modal expressions like 'might' (Veltman's Update Semantics), our approach locates the dynamics in open word classes like common nouns and verbs that are used to express changes occurring in the world.

Dependencies, semantic constraints and conceptual closeness in a dynamic frame theory

Given *only* this information, no information about non-sortal properties is supplied. In order to get such information, a language user applies both local contextual information and global world knowledge to extend this lexical information, e.g. by information about properties of objects.[3]

	sort	color	form	origin	ripeness	taste
object	orange	green	oval	spain	ripe	sweet

Table 1: Tabular representation of the lexical meaning of the common noun 'orange' enriched with contextual information and world knowledge

From a linguistic point of view, the representation in Table 1 provides a *decompositional* analysis of a common noun.

(7) $\lambda x(orange(x) \wedge color(x) = green \wedge form(x) = oval \wedge origin(x) = spain \wedge ripeness(x) = ripe \wedge taste(x) = smooth \ldots)$

However, such a decompositional representation of the meaning of a lexical item is still both a flat and completely static structure in the following sense. First, no distinction is made between admissible values for a particular property. Although these values can be ordered (e.g. say in form a scale, i.e. a partially or linearly ordered set), there is no relation that orders them with respect to plausibility or expectancy. Second, no distinction is made between admissible values for objects to which this object can be related. For example, for the denotation of common nouns: what are the most plausible (expected) events that bring about a change w.r.t. one of its properties? Conversely, for events denoted by verbs: with respect to which sorts of objects does the event most likely bring about a change? Third, 'Does the event have more than one outcome, i.e. it is deterministic or non-deterministic?' Fourth, no information about dependencies between (the values of) properties is expressed. Thus, the problem is *not* only related to getting *more* information, but also to the question of *how* this information is ranked and what dependencies exist between different properties. However, in order to impose both expectancy and

---

[3] Thus, our analysis follows Hagoort's 'Immediacy Hypothesis': *all sorts of information available to the comprehender is immediately used in parallel in order to arrive at a meaningful interpretation.* According to this hypothesis, a language user not only uses the information provided by the lexical meaning of an expression, say it is an orange or a port, but also information from the context in which an expression is processed and his world and/or background knowledge.

dependency constraints a decompositional analysis of the denotations of common nouns and verbs is needed because only then is it possible to explicitly refer to the properties with respect to which those constraints are defined.

Another way of looking at this problem is in terms of the information state of a language user. We follow dynamic approaches and define an information state as a set of possibilities consisting of the alternatives that are still open according to the information available to the language user. In this paper information sets are defined in terms of variable assignments.[4] Following standard practice, sets of assignments will be called *possible worlds*. Consider (7) again. The information state of a language user w.r.t. to this information is given by a set of possible worlds capturing his epistemic uncertainty, which is due to the fact that his knowledge about the values of properties of an orange is only partial and incomplete. As an effect, his knowledge consists of all those possibilities that are compatible with his current knowledge. In the present case the alternatives concern possible expansions of his knowledge about the orange. He then assumes that the actual (correct) description is some subset U of the set W of possible worlds. However, since all possible worlds are assumed to have equal status for the language user, no world is preferred or more expected than any other in the set of all possibilities. As a consequence, updating amounts to intersecting. A further problem concerns the information that a language user can infer from his current information state provided, say, by applying the information given by the lexical meaning plus context information together with world knowledge. If his information state is a flat structure in the sense that all worlds are taken as equal, no information about the values of properties about which no information is provided can (defeasibly) be drawn. By contrast, if a language user has information both about dependency and expectancy relations, he can use this type of information to (defeasibly or non-defeasibly) infer other pieces of information about the situation described by the sentences he is currently processing. For example, knowing only that a melon is ripe, he defeasibly infers a value for its Sound attribute: muffled. Thus, the cognitive significance of dependency and expectancy relations consists in the fact that given part of a sentence, a language user will defeasibly infer as much additional information about the situation described by the sentence as possible. Consider the following example. Suppose there is an input state representing mostly ducks (say, because the topic of a conversation are ducks). Then an event of

---

[4] Or, as sets of sets of assignments. See section 3 for details.

Dependencies, semantic constraints and conceptual closeness in a dynamic frame theory

swimming is more expected than events of jumping or walking. By contrast, if the topic is about deers, swimming is less expected than jumping.[5]

3 Outline of the formalization

3.1 Structures for events, objects and their properties

We start by fixing models for objects and events that capture sortal information which is used in defining the lexical meanings of common nouns and verbs.

Definition 1 (Object structure) *Let CN be a set of object sort symbols like 'orange'. An object structure $\mathcal{O}$ is a quadruple $\langle O, \{P_{cn}\}_{cn \in CN}, \sqsubseteq_o, \sqcup_o \rangle$ s.t. (i) O is a non-empty set of objects like trees and dogs; (ii) each P_{cn} is a subset of O; (iii) $\sqsubseteq_o$ is the material part-of relation on O, which is required to be a partial order and (iv) $\sqcup_o$ is the join operation on O, which is required to be a join-semilattice.*

Definition 2 (Event structure) *Let VERB be a set of event sort symbols like e.g. 'squeeze'. An event structure $\mathcal{E}$ is a quadruple $\langle E, \{P_v\}_{v \in VERB}, \sqsubseteq_e, \sqcup_e \rangle$ s.t. (i) E is a non-empty set of actions and/or events like runnings or readings; (ii) each P_v is a subset of E; (iii) $\sqsubseteq_e$ is the material part-of relation on E, which is required to be a partial order and (iv) $\sqcup_e$ is the join operation on E, which is required to be a join-semilattice.*

Elements of E and O will be called *entities*. At the level of $\mathcal{O}$ and $\mathcal{E}$, entities are taken as elements of the underlying domain of some fixed global model $\mathcal{M}$, which can have parts. Examples are the leg of a table or the tail of a dog for the domain O of persistent objects and a subevent of eating half an apple for the eating of the whole apple in the domain E. Such relations are represented by a part-of relations $\sqsubseteq_o$ and $\sqsubseteq_e$, respectively. In addition, they can be 'summed' to form plural entities. For example, if o, say Fred, and o', say Mary, are elements of the object domain O, then $o \sqcup o'$ is also an element of O. This is modeled by the join operations $\sqcup_o$ and $\sqcup_e$, respectively.

What is missing at this level is the view of an entitiy as a 'bundle' of properties, corresponding to a decompositional analysis at the linguistic and/or conceptual level. Such a view makes it possible to impose constraints on (the values of) properties of entities denoted by common nouns and events. Properties of objects

---

[5] See van Elk et al. (2010) for empirical evidence based on an EEG study and references cited therein.

like 'Ripeness', 'Sound' or 'Age' are represented by partially or linearly ordered sets, called *scale structures*.

Definition 3 (Scale structure) *A scale structure $\mathcal{D}$ is a pair $\langle \Delta, \leq \rangle$ s.t. Δ is a non-empty set of degrees, the set of admissible values for the scale, and $\leq$ is an ordering on Δ, usually either a partial or a linear order. Scales are required to have a least element. Intuitively, the least element means that no information about the value is known or provided.*

Let *PROP* be a set of property symbols like 'sort' or 'ripeness' and let $\{\mathcal{D}_p\} \bigoplus_{p \in PROP}$ be a family of scale structures indexed by elements from *PROP*. Elements of O are assigned a subset of $\{\mathcal{D}_p\}_{p \in PROP}$ by a (subset of a) family of partial functions $\{\gamma_p\}_{p \in PROP}$, which assign to an $o \in O$ the scale structure $\mathcal{D}_p$, if defined. The following condition is imposed on this assignment. If $o, o' \in P_{cn}$, then $\gamma_p(o)$ is defined iff $\gamma_p(o')$ is defined and one has $\gamma_p(o) = \gamma_p(o')$, i.e. objects belonging to the same sort are assigned the same scale structures. If $\gamma_p(o)$ is defined for an object of sort cn, the property p is said to be *admissible* for objects of sort cn.

While processing a common noun, context information and world knowledge provide a language user with the current values of some of the properties assigned to the object denoted by the common noun. This decomposition can be represented as a (finite) conjunction of the form (8).[6]

(8) $\phi_\sigma \wedge \phi_1 \wedge \ldots \wedge \phi_n \ (= \phi)$

In (8), ϕ_σ expresses sortal information (lexical meaning), i.e. information about the property 'Sort' and the ϕ_i non-sortal information (context information and world knowledge), e.g. information about properties like 'Ripeness'. Since in general a language user doesn't know the values of all properties of the object, he is epistemically uncertain about the exact 'status' of the object. For example, suppose that w.r.t. a particular melon the values of the properties 'Form' and 'Origin' are known to be 'oblong' and 'spain' by a language user and that there are exactly two other properties 'Sound' and 'Ripeness', whose possible values are 'dull' or 'muffled' and 'not ripe' or 'ripe', respectively. The set of possibilities can be represented by the following set of assignments. The 'real' melon could be any of the four melons, each corresponding to a variable assignment.

---

[6] Alternatively, the conjunction ϕ can be taken as a set of formulas, i.e. as a knowledge base in theories of belief revision.

object	sort	form	origin	sound	ripeness
m_1	melon	oblong	spain	dull	ripe
m_2	melon	oblong	spain	dull	not ripe
m_3	melon	oblong	spain	muffled	ripe
m_4	melon	oblong	spain	muffled	not ripe

Table 2: A set of possibilities for an object denoted by the common noun 'melon'

3.2 Dependence logic

One way of looking at Table 2 is as a table in a database. In Dependence Logic (Väänänen 2007), such tables are an instance of a *team*. A team is a set of agents, with an agent being defined as a function from finite sets (or tuples) of variables, called the domain of the agent, into an arbitrary set, called the codomain of the agent. In the present context, agents are objects, i.e. elements of the domain O, viewed as bundles of properties.

Definition 4 (Team Dependence Logic) *Let $\langle x_1, \ldots x_n \rangle$ be a finite tuple of property variables such that no two variables are of the same property sort (i.e. each variable has associated with it a sort $p \in$ PROP). Let M be the union of the domains Δ from $\{D_p\}_{p \in PROP}$. An agent is any function from $\langle x_1, \ldots, x_n \rangle$ to M. A team S is a set of agents. A team S is admissible for objects of sort cn if $dom(S) = \langle x_1, \ldots, x_n \rangle$ and for x_i, $1 \leq i \leq n$ the sort of x_1 $v(i)$ is admissible for objects of sort cn.*

Each row in Table 2 is an assignment, or, when viewed from the point of view of an application, a possible description of an object (an agent). Properties of objects (agents) are represented by attributes which are variables in the formal representation. Thus, teams are directly related to the view of an object as a 'bundle' of properties.

An operation on teams is the *supplement* operation, which adds a new attribute to the objects in a team, or alternatively changes the value of an existing attribute.

Definition 5 (Supplement of a team; Väänänen 2007) *If M is a set, S is a team with M as its codomain and $F : S \to M$, $S(F/x_n)$ is the supplement team $\{s(F(s)/x_n) : s \in S\}$, where $s(a/x_n)$ is the assignment which agrees with s everywhere except that it maps x_n to a: $dom(s/x_n) = dom(s) \cup \{x_n\}$, $s(a/x_n)(x_i) = s(x_i)$ when $x_i \in dom(s) \setminus \{x_n\}$ and $s(a/x_n)(x_n) = a$.*

The supplement operation is used to model the combination of the lexical meaning of a common noun with context information and world knowledge about the referent of this noun in a given context. Let $x_n, \ldots, x_m$, $n < m$, be the attributes about which the context and world knowledge provide information. If S is the team corresponding to the lexical meaning of a common noun, then $S(F/x_n)(F/x_{n+1}) \ldots (F/x_m)$ is the team resulting from adding the information aboute the attributes $x_n, \ldots, x_m$.

In Dependence Logic, formulas are interpreted with respect to sets of assignments (teams) and not w.r.t. to single assignments as in first-order logic. In Dynamic Dependence Logic, formulas are interpreted as relations between sets of assignments (Galliani 2014). This shift makes it possible to define dependency relations between attributes. For example, functional dependency between a sequence $\vec{x}$ of variables and a variable y is expressed by the atomic formula $=(\vec{x}, y)$, with the intuitive meaning 'the $\vec{x}$ totally determine y'. The satisfaction clause for this dependence atom is (9a). The constancy atom $=(x)$ requires the value of the attribute x to be constant in a team, (9b). This formula is used to express that a language user knows the value of an attribute.[7]

(9) a. $\mathcal{M} \models_S\, =(\vec{x}, y)$ iff $\forall s, s' \in S (s(\vec{x}) = s'(\vec{x}) \to s(y) = s'(y))$
 b. $\mathcal{M} \models_S\, =(y)$ iff $\forall s, s' \in S (s(y) = s'(y))$
 c. $\mathcal{M} \models_X \exists x \phi$ iff there is a function $F : X \to \exists_M$ such that $\mathcal{M} \models_{X[F/x]} \phi$, where $\exists_M$ is the local existential quantifier defined by $\{A \subseteq M \mid A \neq \emptyset\}$ and $S[F/x]$ is the team $\{s[a/x] \mid s \in S, a \in F(s)\}$.

The interpretation of the existential quantifier is based on the supplement operation, i.e. it either adds a new attribute to all agents in the current team, or alternatively it changes the value of an existing attribute. Thus, the existential quantifier is inherently dynamic in the sense that it changes the current team w.r.t. which it is interpreted (see Galliani 2014, for details on a dynamic interpretation of Dependence Logic).

Using the dependence formula $=(\vec{x}, y)$, it is possible to express dependencies between properties like 'Age' and 'Price' for stamps and 'Ripeness' and 'Sound' for melons.

---

[7] For formulas that do not contain a dependence atom, one has: $\mathcal{M} \models_S \phi$ iff for all $s \in S : \mathcal{M} \models_s \phi$, where $\models_s$ is the usual Tarskian satisfaction relation.

(10) a. $=(age, price)$
   b. $=(ripeness, sound)$

For example, (10b) says that the value of the attribute Sound is functionally dependent on that of the attribute Ripeness. Both examples in (10) are not quite correct because they do not take into consideration that for example (10a) holds for stamps but not for other artefacts or human beings. Second, the value of the price depends in general not only on its age but also on other factors like availability or demand. These shortcomings can be remedied as follows.

(11) a. $x_{sort} = stamp \rightarrow =(age, price)$
   b. $x_{sort} = stamp \rightarrow =(age, availability, demand, \ldots, price)$

A team represents the set of possibilities of a language user in the following sense: $g \in S$ if and only if the language user believes g to be a possible (and complete) description of the object. As noted in Galliani & Väänänen (2014), moving from assignments to teams (or sets of assignments), makes it possible to assign to each formula ϕ and model $\mathcal{M}$ the family of teams $\mathcal{S} = \{S \mid \mathcal{M} \models_S \phi\}$. As a consequence, formulas can be interpreted as *conditions over belief sets*. Knowledge of the value of a property in the sense that this property is assigned the same value in all information states can be expressed by a constancy atom $=(x)$. In Table 2 above, this holds for the attributes 'sort', 'form' and 'origin'.

Definition 6 (Information state w.r.t. to an object) *Given a decompositional formula ϕ representing the beliefs of a language user about an object $o \in O$, his epistemic uncertainty (or his set of possibilities) w.r.t. to o is given by the family of teams $\mathcal{S}$ of teams satisfying ϕ, i.e. $\mathcal{S} = \{S \mid \mathcal{M} \models_S \phi\}$.*

Note that information states are defined w.r.t. the domain O of objects. The domain E of events plays no role. Rather, this domain functions as a state transformer: elements of this domain trigger changes in information states.

3.3 Ranking functions

So far, the information state about an object of a language user is flat in the sense that all teams in this information state are taken as equally plausible. However, a language user also has expectancies about (i) the values of properties about which he so far doesn't have any information and (ii) sorts of events in which an object of the given sort is most plausibly involved. These expectations lead to a ranking of the teams in his information state. Such expectancies are defined in terms of κ-rankings, which are based on the notion of surprise.

Definition 7 (κ-ranking function; Goldszmidt & Pearl 1992, Spohn 1988)
A ranking is a function $\kappa : \Omega \to \mathbb{N}^*$ with Ω a non-empty set such that $\kappa(\omega) = 0$ for at least one $\omega \in \Omega$ and $\mathbb{N}^* = \mathbb{N} \cup \{\infty\}$.

In the present context, Ω is either a set of teams (or possible worlds with each world representing a team in Ω) or the domain E. The numbers can be thought of as denoting degrees of surprise (Halpern 2005, p.43). For example, $\kappa(w)$ is the degree of surprise a language user attributes to team w to be the 'correct' team representing the interpretation of a sentence or a part of it. The higher the number, the greater the degree of surprise. For example, '0' means 'completely unsurprising' whereas greater numbers express increasingly higher degrees of surprise. The value ∞ means 'impossible' or 'so surprising as to be impossible'. In terms of plausibility or expectancy, the value 0 means 'most plausible' or 'most expected'. Though degrees of surprise are assigned to elements of Ω, they can also be defined to formulas ϕ. The rank or degree of surprise of ϕ is the least rank of the set of worlds in which ϕ is true, (12).

(12) $\kappa(\phi) = min_w \{\kappa(w) \mid \mathcal{M} \models_w \phi\}$

One has $\kappa(\phi) < \kappa(\psi)$ if ϕ is less surprising than ψ. For example, given an information state about a melon in which it is known that this melon is ripe it is less surprising to find that its taste is sweet than to find that the taste is not sweet but sour. One therefore has $\kappa(sweet) < \kappa(sour)$.

κ-rankings are not only used for ranking information states and formulas but also to define *defeasible conditionals* that allow to defeasibly infer information ψ from information ϕ. These conditionals have the form $\phi \xrightarrow{\delta} \psi$ and mean 'Typically, if ϕ then expect ψ with strength δ' (Goldszmidt & Pearl 1992). If $\phi \xrightarrow{\delta} \psi$ holds w.r.t. a ranking κ, ψ must be true in all most expected (or least surprising) worlds in which ϕ is true. This condition imposed on $\to$ can be expressed in terms of *conditional ranks*, which have the form $\psi|\phi$. Intuitively, $\psi|\phi$ expresses the degree of surprise of finding ψ given that ϕ is known to be true. The definition of $\psi|\phi$ is given in (13).

Dependencies, semantic constraints and conceptual closeness in a dynamic frame theory

(13) $\kappa(\psi|\phi) = \kappa(\psi \wedge \phi) - \kappa(\phi)$

The inequality $\kappa(\neg\psi|\phi) > \delta$ means that given ϕ it would be surprising by at least $\delta + 1$ ranks to find $\neg\psi$ and is equivalent to $\kappa(\psi \wedge \phi) + \delta < \kappa(\neg\psi \wedge \phi)$ (Goldszmidt & Pearl 1992). Now $\phi \xrightarrow{\delta} \psi$ is defined by (14).

(14) $\phi \xrightarrow{\delta} \psi$ iff $\kappa(\psi \wedge \phi) + \delta < \kappa(\neg\psi \wedge \phi)$.

A ranking function κ is said to be admissible with respect to a set Δ of defeasible conditionals if (15) holds.

(15) $\kappa(\phi_i \wedge \psi_i) + \delta_i < \kappa(\phi_i \wedge \neg\psi_i)$ for all $\phi \xrightarrow{\delta} \psi \in \Delta$.

Each type of (defeasible) inference discussed in the introduction is analyzed in terms of a mapping whose range is a ranking function of a particular kind. These mappings differ w.r.t. (i) the sort of the domain, which reflects what is known by the language user, and (ii) the domain of the ranking function, which reflects the type or sort of knowledge that is defeasibly inferred from this knowledge. The following cases have to be distinguished.

1. given: information about the *sort* of an object;
   inferred: information about the action (event) in which this object is involved.
   Example: given: 'duck'; inferred: 'swim'.
2. given: information about the sort of an action (event);
   inferred: information about the sort of participants (modulo a thematic role)
   Example: given: 'swim'; inferred: 'duck', 'dolphin' or 'fish'.
3. given: information about the value of an attribute a;
   inferred: information about the value of a different attribute a'.
   Example 'The melon is ripe': given: 'Ripeness:ripe'; inferred: 'Sound:muffled'.
4. given: the sort of an ection (event);
   inferred: the values of attributes of objects involved in the event that hold in the consequent state of the event.
   A first example is 'The melon ripened'. There are at least two inferences that can be drawn about the consequent state of the ripening: (i) it is ripe, i.e. the value of the Ripeness attribute is 'ripe' and (ii) the value of the Sound attribute is 'muffled'. Inference (i) is non-defeasible because 'ripen' is a degree achievement that requires the maximum value on the underlying scale to

hold in the end state of the event. By contrast, inference (ii) is defeasible. A second, more complex, example is given by PBV's: 'The melon sounds ripe'. This sentence is based on experiencing a muffled sound of the melon ('The melon sounds muffled'). Next, a most plausible sort of event is looked for such that Sound:muffled holds in its consequent state. In this case an event of ripening is the most expected candidate. Since in the consequent state of such an event Ripeness:ripe holds, 'The melon sounds ripe' follows.

5. given: a change in the value of an attribute a;
   inferred: a change in another attribute a'.
   An example is given by 'The older a stamp, the more expensive it is'.

3.4 Rankings on information states

In a first step, the set of teams W satisfying (part of) a decompositional formula ϕ is ranked.

Definition 8 (Ranking on information states) *A ranking on an information state corresponding to a decompositional formula $\phi = \phi_1 \ldots \phi_n$ is a ranking function $\kappa : W \to \mathbb{N}^*$ s.t. $\kappa^{-1}(0) \subseteq [[\phi_i]]$ iff $\mathcal{M} \models_w =(\phi_i)$ for all $w \in W$.*

The condition $\kappa^{-1}(0) \subseteq [[\phi_i]]$ iff $\mathcal{M} \models_w =(\phi)$ expresses the requirement that a language user knows the value of a property if it is constant in all teams belonging to the information state.[8] Note that it is not required that the whole decompositional formula ϕ be known. For example, if a language user only knows that the object is of sort P_{cn}, only ϕ_σ satisfies the condition $\kappa^{-1}(0) \subseteq [[\phi_\sigma]]$.

The ranking function κ can naturally be interpreted as characterizing the degree to which a language user is willing (i) to predict possible continuations of a sentences with respect to properties of objects and (ii) to accept alternative descriptions which are not in accordance with his current information about the object. For example, in the case of a melon or an orange, the most plausible or least surprising values for the attribute 'Taste' is 'fruity', whereas 'salty' will most likely get the value ∞ because it is deemed to be impossible.

---

[8] It is assumed that an attribute (or a property) has exactly one value, i.e. attributes are functional relations.

3.5 Rankings of information states on events

The first mapping to be defined captures case (1) Since this case concerns the expectancy of particular sorts of events given the sort of an object, it has to be a mapping from the domain W of teams in an information state to a ranking function κ with domain E.

Definition 9 (Event ordering; Boutilier 1998) *An event ordering is a mapping $\mu : W \rightarrow (E \rightarrow N^*)$ that maps each $w \in W$ to a κ-ranking $E \rightarrow N^*$ on the domain of events E. Instead of $\mu(w)$, we will write κ_w. It is required that $\kappa_w(e) = 0$ for some event $e \in E$, i.e. there is at least one most plausible event to occur in a world w. If $\kappa_w(e) = \infty$, this means that an occurrence of e at w is taken to be impossible. In addition we require $\kappa_w(e) = \kappa_w(e')$ for two events e, e' belonging to the same sort P_v, i.e. events of the same sort are assigned identical plausibility for a given w.*

Given μ, each world w has associated with it an event ordering $\mu(w)$ that determines the plausibility of event occurrences at that world.[9] For example, if W is a family of teams of sort 'duck', events of sort 'swim' will be assigned the value 0. By contrast, if the sort is 'deer', events of sort 'jump' are most plausible and hence get value 0. For human beings, the set of most plausible events is in general rather large due to the fact that they can be correlated to a large number of different sorts of events (see van Elk et al. 2010, for details).

Since W represents information about objects, the mapping μ establishes a relation between the domain O and the domain E. The cognitive significance of this mapping is the following. Given an information state w, a language user uses κ_w to defeasibly infer the most plausible events that are likely to occur with an information state of this sort and, in an additional step, expects particular verbs (or verbs stems) to occur farther down the sentence which denote events of those sorts.

3.6 Rankings of information states w.r.t. events

The mapping μ only captures the expectancy of the occurrence of an event given objects of a particular sort. Next we define an analogous mapping that determines the expectancy of a particular sort of object, given information about an event of some sort. It maps elements of the domain E to ranking functions with a domain of teams. This corresponds to case (2).

---

[9] Intuitively, $\kappa_w(e)$ captures the plausibility of the occurrence of event e at w.

Definition 10 (Information state ranking for events) *An information state ranking for events is a mapping* $\mu^* : E \to (W \to \mathbb{N}^*)$ *that is defined by* $\mu^*(e)(w) = \mu(w)(e)$.

Intuitively, μ^* captures the fact of what types of information states are 'preferred' by events of a given sort. The cognitive significance of this mapping is similar to that of μ. If a verb is encountered denoting events of type σ, a language users uses this mapping to predict the most plausible sorts of objects to fill in a role in the event. In contrast to the mapping μ, there is not a single mapping but rather a family of such mappings because this type of mapping must be defined relative to a particular thematic role like actor or patient.

3.7 Event outcome ranking

In a final step, we define the relation between an event and its possible outcomes. This mapping maps an event and a team (the input state) to a ranking function on teams such that an element of this domain functions as the consequent state which results when the event occurs in the input state.

Definition 11 (Event outcome ranking) *An event outcome ranking is a mapping* $\tau : E \to (W \to (W \to \mathbb{N}^*))$ *that assigns to an event* $e \in E$ *and an (input) information state* w *a ranking function on the set of information states. It is required that* $\forall e, e' \in P_v : \tau(e)(w) = \tau(e')(w)$ *hold, i.e. events of the same sort have the same outcome ranking functions relative to a given world* w. *Since* $\tau(e)(w)$ *is a ranking function, one must have* $\tau(e)(w)(w') = 0$ *for at least one event* w' *so that one outcome of* e *is most plausible.*

Intuitively, $\tau(e)(w)(w')$ describes the plausibility that the world w' results when event e occurs in w (Boutilier 1998:292). For example, an event denoted by 'ripen' results in a state in which the object that undergoes the change, say a melon, is ripe.[10] The cognitive significance of τ is the following. If a language user knows the sort of the event, say after having processed the predicate, he can defeasibly infer possible outcomes. Thus the set of possible outcomes (teams) is not a flat set but a ranked set of alternatives. Let $S_{e,w} = \{v \mid \tau(e)(w)(v) \neq \infty\}$ be the set of outcomes that possibly result for a given e and w. The mapping τ then induces a ranking κ on this information state as follows: $\kappa(v) < \kappa(v')$ iff $\tau(e)(w)(v) < \tau(e)(w)(v')$.

---

[10] 'The melon ripened' implies that the melon was ripe at the end of the event since 'ripen' is a so-called degree achievement.

Dependencies, semantic constraints and conceptual closeness in a dynamic frame theory

This mapping is used for case (iv). For example, if the sentence "The melon ripened" is processed, a language user not only knows that an event of sort 'ripen' occurred but in addition, by using τ, he infers that (i) the melon is ripe and (ii) that it sounds muffled. Again, (i) is a non-defeasible inference whereas (ii) is defeasible.

The mapping τ is extended to sequences (or histories) of events in the following way.

(16) $w \xrightarrow{e^n} v$ iff there are $u_0, \ldots, u_n$ s.t. $w = u_0$ and $v = u_n$, $e_1 \ldots e_n$ s.t. $e^n = e_1 \sqcup \ldots \sqcup e_n$ and for each (u_i, u_{i+1}) with $0 \leq i < n$ one has $u_i \xrightarrow{e_{i+1}} u_{i+1}$.

For $w \xrightarrow{e^n} v$, the rank is defined as the sum of the ranks of its component (atomic) transitions.

(17) $\tau^*(e)(w)(v) = \sum \tau(e_{i+1})(u_i)(u_{i+1})$

This rank expresses the degree to which a language user thinks that this history might occur (or has been occurred, using an abductive argument). It is used for case (5). Each history represents a possible evolution of how an outcome ϕ can be brought about by a sequence of events $e = e_1 \ldots e_n = e^n$. For example, if the sort of the events e_i is restricted to events of sort 'ageing', all histories have an outcome in which the object undergoing the change is older than in the input state. The output states can differ w.r.t. other properties, like 'Price' for example, that can also be changed by an event of sort 'ageing'.

4 Applying the formalism to the data from section 1

When processing a sentence, a language users knows that his current information state will be changed to a new one. Using his world knowledge, he also knows that this sentence either describes a change in the world or the persistence of a property of an object. In the former case the event described can either be deterministic or non-deterministic and the sentence can describe a relation between two properties over time that are linked by a dependency relation.

The cognitive significance of ranking functions and dependency relations is grounded in the fact that they allow a language user to anticipate as much information as possible about the potential output information state that results from processing the next upcoming sentence. Using the mappings κ, μ, μ^* and τ, he can already calculate the plausibility of a transition $w \xrightarrow{e} v$ as follows (Boutilier 1998:292).[11]

(18) $\kappa(w \xrightarrow{e} v) = \tau(e)(w)(v) + \mu(w)(e) + \kappa(w)$.

According to (18), the plausibility of a transition $w \xrightarrow{e} v$ depends on the plausibility of w, the degree to which an event e is expected to occur in w and the degree to which event e can bring about an outcome v given input w.[12] Given a condition ϕ that has to hold in the output state v, the set of possible ϕ-transitions is defined by (19) (Boutilier 1998:293).

(19) $Tr(\phi) = \{w \xrightarrow{e} v \mid v \models \phi \wedge \kappa(w \xrightarrow{e} v) \neq \infty\}$.

The most plausible transitions resulting in an outcome state satisfying ϕ are (20).

(20) $\text{mpt}(\phi) = \{v \mid w \xrightarrow{e} v \in \min(Tr(\phi))\}$.

In our application to natural language, the interpretation of a sentence need not involve all three mappings. Consider 'The melon ripened' and 'The duck swam'. After processing the subject a language user is given a ranked set of teams, i.e. an information state, of a particular sort: 'melon' and 'duck', respectively. He noe uses the mappings τ and μ^* to predict a most expected action and/or event together with most expected results in which a melon or a duck are involved. Thus, in this particular case he will calculate $\kappa_w(w \xrightarrow{e} v) = \tau(e)(w)(v) + \mu(w)(e)$ for a given w or, equivalently, $\kappa(w \xrightarrow{e} v) = \tau(e)(w)(v) + \mu(w)(e) + \kappa(w)$ with $\kappa(w) = 0$. For 'melon', an event of ripening has a particular non-defeasible outcome: the melon is ripe. Given this most expected event, there is in addition a most expected (least surprising) outcome: it will sound muffled. As a consequence, the most expected (least surprising) elements of the set $S(w) = \{(e, v) \mid w \xrightarrow{e} v\}$ will be events of sort ripening with a consequent state v in which the melon is both ripe and sounds muffled. By contrast, for 'duck' and 'swim', the corresponding set is larger because a swimming event usually has no single, most expected outcome. For example, there can be a change of location or a loss of energy as well as a combination of such results. However, none of those changes need be salient in a

---

[11] As noted by Boutilier (1998:292), this formula is the qualitative analogue of the probabilistic equation $Pr(w \xrightarrow{e} v) = Pr(v|w, e) \cdot Pr(e|w) \cdot Pr(w)$.

[12] For expectations that involve the passing of time like for instance in 'The older a stamp, the more expensive it is', the mapping τ^* instead of the mapping τ is used.

given context. One way of modelling this lack of salience of particular results is to assume that nothing changes with respect to properties in the input state w by setting $v = w$. Below we will see how this idea can be made precise by using defeasible conditionals.

A drawback of using ranking functions directly is that they involve teams. However, in many cases an expectation only involves two particular properties and not all properties denoted by a complete decompositional formula. For this reason, defeasible inferences based on expectations are better directly expressed in terms of those properties. One way of doing this which is still based on ranking functions, is to formulate defeasible inferences in terms of *defeasble conditionals*. We follow Goldszmidt & Pearl (1992), who define a consequence relation on a set Δ of defeasible conditionals and a distinguished κ-ranking κ^+. This ranking is defined as a ranking function that is minimal in the sense that any other admissible ranking function must be assigned a higher ranking to at least one world and a lower ranking to none.[13] As a consequence, κ^+ assigns to each world the lowest possible rank permitted by the admissible constraint. The exact definition is given below. The parameter δ stands for the strength with which the consequent follows from the antecedent. This takes care of the fact that the inference is defeasible and, at least in general, not strict. The greater δ, the greater the strength with which σ follows from ϕ. In the limiting case if $\delta = \infty$, the defeasible inference is strict. In the sequel, when giving examples of defeasible conditionals, the exact value of δ will be left open since this value has to be determined empirically.

Definition 12 (Plausible inference; Goldszmidt & Pearl 1992) σ *is a plausible conclusion of* ϕ *relative to a set* Δ *of defeasible conditionals, written* $\phi \mathrel{\vert\kern-0.3em\sim}^\delta \sigma$, *iff* $\kappa^+(\phi \wedge \sigma) + \delta < \kappa^+(\phi \wedge \neg\sigma).$

The antecedent contains information about the input information state which expresses information that is known to the language user, i.e. it is required that one has $M \models_S =(\phi)$ for each team S in the input information state. The difference between the two types of information consists in their strength. Whereas the antecedent has to be known, for the information in the consequent this need not be the case.[14] Thus, the consequent contains information that can defeasibly be added to this input information state, resulting in a new (output) information state. This information state not only consists of the information that results

---
[13] Goldszmidt & Pearl (1992) show that any consistent set Δ has a minimal ranking.
[14] How this difference is modelled in the output information state must be left to another occasion.

when semantically processing the (surface) constituents of a sentence but also by adding the information in the consequent of defeasible conditionals whose antecedent matches information that is given by processing a particular constituent or, more generally, by information that is given by the context. The addition of the information in the consequent is modeled by using the supplement operation from Dynamic Logic, expressed by the existential quantifier. In the context of a dynamic semantics defeasible conditionals are used to construct the output information state. For example, if the consequent has the form $\phi_1 \wedge \ldots \phi_n$ with $\phi_i \equiv x_\sigma$, For 'The melon ripened', one gets the defeasible conditional (21a), and for 'The duck swam' the defeasible conditional (21b).

(21) a. $x_{object} = melon \mathrel{\vert\!\!\sim}^\delta x_{event} = ripen \wedge x_{ripeness} = ripe \wedge x_{sound} = muffled$
   b. $x_{object} = duck \mathrel{\vert\!\!\sim}^\delta x_{event} = swim$

The difference between an event of ripening, which brings about particular results and which therefore has a consequent state, and an event of swimming is captured by the fact that for the former but not for the latter there are defeasible conditionals specifying inferences about what holds in the consequent state.

Simple sentences and the N400.

For simple sentences like 'John squeezed an orange', only the mappings μ and μ^* are important. Outcomes play no role because only the expectancy relations between sorts are involved. In (22), two examples of plausible inferences are given

(22) a. $x_{sort} = squeeze \mathrel{\vert\!\!\sim}^\delta x_{theme} = orange.$
   b. $x_{sort} = orange \mathrel{\vert\!\!\sim}^\delta x_{event} = squeeze \vee x_{event} = buy.$

Example (22b) is used to augment the current state with the information that the eventuality is of sort 'squeeze' or of sort 'buy'. If $\delta > 0$ holds, this means that a language user is more reluctant to draw the plausible inference. However, in the present context it is assumed that a language user only uses plausible inferences where $\delta = 0$. In the consequent, the existential quantifier is used, in order to capture the dynamic character of this defeasible inference since a new attribute, here x_{event} has to be introduced.

The *the ... the*-construction and the inferential user of PBVs.

In contrast to simple sentences like 'John squeezed an orange', which can be analyzed in terms of only using κ, μ and μ^*, both the *the ... the*-construction and the inferential use of PBVs involve in addition the outcome mapping τ. This is a direct consequence of the fact that they involve dependencies of (the values of) properties over time.

The *the ... the*-construction.

Consider again example (6a), repeated here as (23).

(23) The older a stamp, the more expensive it is.

The price of a stamp is in general not only dependent on its age but also on other factors such as availibility and demand. In Dependence Logic, this dependency can be expressed by (24), where $\vec{x}$ is a sequence of variables (attributes) containing 'age'.

(24) $=(\vec{x}, \text{price})$

Such a functional dependency is a necessary condition for the truth of a *the ... the*-construction. In addition, a stamp can get older without becoming more expensive at the same time. Thus, one only has 'Typically (normally), a stamp gets more expensive if it gets older'. Therefore, an event of sort 'ageing' (or 'getting older') for a stamp can have at least two different outcomes. In one output only the age of the stamp has increased and in a second output both its age and its price have increased (relative to the input state). As a consequence, events of ageing for stamps are non-deterministic. Since the *the ... the*-construction involves the comparative construction *the ... the*, it is necessary to not only consider single transitions but sequences of such transitions defined in terms of the mapping τ^*.

The output states u_i, $1 \leq i \leq n$, of the (atomic) transitions differ in the value assigned to the outcome mapping τ.[15] Assuming $\tau(e)(w)(v) = 0$, just in case v satisfies both the condition that the value of 'Age' has increased and that the value of 'Price' has increased, the most plausible histories involving a sequence of ageing events for a stamp are those in which both the stamp not only gets older but also gets more expensive.[16]

---

[15] They do not differ w.r.t. κ and μ because an event of ageing leaves these rankings unchanged.
[16] An analogous argument for other sorts of objects need not go through as in this case $\tau(e)(w)(v)$ need not be 0.

In defining a defeasible conditional based on τ^*, one abstracts from the temporal development. Rather, one only uses the information that the value of the given attribute, say Age, in the input information state has increased (decreased) and that there is a corresponding change in the dependent attribute, say Price. Thus, the general form of a defeasible conditional based on τ^* has the form (25a). For (23), one gets (25b). Using this defeasible conditional, one infers that the value of the Price attribute has increased too.

(25) a. $x_{e_{sort}} = \sigma_e \wedge x_{o_{sort}} = \sigma_o \wedge x_{o_{attr}} = \beta \wedge x_{o_{attr'}} = \alpha \overset{\delta}{\mid\sim} x_{o_{attr}} \neq \beta \wedge x_{o_{attr'}} \neq \alpha.$

b. $x_{e_{sort}} = ageing \wedge x_{o_{sort}} = stamp \wedge x_{o_{age}} = \alpha \wedge x_{o_{price}} = \beta \overset{\delta}{\mid\sim} x_{o_{age}} > \alpha \wedge x_{o_{price}} > \beta.$

Inferential use of PBVs.

On its inferential use, the interpretation of a PBV involves a change. We will argue that the interpretation process is similar to an abductive argument (see Boutilier 1998) involving three steps. Consider the example 'The melon sounds ripe'. First, there is an observation (perception): the melon emits a particular sound that is classified as 'muffled'. Second, an explanation for this particular sound value is given by postulating some (most) plausible event or events that could have brought about the observed change in the property expressed by the verb ('sound' in this case). Besides a ripening event, the sound of the melon could have been manipulated mechanically. But the former event is assumed to be more plausible, say due to experience and general world knowledge. Finally, the outcomes of this event are calculated. In this case one gets that the melon is ripe. The defeasible element is the postulation of a (most) plausible event. In the case of PBVs, this is an event related to the property expressed by the predicative complement, e.g. a ripening in the case of 'The melon sounds ripe' where the predicative complement is 'ripe'.

Similar to the *the ... the*-construction, there are two constraints that must be satisfied. First, there must be a functional dependency between the two properties. For example, the value of the 'Sound' property must be determined by the value of the 'Ripeness' property. Second, this condition need only hold in the normal or typical case.[17] Consider (26).

(26) *The melon sounds oval.

---

[17] Gamerschlag & Petersen (2012) and Petersen & Gamerschlag (2014) formulate related constraints in their type-based frame analysis of PBVs.

In this case there is no functional dependency between the value of the property 'Sound' and the property 'Form'. In a team of sort 'melon', the value of the 'Form' property can arbitrarily vary while the 'Sound' property remains constant, say 'muffled'. For 'The melon sounds muffled', the information in the input information state is (27a). The first defeasible inference is based on the mapping μ, (27b). The second step involves the non-defeasible inference that an event denoted by the verb 'ripe' brings about a state in which the object undergoing the ripening is ripe at the end of the event (27c). When taken together, one gets (27d).

(27) a. $x_{o_{sound}} = \textit{muffled} \land x_{o_{sort}} = \textit{melon}$.
b. $x_{o_{sound}} = \textit{muffled} \land x_{o_{sort}} = \textit{melon} \stackrel{\delta}{\leadsto} x_{e_{sort}} = \textit{ripen}$.
c. $x_{e_{sort}} = \textit{ripen} \land x_{o_{sort}} = \textit{melon} \vdash x_{o_{ripeness}} = \textit{ripe}$.
d. $x_{o_{sound}} = \textit{muffled} \land x_{o_{sort}} = \textit{melon} \land x_{e_{sort}} = \textit{ripen} \stackrel{\delta}{\leadsto} x_{o_{ripeness}} = \textit{ripe}$.

5 Summary

In this paper we developed an extension of a dynamic semantic theory for natural language which makes it possible to express both dependency relations between properties of objects and expectancies between nominal and verbal concepts. The theory is based on a decompositional analysis of common nouns in which they are interpreted as 'bundles' of properties, similar to the way objects are represented in database theories. The ranking functions defining those expectancies are used to draw defeasible inferences from information that is provided by the lexical meaning of words in a sentence that have already been processed.

Needless to say, the theory has to be worked out in greater formal detail: (i) The relation between Dependence Logic and κ-rankings must be further explored. E.g., is it possible to define ranking functions directly in Dependence Logic?; (ii) The dynamic component must be made more explicit. In particular, how are information states for various objects modeled and how is it possible to explicitly talk about changes?; (iii) How are the rankings empirically determined? Possible approaches are strategies from n-gram models and techniques used in neuroscience based on the concept of cloze probability; and (iv) Defeasible inferences are simply added to the output information state. As a consequence, there is no distinction between 'hard' and 'soft' (defeasible) information.

References

Baggio, Giosuè & Peter Hagoort. 2011. The balance between memory and unification in semantics: A dynamic account of the N400. *Language and Cognitive Processes* 26(9). 1338–1367.

Boutilier, Craig. 1998. A unified model of qualitative belief change: A dynamical systems perspective. *Artificial Intelligence* 98(1-2). 281–316.

van Elk, Michiel, Hein T. van Schie, Rolf A. Zwaan & Harold Bekkering. 2010. The functional role of motor activation in language processing: Motor cortical oscillations support lexical-semantic retrieval. *NeuroImage* 50(2). 665–677.

Federmeier, Kara D. & Marta Kutas. 1999. A rose by any other name: Long-term memory structure and sentence processing. *Journal of Memory and Language* 41(4). 469–495.

Galliani, Pietro. 2014. Transition semantics: the dynamics of dependence logic. *Synthese* 191(6). 1249–1276.

Galliani, Pietro & Jouko A. Väänänen. 2014. On dependence logic. In A. Baltag & S. Smets (eds.). *Johan van Benthem on logic and information dynamics.* 101–119. Springer.

Gamerschlag, Thomas & Wiebke Petersen. 2012. An analysis of the evidential use of German perception verbs. In C. Hart (ed.). *Selected papers from the 3rd UK Cognitive Linguistics Conference.* Vol. 1. 1–18.

Gärdenfors, Peter. 1988. *Knowledge in flux.* Cambridge, MA: MIT Press.

Goldszmidt, Moisés & Judea Pearl. 1992. Rank-based systems: A simple approach to belief revision, belief update, and reasoning about evidence and actions. In B. Nebel, C. Rich & W. R. Swartout (eds.). *Proceedings of the 3rd International Conference on Principles of Knowledge Representation and Reasoning (KR'92).* 661–672. Morgan Kaufmann.

Hagoort, Peter & Colin M. Brown. 1994. Brain responses to lexical ambiguity resolution and parsing. In L. Frazier C. Clifton Jr & K. Rayner (eds.). *Perspectives on sentence processing.* 45–81. Hillsdale, NJ: Lawrence Erlbaum Associates.

Halpern, Joseph Y. 2005. *Reasoning about uncertainty.* MIT Press.

Kutas, Marta & Kara D. Federmeier. 2011. Thirty years and counting: Finding meaning in the N400 component of the event-related brain potential (ERP). *Annual Review of Psychology* 62(1). 621–647.

Löbner, Sebastian. 2014. Evidence for frames from human language. In T. Gamerschlag, D. Gerland, R. Osswald & W. Petersen (eds.). *Frames and Concept Types.* Vol. 94. Studies in Linguistics and Philosophy. 23–67. Springer.

Naumann, Ralf. 2013. An outline of a dynamic theory of frames. In V. Marra G. Bezhanishvili, S. Löbner & F. Richter (eds.). *Proceedings of the 9th International Tbilisi Symposium on Language, Logic and Computation.* Vol. 7758 LNCS. 115–137. Springer.

Petersen, Wiebke & Thomas Gamerschlag. 2014. Why chocolate eggs can taste old but not oval: A frame-theoretic analysis of inferential evidentials. In T. Gamerschlag, D. Gerland, R. Osswald & W. Petersen (eds.). *Frames and Concept Types.* Vol. 94. Studies in Linguistics and Philosophy. 199–218. Springer.

Spohn, Wolfgang. 1988. Ordinal conditional functions: A dynamic theory of epistemic states. In W.L. Harper & B. Skyrms (eds.). *Causation in decision, belief change, and statistics.* Vol. II. 105–134. Kluwer Academic Publishers.

Väänänen, Jouko A. 2007. *Dependence logic - a new approach to independence friendly logic.* Vol. 70. London Mathematical Society Student Texts. Cambridge University Press.

Author

Ralf Naumann
University of Düsseldorf
nauman@phil.uni-duesseldorf.de

What Cost Naturalism?

Martin Stokhof & Michiel van Lambalgen[*]

The paper traces some of the assumptions that have informed conservative naturalism in linguistic theory, critically examines their justification, and proposes a more liberal alternative.

1 Introduction

In this paper we take up an issue that was touched upon in our earlier paper on abstraction and idealisation in linguistics[1] only in passing, viz., what we there called 'the ideological nature' of certain views about the nature of linguistics as a scientific enterprise. The choice of the term 'ideological' has confused some readers and may have been less fortunate. But apart from the choice of appropriate terminology, there is, we feel, an important issue here, one that needs further investigation. This note is a first step.

What is the issue? To put it in general terms, many approaches in modern linguistics are characterised by an, implicit or explicit, commitment to a concept of language that views it as the kind of natural phenomenon that can be studied by scientific means, with the natural sciences (physics, biology) acting as role models for what proper scientific theorising looks like. Language here is an ontologically homogeneous phenomenon that, in principle, can be captured and explained completely in, broadly speaking, physicalistic terms.

The original remark about the ideological nature of this view is motivated by our concern that it is insufficiently based on a prior and independent conceptualisation of what language is and what an explanatory theory of it would need to account for,

---

[*] We would like to thank the participants in the workshop and an anonymous referee for helpful comments and criticisms.
[1] Stokhof & van Lambalgen (2011a).

with only subsequently an argumentation that such goals can actually be achieved best by a physicalistic theory. Rather, it seems, the reverse has taken place. With the choice of a particular type of theory already in place, the concept of language has been adjusted and changed so as to fit the pre-conceived idea of what a proper theory of language should look like. But such a move can only be inspired by the idea that only the type of theoretical explanation that we know from the natural sciences can count as a proper account of whatever phenomenon we are dealing with. And that, we venture to claim, is not motivated by argument but by ideology.

In order to make good on this claim, we need to do a number things. First of all, we need to provide evidence that this kind of reasoning is indeed used in discussion about what the nature of linguistics is. Second, we need to show that this leads to the ontological homogenisation that we claim it does. That should settle the 'ideology' claim. But if, thirdly, we also are able to show that the resulting picture is deficient, both descriptively and explanatorily as well as philosophically, our investigation will also be able to provide some support for alternative conceptions of language and for other ways of doing linguistics.

2 A quick exploratory dig

One prevalent view on naturalism as applied to linguistics, to which we will turn in the next section, is, we venture, a reflection of what one might call 'Chomsky's shadow', a result of the deep and still present influence of some key assumptions that were infused in modern linguistics with the advent of generative grammar. There are many such elements that continue to shape theoretical thought in the discipline, here we focus on two that we think are directly relevant for the topic of this paper, viz., individualism and the adoption of a particular type of explanation. We realise of course that what follows is only a very rough sketch, one that traces one particular way of thinking, and that does not do justice to some of the alternative approaches that have been developed.[2] Nevertheless, we do think that the underlying assumptions that we discuss are not operative only in one particular paradigm, but that they are around in other frameworks as well.[3]

---

[2] Such as various approaches in functional linguistics and cognitive linguistics. Cf., e.g., Givon (2013) for some discussion of the assumptions underlying functional linguistics that is congenial with the argument developed in this paper.

[3] Cf., below, footnote 13 and 22 for two examples from different frameworks.

What Cost Naturalism?

The individualism that is part and parcel of many approaches in linguistics, past as well as present, can be stated succinctly as follows: 'language is an individual asset, and linguistic ability is an individual property'. The assumption is that in principle, though not de facto, an individual could be a competent language user all by his- or herself. Or to put it slightly differently, in giving a description of what linguistic ability is, and in giving a description of what that ability is about, viz., language, there is no need to refer to anything over and above the individual itself. Language use may be a social art, but language itself and the ability to use it are not. Of course, in real life people do not become language users in complete isolation, nor do they function as such without being part of a social environment. But, or so the idea goes, 'in principle' these social aspects can be bracketed, at least if they themselves are not a topic of study, of course. With regard to individualism, then, the basic divide is not between theories that leave out the social (communicative) dimension as a proper concern for linguistics and theories that include it, but between those that assume that the social dimension can be viewed in terms of the interplay of individual abilities and those that do not view the individual ability as an independent and foundational element.

The second factor that we want to draw attention to is the reliance on a particular form of explanation. There is a tendency in many linguistic theories to assume that explanations of linguistics facts ultimately need to be stated in terms of structural properties, of language, grammar, and of individual language users.[4] This inspires an exclusive focus on structural properties of the human cognitive make-up, ultimately, those of the human brain. This notion of a structural explanation is familiar from the sciences. However, in the case of linguistics actual access to such underlying structural properties never was a substantial part of the enterprise: it remained, rather, an assumption that such access would be possible, i.e., it was a way of formulating explanations, rather than a way of explaining things. This is what Ernan McMullin called 'hypothetico-structural explanation (McMullin 1978, p. 139):

> When the properties or behaviour of a complex entity are explained by alluding to the structure of that entity, the resultant explanation may be called a structural one. [...] Such explanations play only a small role in scientific enquiry. Much

---

[4] This is not to say that the resulting theoretical frameworks will be the same: what counts as the relevant structural properties, what form the system takes, what role semantics and pragmatics have to play in an overall account, are some of the parameters along which different approaches distinguish themselves.

commoner are those where the structure is postulated to account for the observed properties or behaviour of the entity under investigation. [...] [These] could be called 'hypothetico-structural'.

When individualism and the concept of hypothetico-structural explanation are combined the distinction between competence and performance that has been enormously influential, and not just in the generative grammar tradition,[5] seems almost self-evident. And with that the first, decisive step on an ever more abstract construction of the central object of linguistics is taken that we know from the generative tradition: from actual languages, as used in the 'here-and-now', to the concept of 'possible human language', and then to that of 'universal grammar' and ultimately the 'faculty of language in the narrow sense'.

Of course, not all linguistic theories have been travelling that far on the road of abstraction, but many of them have been, and still are, affected by this powerful combination of assumptions.

3 Abstraction and idealisation, once more

Now, one could regard the movement just described also in a positive way, i.e., as a manifestation of the increasing maturity of linguistics as a scientific enterprise. And it has been presented as such in the literature. After all, no scientific discipline engages directly with the continuous stream of experiences of phenomena that we have, they all construct their object of investigation from the endless particularities of phenomena by focussing on what is deemed important and leaving out the rest. Thus any discipline needs to create from the experiental flux a more or less stable set of entities that it aims to investigate.

That much is certainly true, and it is something can be observed in any scientific discipline (as well as in many other branches of human cognitive activity, by the way.) But as we have argued elsewhere,[6] there are crucially different ways of doing this, that have substantially different implications for the relationship between what a discipline is concerned with and the phenomena themselves.

Very briefly, in the paper just referred to, we made a distinction between 'abstraction' and 'idealisation', and characterised the difference in broad terms as follows.

---

[5] It was also a formative element in the development of formal semantics, for example.
[6] Cf., Stokhof & van Lambalgen (2011a, 2011b).

Features of a phenomenon that are abstracted are real features that at some point in time are considered to be too complex or too intractable, or, in some cases, not sufficiently relevant, to be taken into account in conducting a scientific inquiry into the nature of the phenomenon. A decision to abstract away from a feature is thus context-dependent and reflects various types of constraints that may obtain at a particular moment in time, relating to the availability and accuracy of instrumentation, availability and access to data, and so on. What needs to be pointed out is that abstraction is an intentional move: the features that are abstracted from are acknowledged as real, and they do occur, albeit in a special way, in subsequent theories, and, being actual features of the phenomenon, they will manifest themselves in experiment and observation. That holds, of course, also for features of a phenomenon that have not been acknowledged as such, i.e., features that have not been observed. These play a role in experimental and observational results as well, but they are not intentionally left out of the theory. They are simply not taken into account because they have not been observed.

Features that are abstracted from are typically quantitative in nature, and often they concern the numerical value of something that is known to exist, but difficult, or in some cases not particularly relevant, to measure precisely. Examples for the natural sciences would be movement on a frictionless plane; the concept of a perfectly rigid rod, or of perfect vacuum; free space constants, such as the gravitational and magnetic constants; or the concept of a perfectly pure chemical substance. In each of these cases there is a quantitative parameter (friction, the number of molecules in a certain volume, etc) that is set to a particular value (zero, infinity, or a specific number, as the case may be), not because that value is known, which it isn't, but because it is too difficult or too unimportant to actually measure.

What should be kept in mind is that although abstracted from, these parameters not only do turn up in experiment and observation they also are essential ingredients of the theories that are based on them. If we described the movement of an object on a frictionless plane, we are not assuming that friction does not exist; we're only setting its value to zero. That is of crucial importance because it implies that there will always be discrepancies between the predictions made by a theory that is based on the abstraction and what we can observe in the laboratory or in the real world. And it are such discrepancies as we would be able to observe and eventually measure, e.g., when better or new instruments become available, that will allow us to provide richer and better theories that rely on less abstractions.

Thus in the case of abstraction there is always a 'back-and-forth' between the theory based on an abstraction and the real phenomenon as it manifests itself in experiment and observation. And it is this back-and-forth that allows, and, in some cases, forces us to 'undo' the abstraction and come up with a better theory.

So the motivation for abstraction is primarily methodological (in a fairly literal sense, as 'having to do with what methods we have at our disposal') and practical, and hence in principle always temporary and revisable.

What about the second way of constructing an object of investigation, viz., 'idealisation'? The difference with abstraction is that here features that are 'idealised away' literally disappear from view. These are features of the phenomenon that are considered to be irrelevant from the perspective of what the discipline is interested it. Hence an idealised feature no longer plays a role in the empirical investigation: it is declared unnecessary to be considered further. The difference with abstraction may be subtle, but is it fundamental: an idealised feature is not 'merely' too complex or intractable, or not relevant in a specific use case, rather, it is viewed as something that need not be considered in, and may even stand in the way of, an attempt to understand the phenomenon since it is irrelevant for acquiring such an understanding.

Thus idealisation creates an ontological gap between phenomenon and constructed object: an idealised feature is, of course, a real one at the level of the phenomenon, but it is no longer present in the constructed object and has no role to play in the subsequent theories that employ that object. In a quite literal sense idealisation is an ontological move, rather than an epistemological one like abstraction: it changes the subject.

Features that are idealised are typically qualitative features of the phenomenon. Examples from linguistics that suggest themselves are: language as an infinite set of sentences; the competence – performance distinction; or the concept of literal meaning. In each case there is a particular feature of actual language use (e.g., its dependence on non-linguistics aspects of context, or the limitations of cognitive processing power, and so on) that is being discarded. As a result a new concept is formed that lacks this feature, and thus constitutes a different kind of entity than the original phenomenon.

Take the first example: if we look at languages in the 'here-and-now', i.e., as the phenomenon that we actually encounter when people use language, it is obvious that it is a finite object. The total number of utterances of any natural language, past, present and future, is finite, as is the existence of the human species. What is important is that this finite number of utterances appears to be unpredictable in this sense that we constantly encounter utterances of new expressions and that we have no reason to assume that this is bounded purely quantitatively (i.e., there there is some fixed n that serves as the upper bound of the number of utterances we may encounter). Thus 'creativity' of language use/users is a real phenomenon, one that needs to be accounted for. What is important to note is that this creativity in fact is bounded: it does not mean that anything goes and that there are no restrictions, e.g., on the length or the complexity of the structure of utterances (especially embedding) that are operative

And this is were things go wrong. The preferred way of accounting for creativity is to drop the actual feature of language's finiteness and switch to a different concept of language that identifies a language with an infinite number of expressions.[7] But this is an ontological switch that is underdetermined by the observed creativity, and that turns a fact to be explained into a defining feature, and thereby changes the phenomenon that we observe into a different type of entity altogether.[8]

This also means that with idealisations there is no straightforward 'back-and-forth' between the theory containing the idealisation and the actual phenomenon as it appears in experiment and observation. Since the idealised feature is missing from the theory, there is not direct relation between what we learn from experiment and observation and the predictions made by the theory. There is an ontological gap, and that gap needs to be bridged by an additional 'bridging theory' that relates what the theory says to what is actually out there. That means that idealisation comes with an additional epistemological task, viz., to come up with an adequate bridging theory. How to do that is not at all obvious, however, especially because the adequacy criteria for such a theory seem hard to come by.

So unlike abstraction, which is clearly motivated by practical and methodological concerns, the motivation for idealisation is different: it does not derive from empirical considerations, but rather is motivated by conceptual-philosophical ones. Where these are based on pre-conceived ideas about what constitutes a proper scientific investigation, –and as we shall argue, such ideas are indeed

---

[7] A move that is inspired by the concept of a language that comes from the deductive sciences.
[8] For another example, viz., the celebrated 'competence – performance' distinction, cf., Stokhof & van Lambalgen (2011a, section 8).

behind idealisations that we find in linguistics,– they can be properly be called 'ideological'.

4 Naturalism in linguistics: a specific case

Before turning to a more general outline of naturalism in linguistics, we first briefly discuss a specific way of arguing for this general view. It draws on the work of Chomsky, arguably one of the most influential thinkers in this area, and not just in the generative tradition.[9] Chomsky has argued extensively that linguistics is a science like other sciences, and hence that it should follow the same leads in the construction of its objects as well as in the methodologies it employs in studying them. That means not only that linguistics should be held to the same standards as any other empirical discipline, but also that it should be judged by similar criteria. This, Chomsky claims, is not always the case, especially in philosophy, where what is accepted as normal and appropriate in the other sciences is judged by other standards if it occurs in linguistics (Chomsky 1995, p. 7):

> [...] it is a rare philosopher who would scoff at its [i.e., physics', MS-MVL] weird and counterintuitive principles as contrary to right thinking and therefore untenable. But this standpoint is commonly regarded as inapplicable to cognitive science, linguistics in particular. Somewhere between, there is a boundary. Within that boundary, science is self-justifying; the critical analyst seeks to learn about the criteria for rationality and justification of scientific success. Beyond that boundary, everything changes; the critic applies independent criteria to sit in judgment over the theories advanced and the entities they postulate.

The message here is clear. According to Chomsky philosophers accept what is done in physics and related areas of research at face value, and they study it in order to understand it the way it is. But when it comes to linguistics and similar disciplines the subject matter is not studied 'as is', but it is judged, and apparently by criteria that are germane to the disciplines in question.

---

[9] The 'present relevance' of Chomsky's thought is a matter of debate. It is certainly true that the landscape of theoretical linguistics is much more heterogeneous now than it was in the sixties, seventies and eighties of the previous century. And many approaches are self-proclaimed 'non-' or even 'anti-'Chomskyean. However, there is still a strong tradition in theoretical linguistics that subscribes to some of the fundamental principles discussed here. Cf., below for some examples. And we would claim that even in alternative theoretical approaches one can find assumptions that derive from the generative tradition. For more discussion and concrete examples, cf., Stokhof & van Lambalgen (2011b, pp. 80–85).

But clear as it is, what Chomsky claims here is not beyond dispute. There is a lot of critical discussion of various aspects of physics, or at least of the conceptual understanding of it, both in philosophy as well as in physics itself. The ongoing debate on the proper interpretation of quantum mechanics immediately comes to mind (and we will see a bit of that later on), but also more generally there is critical engagement with the natural sciences and their self-understanding.[10] So it is definitely not true that philosophers do not criticise basic concepts and fundamental principles in the sciences.

Likewise, the charge brought against philosophy that it judges linguistics by 'outside' criteria does not seem completely justified either. Of course, as in any area of investigation, here too there is no doubt that examples can be found of analyses and criticisms that are 'off the mark'. But that is not particularly interesting. Rather, what Chomsky seems to take issue with is criticisms that start from other assumptions regarding what is the proper methodology in linguistics than he deems relevant, and that hence accept methodological pluralism. This is mocked by Chomsky as follows (Chomsky 2000, p. 76):

> We must abandon scientific rationality when we study humans 'above the neck' (metaphorically speaking), becoming mystics in this unique domain, imposing arbitrary stipulations and a priori demands of a sort that would never be contemplated in the sciences.

It is here that a central element of Chomsky's particular form of naturalism comes to the fore. As the passage just quoted strongly suggests, there is, according to him, no special methodology that needs to be employed when studying the human mind, including language. Such an assumption can only lead to 'mysticism', not to explanatory theories. Rather, there is every reason to extend the methodology employed in the study of humans as physical (biological) entities to the study of mind and language.

Thus it appears that Chomsky's main gripe with his philosophical opponents is that they do not share his assumption that, linguistics being an empirical discipline, it should employ the same methodology as any other empirical science, i.e., that they do not, as he does, subscribe to methodological monism.[11]

---

[10] A nice example is Hartry Field's discussion of the role of mathematics in physics (Field 1980); an example in biology is the debate concerning the unit of selection in evolution.

[11] That Chomsky's ideas are still with us is testified by the way in which the nature and goals of linguistic theory are described in more recent work. Here is an example from Culicover and Jackendoff (Culicover & Jackendoff 2005):

5 Naturalism in linguistics: three characteristics

The methodological monism that we identified in the previous section as the rock-bottom of Chomsky's distinct view on the nature of linguistics, is an important characteristic of a naturalistic stance in linguistics (as it is in many other disciples). In this section we briefly review three distinct such characteristics. Of course, in real life naturalism comes in many different forms and guises, and with different motivations and justifications. However, we do claim that these three features are characteristic in the sense that they can be found, perhaps in mixed composition, i.e., with different emphasis and motivation, in most naturalistic views.

The three characteristics are methodological monism, already introduced; ontological monism; and explanatory monism. The first is the assumption that all of science employs the same methodology. This should be read in a broad sense, since, obviously, not all concrete methods are equally relevant, or even applicable in every discipline. The second characteristic embodies the conviction that there are no major distinct ontological categories, i.e., that everything is basically made of the same 'stuff'. Again, this is a claim that should be interpreted with some caution, it is not necessarily a denial of any form of categorial distinction between entities, but embodies the claim that all of them are part of the same ontology. The third characteristic, finally, comes with the claim that there is one model of explanation that fits all phenomena, i.e., that all scientific disciplines employ the same requirements for what constitutes an adequate explanation of the phenomena that constitute their subject matter.

The relations between these three characteristics are complex. It is important to note that they are not merely three sides of one and the same (thick) coin, i.e., they do not imply one another. For example, one could subscribe to ontological monism,

---

We begin a more thorough examination of the situation [in syntax, MS-MVL] by reviewing the first principles of generative grammar, articulated in detail by Noam Chomsky in *Aspects of the Theory of Syntax* (1965) and many subsequent works. With only minor modulation and reinterpretation, these principles have stood the test of time and have received further confirmation through the flood of research in cognitive science in the past forty years. [...] Generative grammar is grounded in the stance that the object of study is the instantiation of language in the context of the human mind/brain, rather than an abstract phenomenon that exists 'in the community' [...] The fundamental linguistic phenomenon is a speaker producing an utterance that is understood by a hearer, and the fundamental question is what is present in the speaker's and hearer's mind/brain that enables this interchanges to take place.

From there Culicover and Jackendoff proceed to identify 'productivity' and 'competence' as core concepts.

yet acknowledge distinctly different methodologies as required by different sets of ontologically non-distinct phenomena. What does follow is that in such a case the motivation for the methodological pluralism can not be ontological. But other justifications can be thought of.

Of course, despite the conceptual independence of these three forms of monism, there are in fact strong affinities between them, and people tend to embrace them as a kind of package deal. But their unification does require some additional assumptions. One such assumption that enables further identification of these three forms of monism is that nature is material. Ontological monism then entails that all entities are material, which in its turns lends much plausibility to methodological monism: if what we study is basically of the same kind, then obviously the same methodology applies across the board (of disciplines, not entities). A further assumption then comes into view, viz., that there is a basic level of material constitution at which all relevant phenomena can be studied. This reductionism then further motivates explanatory monism: if what we study with the same methodology takes place at the same level of material constitution, how could the explanations we are after be different?

Thus arises the idea of a unified science, based on material reductionism. With physics arguably being the most successful science we have, it would stand to reason that this unified science employ the methodology of physics, and if we accept that, we find ourselves engaged with some form of physicalism.

In order to make this a plausible account for linguistics, we actually also need as some form of (methodological) individualism as an additional assumption. This individualism was identified in section 2 as one of the core contributions that Chomsky has made to linguistic theory. It seems to work because the physical realisations of all entities appear to be individual in nature. That holds in general, and for linguistics it seems to imply that it is individual language users that are the core entities that linguistic theory should be concerned with. Thus the individualism appears to guarantee ontological homogeneity, and thereby it also seems to guarantee explanatory unification.

As we have argued elsewhere,[12] some strong idealisations, in particular the competence – performance distinction, are needed to make this work in the case of language. However, as pointed out above, the argumentation for these assumptions is conceptual, and not (or at least not exclusively) empirical. And that suggests

---

[12] Cf., Stokhof & van Lambalgen (2011a, section 8).

that at least in linguistics this form of naturalism is ideologically motivated. It is not based on empirical arguments for methodological monism, nor does it give a sound empirical argumentation for the necessity of methodological individualism. Rather, these two crucial assumptions are embraced on the basis of what ultimately is a scientistic ideology.[13]

6 Naturalism: an alternative view

At this point it might be good to pause for a moment and ask ourselves what this scientistic form of naturalism has bought us in linguistics, and whether there might be an alternative way of being a naturalist and a linguist.

As for the first question, we would venture that the answer is: 'Actually, not that much.' It is true that linguistics enjoys considerable academic prestige, and in part (but admittedly, only in part) this is due because it conceives itself, and is conceived by others, as being the most scientific (rigorous, formal, ...) of the humanities. The adoption of a naturalistic stance no doubt contributes to that. But in actual practice it has led, or so we would argue, initially to an unjustified restriction of the domain of inquiry, and later, when those restrictions became too stringent, to a confusing variety of approaches and methodologies. The continuing adherence to individualism and the model of hypothetico-structural explanation have played a major role here.

---

[13] To further counterbalance the impression that we are only after Chomsky, or generative grammar, we illustrate very briefly how similar ideas have crept into our own work in semantics. In our use of the event calculus, which uses closed world reasoning in the description and explanation of a range of phenomena, from tense and aspect to coercion and logical reasoning, some assumptions about individualism and materialism can be discerned. Cf., the following passage from Stenning & van Lambalgen (2008, p. 161–162):

> Systems of closed-world reasoning are logics of planning. [...] Maintaining a model of the current state of the immediate environment relevant to action is a primitive biological function. [...] The planning logics are just as much what one needs for planning low-level motor actions such as reaching and grasping, as they are for planning chess moves.

> Approaching from the direction of the syntactic and semantic analysis of temporal expressions of natural languages also directs attention to planning as underlying our faculties for language. More generally, a main human brain innovation is the increase in neocortex, and specifically in frontal areas of neocortex. These frontal areas are involved in planning and 'executive functions', among other things.

Clearly the assumptions that are operative here are that language originates from non-linguistic structural properties of the human brain; and that, hence, core aspects of linguistic meaning can be explained in terms of such individual structural properties.

What Cost Naturalism?

But what about the second question, about the possibility of an alternative? If we bracket our commitment to individualism combined with hypothetic-structural explanation, the most intuitive way of explaining the human ability to use language would seem to be one that proceeds in terms of dispositional properties of language users. Instead of postulating 'underlying' structural properties that explain what we can observe about language and its use, – a postulate that would seem to bring along a mechanistic picture of language and language users –, we would try to explain what we can observe in terms of dispositions to verbal and relevant non-verbal behaviour that are triggered in a complex setting of natural, individual, and social conditions.

Such a dispositional account has a number of attractive features. First, it would provide an intuitive account of the voluntary nature of language use. This intentional aspect is hard to give a place in the structure-based, mechanistic view, but comes natural in a dispositional account. After all, dispositions need additional conditions to manifest themselves, and an intentional volitional act would appear to be a prime candidate for such a condition. (Which is not to say that it would be a necessary condition.)

Secondly, it would provide space to accommodate a number of factors other than the individual itself that play a role in a comprehensive account of language and language use. One example here would the communicative purposes of language users, that are relevant input for determining the manifestations of their dispositions to use language. That is still at the level of language users and their interactions. But the dispositional view could also accommodate other factors, such as external determinants of (lexical) meaning, or institutions and other social entities. Since the manifestation of a disposition is something that 'takes place', i.e., is a spatio-temporally located event, the role of both physical and social reality as (co)determining meaning can be incorporated in a fairly straightforward manner.

And thirdly, unlike the competence – performance distinction, which isolates competence from performance limitations, such as constraints on working memory, or limited attention span, the dispositional view prepares a natural setting for such limitation to operate in. After all, as noted above, the manifestations of a disposition take place in concrete situations, and features of these situations may not only contribute to the content of these manifestations, they may also set limits to them, in various ways.

So, all in all, it seems much more intuitive to look at what is individual about language and language use in terms of dispositions than in terms of structure, and to account for them as embedded in a rich and varied social ontology.

However, enter the commitment to hypothetico-structural explanation, again. It is this commitment, that postulates that, 'in the end', explanations will refer only to structural properties, that forces us to consider an explanation in dispositional terms as 'provisional', at best. If not outright non-explanatory,[14] then minimally these are explanations that contain terms, viz., the ones referring to dispositions, that will need to be analysed further until they are eliminated and only reference to structure and structural priorities remains.[15] And this is because, so the argument goes, structure is real and dispositions are not.

As was already mentioned, a key element in the justification for this assumption, and hence for the commitment to hypothetico-structural explanations, is the conviction that physics works that way. And given that physics is the most successful scientific discipline there is, the idea is that linguistics should follow its lead. This raises two questions. First of all, does physics really work that way? And secondly, and this is an issue that is quite independent from the answer to the previous question, what is the justification for linguistics to follow suit?[16]

The first question is a complicated one. The idea that structural explanations are the *nec plus ultra* of all scientific inquiry is based on what is often called the 'Groundedness Thesis', i.e., the view that all dispositions are ultimately grounded in structural properties of the entities involved. As said physics is often assumed to conform to this assumption, but there are dissenting voices. More specifically, it has been argued that at the level of quantum phenomena we find properties that are

---

[14] Arguments to that effect are, by the way, more often than not quite rhetorical in nature, and consist mainly of obligatory references to the circular nature of, e.g., an explanation of the effect of opium in terms of its 'dormative' power.

[15] Getting rid of the non-individual entities would be another task.

[16] It is good to note at this point that although naturalism is very much the default position among linguists in the generative tradition, there are exceptions. An example is provided by Hinzen and Uriagereka, who defend a non-naturalistic interpretation along the following lines (Hinzen & Uriagereka 2006, p 71–72):

> In our view the metaphysics of linguistics points to a radically different ontology of the mind that invites a rather novel reflection on the constraints that delimit the human conceptual edifice, and which to this day have no plausible biological or even physical explanation. As a consequence of that, the human faculty poses much the same explanatory problems for contemporary physicalism as the mathematical faculty does.

This is an unorthodox position that deserves further scrutiny. Unfortunately to do so is beyond the scope of this paper and has to be deferred to another occasion.

inherently dispositional, i.e., not reducible to structural properties that can serve as their causal basis. One example is spin of an electron. Cf., Bigaj (2012, p. 212):

> Orthodox quantum mechanics does not seem to identify any property which could play the role of the causal basis for spin.

But also position arguably needs to be considered as a disposition, rather than a classical property, in view of the probabilistic nature of quantum phenomena. In fact, this holds across the board, given the very nature of quantum phenomena (Bigaj 2012, p. 214)]:

> The dispositional interpretation of quantum properties is a direct consequence of the probabilistic character of quantum states.

Thus the defining characteristic of quantum theory, viz., it is inherently probabilistic character, enforces a dispositional view of its basic objects and their properties. And according to some this even applies to the very existence of quantum objects. Cf., Thompson (1988, p. 77):[17]

> In quantum field theory (a more complete form of quantum physics), even the existence of objects is a dispositional property that may or may not be manifested, as, for example, pairs of particles and anti-particles may or may not be formed.

So, taking the lead of science does not force one to do away with dispositions: even the most fundamental theory of physics does not obey the model of hypothetic-structural explanation, because, as one might put it, 'physical reality is dispositional'.

Now this view on physics and its explanatory model is not uncontroversial, and one might very well maintain that ultimately a fully explanatory theory of the physical world must satisfy the Groundedness Thesis. Which brings us to the second question raised above: Even if physics could rely solely on structural explanations, what reason is there to think that linguistics can too? In order to answer this question, we need to take a step back and look at what motivates naturalism in the first place.

7 The basic claim of naturalism

The core of the naturalistic stance, i.e., the assumption that different forms of naturalism all subscribe to, is that there are no supernatural entities that we

---

[17] Cf., also Suarez (2007) for some further discussion.

need to appeal to in the construction of adequate, explanatory theories of natural phenomena. Or, to put it in the form of a slogan: 'Nature can be explained on its own terms.'

The reasons for making this claim fall in two broad categories. One is ontological/metaphysical: we need not appeal to supernatural entities because such entities do not exist, i.e., they are not part of the ontological furniture of the world. The other is epistemological/methodological: an appeal to supernatural entities is not needed because such entities do not appear in our explanations, i.e., they do not belong to the ontological furniture of our theory of the world. These two types of motivation are not completely independent, of course.

But what counts as a supernatural entity? One way to define the concept would be to give a list of what it applies to, i.e., a list of supernatural entities that have been assumed, conceptualised, or otherwise 'identified' over the ages. It would contain not only well-known concepts from religion, magic and kindred realms, but also some that did occur in scientific explanations at some point in time: phlogiston, vital force, ... Such an enumeration suggests also a more general characterisation, which typically proceeds in terms of what a supernatural entity is *not*:

> x counts as a supernatural entity if and only if x lacks relevant features of physical entities, such as having material constitution, being situated in space-time, being subject to laws, ...

To be sure, this is still a fairly general and 'open' characterisation, but it will do to illustrate that the driving force behind naturalism, at least initially, is to avoid ontological and/or epistemological excess. What does not share basic characteristics with what nature has on offer does not belong to nature but is (or rather: would be) of an entirely different order.

The reference to physical entities in this characterisation might suggest that naturalism and physicalism, which holds that all sciences can be reduced, in some sense, to physics, are actually two sides of the same coin, but that would be too hasty a conclusion. For note that being a naturalist comes with the commitment to eschew reference to supernatural entities, not with the much stricter injunction to refer only to physical entities. What makes its appearance in one's naturalistic explanations must have a physical realisation, but that falls short, or so we will argue, of being a physical entity.

8 Two flavours of naturalism

In order to bring out the difference we distinguish between two types of naturalism: conservative, and liberal.[18]

Conservative naturalism represents the more strict view that not only all natural entities need to have physical realisations, but that all entities *are* indeed physical entities. It is in that respect that liberal naturalism takes a different stance: it agrees with conservative naturalism that all entities need physical realisations, but nevertheless maintains that not all such entities are therefore physical entities, or can be reduced to such entities. In other words, liberal naturalism leaves open the possibility that there are natural entities that are not 100% physical in this sense that, although they do depend on physical entities that realise them, they can nevertheless not be reduced to their physical realisations.

It will be clear from the above that there are natural affinities between conservative naturalism and ontological monism, in particular physicalism, and, in its wake, with methodological monism and explanatory monism. The conservative naturalist position is indeed, as De Caro and MacArthur quite rightly note, a classical one. It is strongly committed to the 'unified science' ideal of logical positivism in a physicalistic form: there are no other entities than physical objects and their properties and relations; everything natural can ultimately be viewed in just those terms; and hence it is the methodological and explanatory canon of physics that defines the scientific enterprise as a whole.

Liberal naturalism, on the other hand, embodies a specific kind of ontological pluralism. It does not recognise any supernatural entities, since it abides with the core commitment of a naturalistic stance. But it does allow natural entities to come in different kinds which are not reducible one to the other. So liberal naturalism subscribes to ontological pluralism within the natural world: it recognises different kinds of natural entities as entities in their own right. With that comes the possibility of methodological and explanatory pluralism: ontological pluralism can not rule out, but it does not imply it either of course, that the study of different kinds of natural entities calls for different methodologies, and also that these different kinds of entities need to be explained in different ways.

---

[18] 'Conservative naturalism' comes close to what is also called 'classical' or 'scientific' naturalism; cf., De Caro & MacArthur (2004).

It will be clear what determines the choice between conservative and liberal naturalism: Are there natural phenomena that require for their proper explanation reference to entities that need physical realisations, so are not supernatural, but that can not be exhaustively characterised in terms of their physical realisations and their properties? If no, than conservative naturalism is a viable stance; if yes, then liberal naturalism is vindicated.

In the next section we will give a number of examples from a variety of disciplines that suggest that, yes, such entities do exists, and that hence, no, conservative naturalism is not a viable option in those disciplines. Moreover, we claim that linguistics is one of these disciplines, so after this brief review we will go into the question what this means for linguistics as a discipline.[19]

9 Groups on active duty: some examples

The first two examples come from biology. The first concerns the role that groups might play as vehicles of selection in the evolutionary process. Where the standard conception of evolution views individuals as the sole instruments in the selection process, some have argued that we need also to take into account the groups to which individuals belong, since the effects of behaviour on groups may be significant, and hence groups themselves may act as selection vehicles as well. Although the idea of group selection was entertained by Darwin, it had fallen in disrepute for a long time. It was revived by Wilson and Sober some twenty years ago, and since then it has been the subject of a lively debate. This is how Wilson and Sober motivate the idea in one of their earliest papers (Wilson & Sober 1994, p. 605–606):

> There are compelling intellectual and practical reasons to distinguish between behaviours that succeed by contributing to group-level organisation and behaviours that succeed by disrupting group-level organisation. [...] A concern for within-group versus between-group processes characterises the human mind and should characterise the study of the human mind as well.

Since its original formulation, the theory of group selection has gone through some revisions and the debate about has not subsided. But the point for our discussion is

---

[19] To avoid misunderstanding, the examples from other disciplines serve to illustrative the viability of liberal naturalism as such, not as (additional) arguments for a liberal naturalistic stance in linguistics. Whether the latter is plausible or not does not depend on the former, of course.

that if this is on the right track, then selection is a 'multi-level' process. It involves not just individuals, but also groups, which hence have to be regarded as basic, non-reducible entities: physically realised in their constitutive individuals, but nevertheless with properties of their own.

The second example from biology concerns trait inheritance. Again, the standard theory is individualistic, as it locates the inheritance mechanisms solely in the individual genome, and thus considers that to be the only relevant factor for phenotypic expression. However, this view arguably ignores the obvious and important role of other contributing factors. This is how Dupré characterises the situation (Dupré 2014, p. 81–82):

> To expect in general that identifiable bits of the genome will have privileged relations to particular traits of the phenotype, given that they do not typically even have unique relations to particular functional proteins, would be hopelessly unrealistic.The notion of the genome as composed of a series of genes 'for' particular phenotypic traits has gone the way of phlogiston. [...] The classificatory division of the genome within genomics proper, therefore, is one driven very much by theoretical considerations, and is little effected by social factors in the interesting sense of 'social'. If genomics eventually gives us a good understanding of development, then we might expect to derive real abilities to control developmental outcomes, human and otherwise. But given the demonstrable complexity of development and of its joint dependence on internal and environmental factors, the task is a daunting one.

This goes against a widespread belief that phenotypic expression of inherited traits is a matter of the individual only, whereas it is quite obvious that environmental factors of various kinds also play a key role.[20] And it seems quite likely that among these environmental factors are entities that are not individual in nature, such as kinship and other social groups, economic and social institutions, and so on.

Other scientific disciplines also provide arguments against the individualistic bias that is a characteristic feature of conservative naturalism. For example, in

---

[20] On the widespread nature of the individualistic bias, cf., Lobo & Shaw (2008):

> In an age in which scientists and the public are excited about the sequencing of the entire human genome, we need to temper that excitement, at least a little, and be careful not to believe all the hype surrounding genes' involvement in determining development and behaviour. While an organism's genetic makeup plays a critical role in its development, there is also a rich and complex interplay between the genome and cues from the environment.

economics and decision theory the importance of the role of groups, in particular of such factors as group knowledge and rationality, group intentionality and action, is increasingly acknowledged. And more and more it becomes clear that the group properties mentioned can not always be reduced to their individual counterparts. Witness the 'Diversity Prediction Theorem', a mathematical result concerning the accuracy of group and individual prediction:[21]

> The squared error of the collective prediction equals the average squared error minus the predictive diversity

What this says is that the prediction of the group as a whole becomes better as the diversity of the predictions of its members increases. Again, what we have here is a property of an entity that can not be reduced to properties of its constitutive members, which means that groups as entities need to be taken on board. And unlike its conservative counterpart, liberal naturalism allows for that.

And then of course there is an entire tradition in the social sciences that is naturalistic in its basic stance, yet embraces a social ontology in which such entities as communities, institutions, practices, and the like play an essential role. That tradition has many different faces, as the works of authors such as Foucault, Bourdieu, Giddens, Schatzki, and many others illustrates. But they all subscribe to the starting point that was formulated already in the nineteenth century by one of the founders of modern sociology, Emile Durkheim (Durkheim 1895):

> Here, then, is a category of facts which present very special characteristics: they consist of manners of acting, thinking and feeling external to the individual, which are invested with a coercive power by virtue of which they exercise control over him. Consequently, since they consist of representations and actions, they cannot be confused with organic phenomena, nor with psychical phenomena, which have no existence save in and through the individual consciousness. Thus they constitute a new species and to them must be exclusively assigned the term social. It is appropriate, since it is clear that, not having the individual as their substratum, they can have none other than society, either political society in its entirety or one of the partial groups that it includes – religious denominations, political and literary schools, occupational corporations, etc.

We take it that these examples, coming from a range of different fields, though not always uncontroversial within the respective disciplines, do illustrate the point

---

[21] Cf., Page (2007).

that the strict conservative naturalism that many would subscribe to as a matter of course is not the only option, and in some cases arguably not the right one. Liberal naturalism seems the way to go.

10 And in linguistics, too

In this section we list just a few of the many phenomena that substantiate the claim that what was claimed in the previous section holds for linguistics as well. The point here is not to introduce anything new, as these phenomena are well-known and extensively studied. Rather it is to emphasise that social entities, used here as a catch-all phrase to refer to groups, communities, social practices, institutions, and sundry entities, play a key role in an account of them. And that means that if we are to explicate the ontological implications of such accounts in a naturalistic setting we need a liberal naturalism.

First of all, there is the area of speech act theory from which reference to institutions and institutional practices can not be eliminated. Despite the fact that in most classical formulations the focus in the analysis of linguistic actions, and of the intentionality that is involved in them, remains at the individual level, it is also true that the institutional level is a necessary ingredient of a proper understanding of many speech acts. A similar argument can be made for the analysis of linguistic performativity, which also requires the acknowledgement of institutional frameworks. The ensuing ontological diversity is usually not spelled out very explicitly, but it is there.

A second example comes from semantics, and is provided by various forms of semantic externalism and by the phenomenon of the division of linguistic labour. By its very presuppositions, semantic externalism is at odds with the cognitivist conception of meaning that locates meaning in the individual's mind (or brain, as the case may be). It brings in other factors that co-determine meaning, such as the physical world in the case of natural kind terms, or the social or cultural environment in other cases. Especially the latter are hard to account for on a strictly individual basis. And the same holds for the phenomenon of division of linguistic labour, with it associated references to different subgroups in a linguistic community. The commitment to a social ontology and the concomitant failure of a conservative naturalistic stance may not always be very clear from the formal accounts that have been proposed, but they are there.

At the interface between semantics and pragmatics we find a third phenomenon: that of meaning contextualism. The assumption of stable ('literal') meanings is a prerequisite for the classical individualistic sender – receiver model of linguistic communication to make sense. It does provided that meanings can be regarded as individual assets. For only on that assumption does it make sense that meanings are used (expressed, transmitted) in context. But if meanings themselves depend on context, such an account is no longer an option. Meaning contextualism reverses the order of explanation: it is not individual, stable meanings that explain communication, rather it is the other way around, it is communicative practices that produce meanings that have (limited) stability. This is how Medina puts it (Medina 2004, p. 571):

> [S]emantic determinacy is the always fragile and relative accomplishment of communicative interactions which rest on a tacit agreement in action that is always undergoing transformation. Meanings become contextually determinate through the practical consensus achieved by participants in situated linguistic interactions against the background of shared practices.

And again, it is only when we spell out meaning contextualism that we find that we can not make do with a strictly individualistic model, but that we need to accept communicative practices and the communities in which they exists as bona fide denizens of our theoretical framework. The point can be strengthened further by pointing to such a phenomenon as successful communication with incomplete understanding. Just like the phenomena just mentioned this is something that lies outside the grasp of a linguistic theory that embraces conservative naturalism and its strict individualism.[22]

---

[22] At this point it may be good to point out that in many explicitly non-Chomskyean paradigms, in which semantics and pragmatics are considered to be intrinsic parts of linguistic theory, methodological individualism still plays a role. Here is an example from construction grammar, cf., the following passage in Goldberg (1995):

> Theorists working in this theory [i.e., construction grammar, MS-MVL] share an interest in characterising the *entire* class of structures that make up language, not only the structures that are defined to be part of 'core grammar'. This interest stems from the belief that fundamental insights can be gained from considering such non-core cases, in that the theoretical machinery that accounts for non-core cases can be used to account for core cases. [...] Construction Grammarians also share an interest in accounting for the conditions under which a given construction can be used felicitously, since this is take to be part of the speakers' competence or knowledge of language; from this interest stems the conviction that subtle semantic and pragmatic factors are crucial to understanding the constraints on grammatical constructions.

11 Liberal naturalism and the dispositional view

So it seems that a comprehensive account of language needs the liberal naturalistic perspective, i.e., a framework that can accommodate both individual and social dimensions of language and language use, and that is not committed to the hypthetico-structuralist model as the only respectable type of explanation, and that thus makes room for the incorporation of dispositional properties at the individual level and for social entities as autonomous elements in its ontology.

Of course groups, social practices, and so on, are not not supernatural entities, they have physical realisations in the natural world. What is important to note here is that, in general, the physical realisations of these social entities are not ontologically homogeneous. In some cases, specific parts of such a realisation may be identified with individual language users. But others pertain to quite different kinds of entities, such as implements, historical records, spatial configurations, and other material aspects. And yet others need to be explained in terms of properties of collectives, such as group intentionality and group knowledge.

This has important consequences, since it paves the way for ontological pluralism, viz., the acknowledgement of different categories of natural entities that are irreducible one to the other. Reduction of behavioural and psychological properties of groups and institutions and their practices, to properties of the individuals that realise them is not always possible. And even the individual behavioural and psychological properties that are involved cannot be reduced, as conservative naturalism would require, to underlying structural properties at the neurophysiological level, at least not in a significant sense.

Thus the picture that emerges is pluralistic in a number of ways. First of all, it comprises different kinds of individual entities, not just human language users. Second, it acknowledges collectives of such individuals, such as linguistic communities, as entities in their own right. And thirdly, it allows not just for the structural properties of the entities involved to play an explanatory role, but also for their dispositions.

This requires an explanatory model that can integrate these various aspects in such a way that the different components and their interactions can all be

---

Obviously, the scope of linguistic theory as it is conceived of here is wider than in the generative paradigm. But note that the central role of the individual is still present: linguistic competence may be a more encompassing notion but it still remains an individual affair

accounted for. An example of such a model, taken from Vanderbeeken & Weber (2002), is given in figure 1.

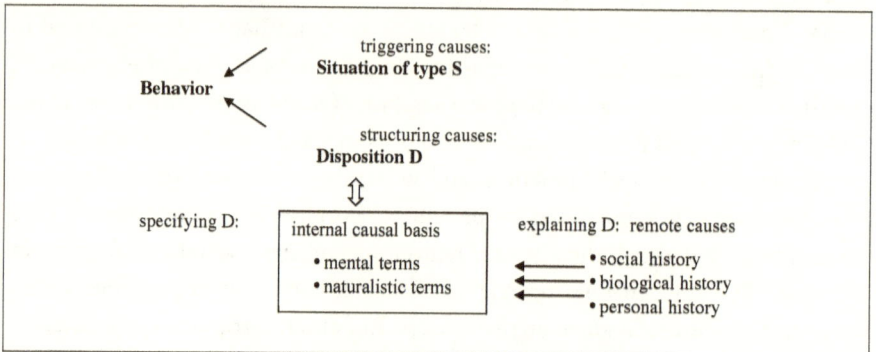

Figure 1: Dispositions in explanations

Not only does a model such as this make room for dispositions as an explanatory factor, it also allows for an account of the complex interactions between different kinds of causal factors, among which are dispositions, structural factors, and environmental factors. A model along these lines thus seems much more adequate for dealing with the rich and varied phenomena that language and language use are.

12 The role of linguistic theory in liberal naturalism

But what, one may (and should) ask, is the role of linguistic theory in such a complex model?

Marr (Marr 1977) usefully distinguished between two types of theories of cognitive phenomena. 'Type 1' theories are theories in which one can distinguish Marr's famous three levels. The top level is like the competence models of linguistics – it specifies in mathematical terms the inputs and outputs of a cognitive process (such as, on one view, language production and comprehension) viewed as an information processing task. Once the top level is specified one can construct algorithms meeting the specifications and compare these algorithms with respect to neural implementability. It is characteristic of a type 1 theory that its inputs and outputs can be described formally, and this makes it doubtful whether linguistics can be regarded as a type 1 theory. Before we substantiate these doubts, we quote

What Cost Naturalism?

Marr's very interesting description of the alternative, 'type 2' theories, which apply when (Marr 1977, pp. 38–39):

> [...] a problem is solved by the simultaneous action of a considerable number of processes, whose interaction is its own simplest description.[...] At each moment only a few of the possible interactions will be important, but the importance of those few is decisive. Attempts to construct a simplified theory must ignore some interactions; but if most interactions are crucial at some stage [...] a simplified theory will prove inadequate.

Indeed, in language comprehension, the input may itself be the product of interacting processes, in the following sense: a piece of discourse may seem uninterpretable gibberish (even though not obviously ungrammatical), until interaction with a non-verbal information source restores sense to the discourse. A classic example of this phenomenon is the experiment in Bransford & Johnson (1972), in which subjects were presented with the following discourse, supposedly from a man muttering to himself:

> If the balloons popped, the sound wouldn't be able to carry since everything would be too far away from the correct floor. A closed window would also prevent the sound from carrying, since most buildings tend to be well insulated. Since the whole operation depends on a steady flow of electricity, a break in the middle of the wire would also cause problems. Of course, the fellow could shout, but the human voice is not loud enough to carry that far. An additional problem is that a string could break on the instrument. Then there could be no accompaniment to the message. It is clear that the best situation would involve less distance. Then there would be fewer potential problems. With face to face contact, the least number of things could go wrong.

Some subjects were shown figure 2 before they had to interpret the discourse.

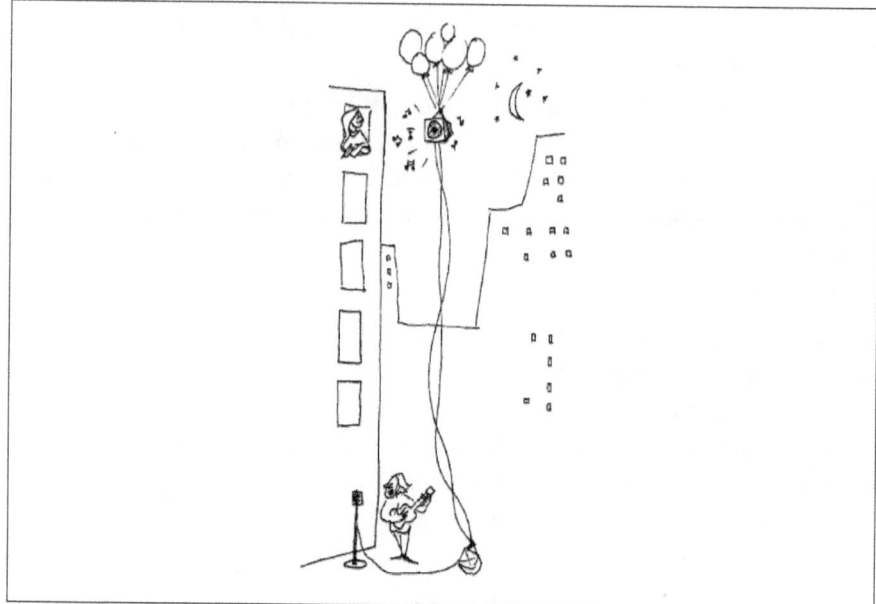

Figure 2: A modern serenade

These subjects could adequately recall and summarise the discourse. By contrast, subjects who were shown the picture after the discourse or not all, were unable to summarise or even recall the discourse. Thus the hearer must have access to the speaker's 'situation model' to be able to interpret the discourse. Realistically, this means that the hearer, starting from a few clues concerning the speaker's situation model, elaborates the situation model and interprets the discourse in an interactive and defeasible manner. Since making the picture available after the speaker has stopped talking does not benefit the hearer, processing must obey the 'principle of immediacy', i.e., 'all available information will immediately be used to co-determine the interpretation of the speaker's message' (Hagoort & Berkum 2007, p. 801). If one adopts this processing principle, linguistics cannot be a type 1 theory.

13 Conclusion

Although much more detail needs to be added, we do think that the considerations given in this paper support the conclusion that an adequate account of language and language use needs a liberal naturalistic perspective. The main reason is that language manifests itself in categorically distinct ontological entities, and methodological individualism does not succeed in constructing an ontologically homogeneous base for this variety. We have to accept that language is ontologically heterogenous and explanatorily not uniform. And the way in which a conservative naturalistic view is defended in the literature supports the claim that theories that aim to give a uniform explanation based on a homogeneous ontology are informed by some form of ideologically informed reductionism.

An alternative, liberal naturalistic view, which is ontologically, methodological and explanatory heterogeneous seems to be called for, and a dispositional account of several aspects of language and language use needs to be incorporated in such a view. The role of linguistic theory in this alternative view is to provide a systematic description of certain properties of linguistic expressions that can be part of such an encompassing account of language and its use. This means that linguistic theory must be viewed as one methodology among many, that deals with one particular aspect among many, of a heterogeneous phenomenon. Viewed in this way linguistic theory offers a conceptual reconstruction of certain aspects of language that also may suggest further empirical investigations. That is an important element of our investigations, but not the final word: linguistic theory is not an explanatory theory of a distinct empirical phenomenon.

References

Bigaj, Tomasz. 2012. Ungrounded dispositions in quantum mechanics. *Foundations of Science* 17. 205–21.

Bransford, J.D. & M.K. Johnson. 1972. Contextual prerequisites for understanding: Some investigations of comprehension and recall. *Journal of Verbal Learning and Verbal Behavior* 11. 717–26.

Chomsky, Noam. 1995. Language and nature. *Mind* 104(413). 1–61.

Chomsky, Noam. 2000. *New horizons in the study of language and mind.* Cambridge: Cambridge University Press.

Culicover, Peter W. & Ray Jackendoff. 2005. *Simpler syntax.* Oxford: Oxford University Press.

De Caro, Mario & David MacArthur. 2004. Introduction: The nature of naturalism. In Mario De Caro & David Macarthur (eds.). *Naturalism in question.* 1–17. Cambridge, MA: Harvard University Press.

Dupré, John. 2014. What's the fuss about social constructivism? *Episteme* 1(1). 73–85.

Durkheim, Émile. 1895. *Les règles de la méthode sociologique*. Paris: Librairie Felix Alcan.

Field, Hartry. 1980. *Science without numbers: A defense of nominalism*. Princeton, NY: Princeton University Press.

Givon, Talmy. 2013. The intellectual roots of functional linguistics. In Shannon Bischoff & Carmen Jany (eds.). *Functional approaches to language*. 9–30. Berlin: De Gruyter Mouton.

Goldberg, Adele. 1995. *A construction grammar approach to argument structure*. Chicago, Ill.: The University of Chicago Press.

Hagoort, Peter & Jos van Berkum. 2007. Beyond the sentence given. *Philosophical Transactions of the Royal Society B* 362. 801–11.

Hinzen, Wolfram & Juan Uriagereka. 2006. On the metaphysics of linguistics. *Erkenntnis* 65. 71–96.

Lobo, Ingrid & Kenna Shaw. 2008. Phenotypic range of gene expression: Environmental influence. *Nature Education* 1(1). 12.

Marr, David. 1977. Artificial intelligence: A personal view. *Artificial Intelligence* 9. 37–48.

McMullin, Ernan. 1978. Structural explanation. *American Philosophical Quarterly* 15(2). 139–47.

Medina, José. 2004. Anthropologism, naturalism, and the pragmatic study of language. *Journal of Pragmatics* 36(3). 549–73.

Page, Scott E. 2007. *The difference: How the power of diversity creates better groups, firms, schools, and societies*. Princeton: Princeton University Press.

Stenning, Keith & Michiel van Lambalgen. 2008. *Human reasoning and cognitive science*. Cambridge, MA: MIT Press.

Stokhof, Martin & Michiel van Lambalgen. 2011a. Abstraction and idealisation: The construction of modern linguistics. *Theoretical Linguistics* 37(1–2). 1–26.

Stokhof, Martin & Michiel van Lambalgen. 2011b. Comments-to-comments. *Theoretical Linguistics* 37(1–2). 79–94.

Suarez, Mauricio. 2007. Quantum propensities. *Studies in History and Philosophy of Science Part B: Studies in History and Philosophy of Modern Physics* 38(2). 418–38.

Thompson, Ian J. 1988. Real dispositions in the physical world. *The British Journal for the Philosophy of Science* 39. 67–79.

Vanderbeeken, Rob & Erik Weber. 2002. Dispositional explanations of behavior. *Behavior and Philosophy* 30. 43–59.

Wilson, David Sloane & Elliot Sober. 1994. Reintroducing group selection to the human behavioural sciences. *Behavioural and Brain Sciences* 17(4). 585–654.

Authors

Martin Stokhof
ILLC/Department of Philosophy
University of Amsterdam
m.j.b.stokhof@uva.nl

Michiel van Lambalgen
ILLC/Department of Philosophy
University of Amsterdam
m.vanlambalgen@uva.nl

Measuring out the relation between formal and conceptual semantics

Tillmann Pross & Antje Roßdeutscher[*]

In this paper, we argue that contemporary approaches of constructionalist syntax in which there is no generative lexicon provide an interface between formal and conceptual semantics with which the gap between formal and conceptual semantics can be bridged. We introduce the framework with the discussion of formal and conceptual aspects of meaning in German spatial denominal prefix- and particle verbs. We then show the representation of both formal and conceptual semantics in the same framework that allows to measure out the relation between formal and conceptual semantics in terms of the distribution of direct objects over verbs and corroborate our proposal with a corpus study.

1 Introduction

In this paper, we perceive the 'gap' between formal and conceptual semantics as pertaining to the different principles according to which the formal semantics of sentences and the conceptual semantics of lexical items is derived. On the one hand, the formal semantics of a sentence is determined compositionally from the meanings of the constituents of the sentence according to the syntactic analysis of the sentence. On the other, the meaning of a word is determined by the arrangement of elements from a fixed set of basic concepts in a lexical entry where the arrangement is not governed by syntactic structures similar to that of sentences.

---

[*] This work was supported by a DFG grant to the project B4 'Lexikalische Information und ihre Entfaltung im Kontext von Wortbildung, Satz und Diskurs', as part of the Collaborative Research Center 732 *Incremental Specification in Context* at the University of Stuttgart.

In order to bridge the gap between formal and conceptual semantics, we propose to make use of a logical form framework in which the perceived gap between formal and conceptual semantics does not manifest itself in a difference of the derivation of meaning in words and sentences. Instead, in the proposed framework, word meaning, and in particular the meaning of morphologically complex words, is structured according to the same syntactic principles underlying the structure of sentence meaning. Our approach is introduced with the discussion of spatial German denominal prefix- and particle-verbs (henceforth short 'p-verbs') as in (1).

(1) *abstützen* (to support), *aufbahren* (to lay sb. out), *aufbocken* (to jack up), *aufkanten* (to tilt sth.), *aufstocken* (to ramp up), *einlagern* (to put in a store) *einsacken* (to bag sth.), *einkellern* (to store), *einkerkern* (to incarcerate), *einsperren* (to cage), *überbrücken* (to bridge), *überdecken* (to cover), *überdeckeln* (to cover with a lid), *überpflastern* (to cobble), *ummauern* (to wall), *umzäunen* (to fence in), *unterfüttern* (to reline), *untermauern* (to support), *untertunneln* (to tunnel under), *verstreben* (to strut)

Based on a detailed analysis of the p-verbs in (2) at the syntax-semantics interface, we show how in our approach the formal components of word meaning can be separated from the conceptual components of word meaning.

(2) a. *eine Terrasse überdachen*
    a   terrace over.prfx.roof
    to roof a terrace
 b. *einen Dachstuhl abstützen*
    a   truss   up.prtc.stilt
    to prop up a truss
 c. *eine Flasche in den Keller einlagern*
    a   bottle in the cellar in.prtc.store
    to put a bottle in the cellar

Furthermore, we argue that the separation of formal and conceptual meaning in a word allows to correlate the relation between formal and conceptual meaning in a p-verb with the restrictions on fillers of argument slots imposed by the p-verb. More specifically, we propose that the relation between formal and conceptual meaning in a given p-verb can be measured out in terms of the distribution of possible fillers of argument slots over p-verbs which in turn provides a linguistic

Measuring out the relation between formal and conceptual semantics

characterization of conceptual meaning independent of assumptions about the cognitive structures underlying conceptual meaning.

The paper is structured as follows. In section 2, we provide some background on the syntax-semantics framework that we employ and relate it to previous approaches to p-verbs in the tradition of lexical decomposition grammar. We illustrate our syntax-semantics interface with the discussion of the three examples of p-verbs in (2) in section 3. The focus of our analysis is on emphasizing the differences between the formal and conceptual constituents of the meaning of those p-verbs. Next, in section 4, we relate the differences in the meaning of p-verbs to the restrictions which these p-verbs impose on the selection of direct objects. We generalize the observations about divergence in selectional preferences with a statistical measure known as selectional preference strength in section 5 and discuss the results of a proof-of-concept corpus study in section 6. We conclude in section 7.

2 Pervasive semantics

2.1 Decomposition in the lexicon

The assumption that the representation of word meaning in the lexicon is structured (and not purely denotational) proved to be a fruitful starting point for the decomposition of meaning in the lexicon to conceptual structures such as 'semantic forms' (Bierwisch 2007, Wunderlich 2012), 'event structure templates' (Rappaport Hovav & Levin 1998), 'dot-types' (Asher 2011, Pustejovsky 2001), 'frames' or 'scenarios' (Fillmore 1982, Hamm et al. 2006). But what all these approaches share is the assumption that word meaning is determined in the lexicon according to principles different from the principles which apply to the determination of sentence meaning in the syntax. It is the assumption of a principal difference between the structure of meaning in the lexicon and the structure of meaning in sentences which we think causes the gap between conceptual and formal meaning. In formal semantics, sentence meaning is determined by the compositional interpretation of the syntactic structure of the sentence. In lexical semantics, word meaning is determined by 'flat' conceptual structures built from a set of basic concepts or fundamental constituents of meaning. Denominal p-verbs in particular have been in the focus of interest for lexical decomposition approaches, where it is assumed that a noun is incorporated with a lexical process into an abstract verbal template (Kaufmann 1995, Stiebels 1998). As an illustration, consider the semantic form that (Stiebels

1998, p. 289) proposes for the denominal spatial p-verb *unterkellern* (build a cellar under sth.) in (3), see also (Roßdeutscher 2011,2013a) for a comparison of lexical decomposition with the present approach.

(3) Lexical entry for *unterkellern*:
$\lambda y.\lambda x.\lambda s.CAUSE(x, BECOME(POSS(y, CELLAR)))(s)$
$\wedge BECOME(LOC(CELLAR\ UNDER[y]))(s)$

The semantic form (3) involves six different conceptual predicates *CAUSE, BECOME, POSS, CELLAR, LOC* and *UNDER*. *unterkellern* itself does not indicate the arrangement of these predicates. Also, the meaning of the conceptual predicates must be given in terms of a pre-theoretic language grounded in assumptions about the structure of human cognition such that paraphrases of the meaning of *unterkellern* as *provide an object x with a cellar such that the cellar is located under x* can be provided a reasonable interpretation. It is also assumed that each of the conceptual predicates encodes a number of additional constraints on the type of arguments it takes, e.g. that for a cellar to be located under an object, this object must provide a region in its underground (see (4a)). Similarly, the combinatorics of conceptual predicates must prevent an incoherent combination as in (4b). Furthermore, the conceptual predicates must license only appropriate modifications and rule out examples such as (4c). Taken together, the constituents (conceptual predicates) and principles of meaning formation (cognitively motivated processes) in the lexicon are fundamentally different from those constituents (words) and principles of meaning formation (compositional interpretation of syntactic structure) that have been employed with great success in the analysis of sentence meaning.

(4) a. *ein Flugzeug unterkellern*
       an airplane under.prfx.cellar
   b. *ein Haus überkellern*
       a house over.prfx.cellar
   c. *ein Haus mit Wasser unterkellern*
       a house with water under.prfx.cellar

Acknowledging these differences in scope and motivation and grossly generalizing, formal semantics is concerned with how meaning is derived compositionally from sequences of words but not what the fundamental constituents of meaning are and how they pattern in words. Lexical semantics is concerned with how the fundamental constituents of meaning pattern in words under the assumption that the meaning of words must be explained with the help of non-linguistic conceptual knowledge. In the following, we propose that bridging the gap between formal and conceptual semantics can be accomplished in an account of word-formation in which there is no generative lexicon but word-formation is entirely syntactic and consequently, the same semantic principles apply to words and sentences.

2.2 Pervasive Syntax

In pervasive syntax approaches to word formation (e.g. Hale & Keyser 1993, Marantz 1997, Alexiadou 2001, Borer 2005), the same syntactic principles are assumed to be at work below and above the 'word level'. Words are formed from 'roots', atomic, non-decomposable and category-neutral elements associated with encyclopedic knowledge. Roots combine with features to build larger linguistic elements. Consequently, the term 'lexical item' has no significance in the theory and nothing can be said to 'happen in the lexicon'. We take the idea of pervasive syntactic structure all the way down as an inspiration for the development of a similarly pervasive semantics. We assume a fairly standard minimalist syntax of phrase structure with move and merge (Chomsky 1995, Adger 2003) and that incorporation is governed by the head movement constraint (Travis 1984). We also assume a minimalist approach to argument structure, where argument structure is determined in the syntax (Hale & Keyser 1993) and a structural parallelism across the nominal (cf. Alexiadou 2001), verbal (cf. Harley 2011) and prepositional (cf. Svenonius 2003) domain.

The basic – and fairly standard – syntax of denominal verbs which we take as the starting point for our discussion is given in (5), (6) and (7).

(5) eine Terrasse bedachen
    to roof a terrace

(6) eine Flasche lagern
    to store a bottle

(7) einen Patienten stützen
    to support a patient

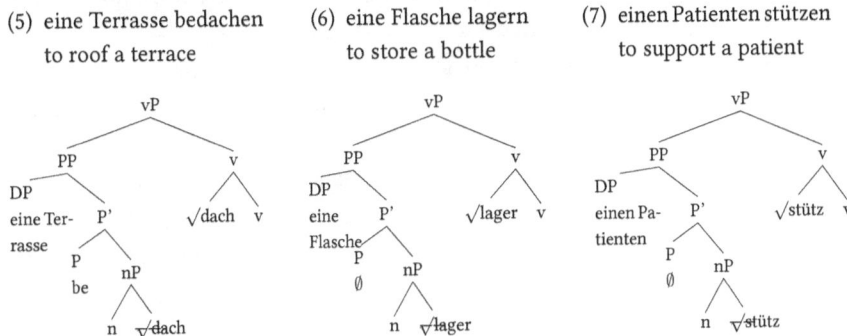

The structure of each of the examples (5), (6) and (7) evolves from the insertion of a root $\sqrt{}$ into a nominal phrase template. The nominal phrase is merged with a prepositional head P which projects a phrase structure the specifier of which is a DP. Independent of whether P is overtly realized with the prefix be- (as in (5)) or not (as in (6), (7)) P has the same syntactic and semantic function. Finally, the prepositional phrase is merged with a verbalizer head v, into which the nominal root incorporates via head movement.

2.3 Pervasive Semantics

In our approach of pervasive semantics, the semantics of (morphologically complex) words is not reconstructed in the lexicon but in the syntax. The starting point of our reconstructions is the insertion of a root into a syntactic context which determines the category of the root. The semantics of the root in that particular insertion context is incrementally specified by the semantic interpretation of the syntactic structure of the insertion context. That is, one and the same root can have different meanings, depending on the syntactic context in which it is inserted and interpreted. For example, the same root $\sqrt{lager}$ can show up in the verb lagern (to store) and the noun Lager (the store), depending on the syntactic context into which $\sqrt{lager}$ is inserted. As we have seen in the examples (5)-(7), syntactic contexts for root insertion have a functional structure determined by the layering of functional heads and their projections. In fact, functional heads have a categorizing function in the syntax we pursue. Heads of verbal phrases vP categorize verbs, heads of nominal phrases nP categorize nouns and heads of prepositional phrases PP categorize prepositions. The layering of functional structure also implies that in "a 'pervasive syntax' approach to morphologically complex forms [...] the analysis and structures proposed for a form must also be contained within the analysis of any structure derived from that form" (Harley 2009, p.320).

The hierarchy and modular organization of functional structure determined in the syntax requires a similar organization of the compositional semantic interpretation of the syntactic structure. Consequently, we propose that each functional head in the syntax is responsible for the introduction and predication of a particular sort of discourse referents. Put another way: functional layers in the syntax correspond to the ontological building blocks of word meaning. For example, v introduces events: e, P introduces states: s, n introduces invididuals: x,

Place introduces regions (sets of bounded directed vectors): r and K(ase) introduces Eigenspace-vectors: r_{id} (Wunderlich 1991). We also propose that the same close-knit connection between syntax and semantics holds for the introduction of conceptual predicates such as that between an event and its result state, i.e. the conceptual predicate CAUSE. Roßdeutscher & Kamp (2010) argue that the syntactic configuration which gives rise to the CAUSE predicate is one in which a verbalizer v is merged with a state-denoting XP to the effect that the event introduced by e is conceptualized as that event of which the state denoted by the XP is its result. Of particular interest to this paper are those conceptual relations that arise from the syntactic configuration of a merge of a P head with an XP, among them the application of one object to another object APPLICATION, the support of one object by another object SUPPORT, and the relative location of an object AT. To identify the conditions for the introduction of conceptual predicates from a merger of P and an XP, we need to make precise what exactly it is that application, support or location is a conceptualization of, i.e. how the denotation of the XP with which P merges influences the conceptual predication over the merge of P and the XP. To this end, we propose to take into account that the denominal verbs which we focus on in this paper involve an additional meaning component. Verbs like *überdachen* or *einlagern* identify a spatial configuration of the nominal root of the verb and the direct object of the verb. For example, *überdachen* in (8a) describes an event in which an object – the roof – is brought into the region above some other object – the terrace. *einlagern* as in (8b) describes an event in which an object – the bottle – is brought into a location inside of another object – the store. *abstützen* as in (8c) describes an event in which an object – the truss – is provided with pillars in its below region.

(8) a. *eine Terrasse überdachen*
    a   terrace over.prfx.roof
    to roof a terrace
b. *eine Flasche einlagern*
    a   bottle   in.prtc.store
    to store a bottle
c. *einen Dachstuhl abstützen*
    a   truss   up.prtc.stilt
    to prop up a truss

(9)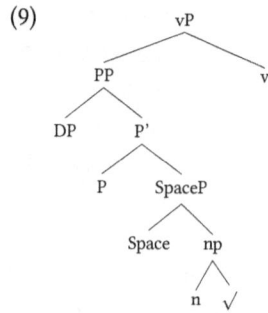

Spatial configurations of the type described in (8a)-(8c) can be represented as conditions on vector spaces: (Zwarts 1997, 2005, Zwarts & Winter 2000) proposed a formal semantics for spatial expressions built from vector spaces in which the denotation of objects is their Eigenspace and spatial configurations are formally defined in terms of structural constraints on sets of vectors such as spatial inclusion (represented as "⊆") or being a set of vectors which point upwards from a reference object x (represented as "↑(x)"), giving the 'above region' of x. For example, in terms of vector space semantics, (8a) is true iff the Eigenspace of the roof used to cover the terrace is located in the above region of the terrace and the above region of the terrace is covered by the Eigenspace of the roof. Similarly, (8b) is true iff the Eigenspace of the bottle is a subset of the vectors defining the interior space of the store. Finally, (8c) is true iff the Eigenspaces of the pillars have contact with and are located in the below region of the truss.

It is obvious even from these informal elaborations that just the spatial configurations described by (8a)-(8c) are not sufficient as characterizations of the meaning of (8a)-(8c). What is necessary in addition is a conceptualization of the spatial configuration *as* a configuration of support, application or inclusion. Earlier we said that the conceptualization of support, application or inclusion is realized with the merge of P and an XP and we are now in a position to make more precise what the XP with which P merges is about. P merges with an XP describing a spatial configuration. To keep the formal characterization of the spatial configuration in terms of vector space semantics apart from the conceputalization of a spatial configuration as a certain relation holding between objects, we call the functional head of the XP with which P merges 'Space'. The syntactic structure of denominal verbs taking into account their spatial semantics is thus a refinement of the basic structure in (5), (6) and (7): it contains an additional functional layer SpaceP inbetween the functional PP layer and the root nP, see (9).

The syntactic structure in (9) provides two main switching points for the semantic interpretation. On the one hand, there is the Space functional layer responsible for the computation of the spatial configuration of vectors described by the verb. On the other, there is the P functional layer responsible for the conceptualization of the spatial configuration of vectors *as* a certain conceptual relation between objects. The difference is that not any vector space object can be conceptualized as a roof or a terrace, because a roof or a terrace is more than just their geometry and location, a roof is associated with a certain concept and so is a terrace. Conceptually, a roof is "a protective covering that covers or forms the top of a building" (Wordnet search, Fellbaum 1998) and a terrace is a "usually paved outdoor area adjoining a residence" (Wordnet search). That is, the function of P conceptualizing a spatial configuration is to check whether the concepts associated with the vector-space object can be coherently predicated as standing in a conceptual relation of support, application or inclusion based on the contribution of SpaceP. This is the syntactic 'locus' where the incoherent examples in (4a), (4b) and (4c) are filtered out. The structural split of formal and conceptual aspects of meaning has two welcome consequences. First, formal and conceptual aspects of meaning are not located in different places as in customary approaches that distinguish a lexicon and the syntax-semantics interface. Second, the unified treatment of formal and conceptual aspects of meaning in the same system of linguistic interpretation allows to assess the distinction between formal and conceptual aspects of meaning from a perspective that is based on linguistic evidence rather than on the distinction between lexicon and sentence that must be motivated by different evidence, e.g. assumptions about the architecture of the human cognitive system à la lexical decomposition grammar. Before we explore the issue of the relation between formal and conceptual semantics in full detail in section 4, we now turn to an in-depth analysis of three examples of spatial denominal p-verbs.

3 Example analyses

3.1 überdachen

The first example of a denominal spatial p-verb which we would like to discuss in more detail is *überdachen* as in (10). (10) is exemplary for a class of spatial denominal p-verbs involving a conceptual relation of application. This class includes verbs such as *ummauern* (to wall), *überpflastern* (to cobble), *umzäunen* (to fence in), *aufstocken* (to ramp up), *überdeckeln* (to cover with a lid), *überdecken* (to cover), *untertunneln* (to tunnel under) and *überbrücken* (to bridge).

(10) *eine Terrasse überdachen*
    a   terrace over.prfx.roof

The reconstruction (11) of (10) at the syntax-semantics interface contains only the main steps of interpretation and is thus grossly simplified. In particular, we use free variables in the lower parts of the structure that would enter the representation only higher up in a compositional analysis. The representations we use are to be understood in the spirit of those representations used in Discourse Representation Theory (Kamp et al. 2011). For *überdachen* and the next example *einlagern*, a detailed reconstruction making explicit all step of composition is given in the appendix. In (11), all constituents in the syntactic representation are in situ. Under the assumption of a functional split between formal and conceptual semantics in the syntax, we distinguish two aspects of the compositional semantic structure of p-verbs.

Measuring out the relation between formal and conceptual semantics

(11) eine Terrasse überdachen

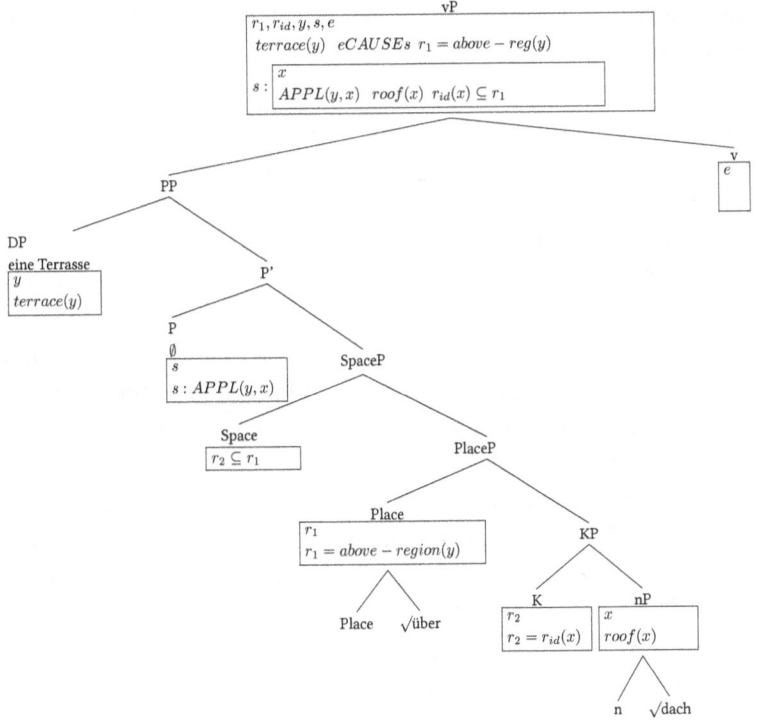

Starting at the bottom of the representation, the root √über introduces a region (indicated by the head Place) which is the above-region of the terrace. The root √dach is inserted into a nP context which is selected by KP so as to reconstruct the Eigenspace r_{id} of the entity denoted by nP. SpaceP relates the region denoted by PlaceP with the Eigenspace denoted by √dach + KP so as to express the spatial truth-conditions expressed by the phrase consisting of the p-verb and its direct object, i.e. that the Eigenspace of √dach is contained in the above region of the reference object.

On top of SpaceP, P is responsible for conceptualizing the vector space semantics calculated at SpaceP. In the present example, P conceptualizes the containment of the Eigenspace of √dach in the above region of the reference object as the application of a roof to the reference object. Conceptualization of the abstract truth-conditions at SpaceP *as* an instance of application requires that roofs and terraces are not just geometrical objects. In order to enter the conceptual application relation in a coherent way, the geometrical objects representing terrace and roof must be conceptualized *as* a terrace or roof. We will discuss our implementation of conceptual coherence in more detail in section 4.

Finally, the representation of the vP-node is to be read as follows: the state-denoting PP is merged with v, giving rise to the conceptualization as $eCAUSEs$, i.e. that the result state of the event of application described consists in the terrace y having a roof x and that the *eigenregion* of the roof, $r_{id}(x)$, is a included in the *above*-region r_1 of the terrace. The variable x and its characterising condition roof(x) are part of an inaccessible sub-DRS, representing incorporation.

What is important for the argument we want to put forward in this paper is that both conceptual and formal aspects of meaning are encoded by the same principles of semantic composition. Consequently, the difference between conceptual and formal meaning does not manifest in the same way as it does in the opposition between lexical and sentence meaning. Rather, what the analysis of *überdachen* suggests is that the distinction of conceptual and formal meaning is more fine-grained than the binary lexical vs. sentence distinction. In particular, the way in which we represented the semantics of *überdachen* encodes both formal and conceptual aspects of meaning linguistically, i.e. without recurse to a language-independent structuring of conceptual predicates. For *überdachen*, we located the contribution of conceptual meaning in the constraints that conceptualization puts on the interpretation of formal meaning, i.e. in the selection of appropriate denominal roots, prefixes and direct objects. *überdachen* constitutes a case in which such selection restrictions are relevant to all constituents of verbal phrases in which *überdachen* occurs. We will see in the next two examples that this does not always need to be the case.

3.2 einlagern

The next example which we would like to discuss in more detail is *einlagern* (to store). (12) is exemplary for a class of p-verbs involving the conceptual relation of location, among them *einsacken* (to bag sth.), *einsperren* (to cage), *einkellern* (to store), *einkerkern* (to incarcerate).

(12) *eine Flasche (in den Keller) einlagern*
    a   bottle (in the cellar) in.prtc.store
    put a bottle in the cellar

einlagern is a particle verb, see (13).

(13) Peter lagert die Flasche ein
     Peter store.V a   bottle   in.prtc
     Peter stores a bottle

Syntactically, the particle verb *einlagern* has a particle-phrase *p*P on top of the denominal vP, see (15). This construction prevents the incorporation of the particle *ein* into the verb via the head movement constraint. The *p*P contributes the information that the bottle becomes stored inside a location. It should be noted that even if the location in which the direct object of *einlagern* ends up is not mentioned explicitly, it is nevertheless presupposed part of the meaning of *einlagern* that there is a distinct location inside of which the object to be stored ends up. The interior space of the denominal root can be picked up with a locative PP such as *in den Keller* (in the cellar), compare (12). To see why the constraint that the final location of the direct object ends up inside the space provided by the nominal root is contributed by the particle *ein*, consider the verb *lagern* without the particle as in (14).

(14) Peter lagert Holz auf dem Boden
     Peter store.V wood on the ground
     Peter stores wood on the ground

Lagern on its own does not come with the requirement that its direct object must be located inside the space provided by its nominal root, because any distinct place will be suitable to store an object. Geometrically, *lagern* requires that its direct object is located in space relative to another object or landmark. This boils down to the requirement that the direct object has an Eigenspace and that this Eigenspace can be located in space. In contrast, the contribution of *ein* in *einlagern* is that it additionally requires that the direct object is located inside a store and not just at a certain location. That is, the difference between *lagern* and *einlagern* is that *lagern* only requires a specified location of the direct object where it remains for some contextually specified time whereas *einlagern* makes explicit that the direct object is moved into a certain place. Consequently, in the *p*P structure, we have a figure-ground relation between the bottle and the cellar, where the bottle ends up in the cellar.

Semantically, the specific syntax of the particle construction in which the contribution of the particle *ein* is considered only above the denominal vP leads to a configuration in which there are two states s_1 and s_2 responsible for the conceptualization of two dependent geometrical configurations. s_2 represents that state which conceptualizes the location of the direct object with respect to the denominal root. s_1 further specifies this location as a location inside the space provided by the denominal root. However, the states s_1 and s_2 are result states of the same event event e. That is, particle constructions of the type exemplified by *einlagern* involve a 'double predication' of the result state relative to the denominal root. We thus assume that s_1 and s_2 are unified as results of the event defined by the merge of *p*P and vP but are semantically distinct.

What is important to the goals of this paper is that in (12) the conceptualization of the geometry with LOC resp. IN does not impose restrictions which are not already structurally conveyed at SpaceP, namely that the location of the bottle is fixed with respect to a certain region or place: $at(r_1, r_2)$ and that the Eigenspace of the bottle is included in the Eigenspace of the store $r_1 \subseteq r_2$. In other words, unlike in (*überdachen*), the conceptual meaning of *einlagern* does not effect interpretation in the form selection restrictions on possible fillers of the argument slot for the direct object.

Measuring out the relation between formal and conceptual semantics

(15) eine Flasche in einen Keller einlagern

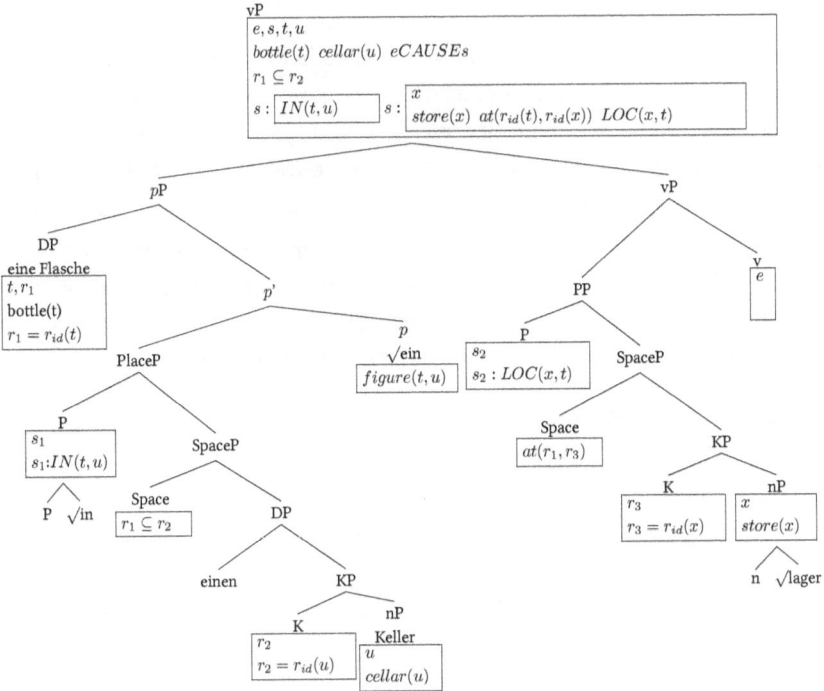

3.3 abstützen

The final example (16) is exemplary of a class of denominal p-verbs which involves the conceptual relation of SUPPORT, among them *aufbocken* (to jack up), *verstreben* (to strut), *untermauern* (to support), *unterfüttern* (to reline), *aufkanten* (to tilt sth.) and *aufbahren* (to lay sb. out).

(16) einen Dachstuhl abstützen
    a   truss   under.prtc.stilt
    to prop up a truss

Like *einlagern*, *abstützen* is a particle verb and thus has a similar syntax and semantics in which a particle phrase is merged with a denominal verb phrase and the denominal root is subject to double predication by both the verb and the particle. Despite these structural similarities, the the contribution of the particle

135

structure with √ab as its prepositional element is of a different nature than the contribution of *ein* in *einlagern*.

We propose that the geometrical relation involved in the reconstruction of (16) is a relation of contact between an object x and a face r of another object. We represent contact between x and r as $x@r \rightsquigarrow (r_{id}(x) \bigcap r \neq \emptyset))$. But for the conceptualization of SUPPORT, geometrical contact between objects is not enough because there are lots of geometrical contact relations which are not relations of support, e.g. a bubblegum adhering at the bottom of a table has contact with a face of the table but it does not support the table. Instead, the conceptualization of SpaceP with the relation $SUPPORT$ between the nominal root √stütz (pillar, stilt), the particle *ab* and the direct object *Dachstuhl* is quite complex in (17).

(17) einen Dachstuhl abstützen

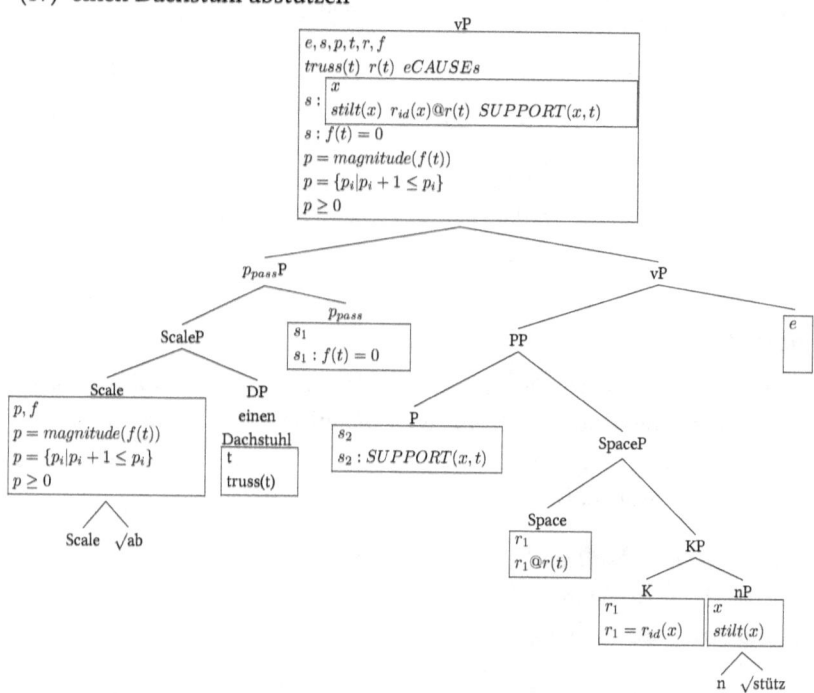

To identify the specific contribution of the particle *ab*, let us consider the vP branch of the structure representing the contribution of the nominal root √stütz. The vP branch derives the verb *stützen* (to support) as in (18).

Measuring out the relation between formal and conceptual semantics

(18) einen Patienten stützen
 a   patient   stilt.V
 to support a patient

stützen does not imply that the force exerted on the direct object is completely absorbed but the direct object itself absorbs some portion of the forces exerted on it. In contrast, the contribution of the particle *ab* in *abstützen* is that the forces exerted on the direct object are completely absorbed in the course of the event described. Conceptually, we model this contribution of *ab* in terms of *ab* contributing a decreasing scale $p = \{p_i | p_i + 1 \leq p_i\}$ of magnitudes of the net force $f(t)$ exerted on the direct object t. From this point of view, what *abstützen* describes is an event which is made up from a sequence of change of states each of which results in a lower point on the scale of net forces exerted on the truss. In plain words, *abstützen* describes an event of incremental reduction of the net force exerted on its direct object. This event is bounded by a particular state, namely that state in which the net force exerted on the truss becomes zero. The approach we just sketched receives further support from constructions in which the incremental nature of the supporting event and its boundedness is made explicit with a *mit*/(with)-PPs involving *genügend* (sufficient) as a description of the event boundary, see (19)

(19) den Dachstuhl mit genügend Balken abstützen
 the truss   with sufficient timber under.prtc.stilt
 to support a truss sufficiently with timber

We render the intuitions about the contribution of the *ab*-particle with a construction in which a p_{pass} head quantifies over a sequence of states of decreased net force and the event modified with *ab* pertains to the sum of the states quantified by p_{pass}. Formally, our analysis in (17) is based on (Roßdeutscher 2012,2013b)'s proposal for such 'passive' *p* constructions. In analogy to verbal passives where the agent is demoted and the theme is promoted, in passive *p*-constructions the figure is demoted and the ground is promoted. For *einlagern*, the direct object is the figure whereas the nominal root plays the role of the ground. In *abstützen*, there is no explicit figure. Instead, the ground (if we would still call it like this) – the truss – is promoted as the direct object of *abstützen*: different from *einen Keller* in (15), which receives prepositional accusative case, *einen Dachstuhl* does not and leaves the p_{pass}-phrase in order to receive accusative case in vP.

The semantic effect of p_{pass} is a quantification over the elements of the implicit resp. demoted figure, i.e. the decrease in net force on the truss that the timber stilts that are moved into the below-region of the truss bring with them. The effect of this quantification is boundedness of the event description: the totality of timber stilts exerts a force on the truss which renders the net force on the truss zero and thus, as a result of the event described, the truss is supported in upholding against gravity. (17) represents the semantic constribution of p_{pass} in a simplified manner, leaving out the details of the quantification over states represented on the scale of net forces exerted on the truss. Additional complexity is introduced in the analysis by the fact that *abstützen* is, just like *einlagern*, a particle verb and thus the semantics involves the same kind of 'double-predication' of the result state of the event predicated in vP. That is, similar to the predication of the nominal root $\sqrt{}$lager in *einlagern* (12), the *mit*-PP in (19) reintroduces the incorporated nominal root $\sqrt{}$stütz.

What is important to note from the discussion of *abstützen* and the involved conceptualization with SUPPORT is that formal meaning is by far not enough to capture what the conceptual meaning of SUPPORT is about. For SUPPORT, the additional conceptual machinery of force dynamics has to be invoked to grasp the meaning of constructions involving *abstützen*, which sets it apart from the relation between formal and conceptual meaning in both *einlagern* and *überdachen*, an observation which we explore in full detail in the next section.

4 Selection Restrictions

With respect to the case under consideration, in our discussion of the relation between formal and conceptual semantics, we focus on conceptual coherence pertaining to the restrictions imposed on the selection of appropriate fillers of a conceptual relation, in the case under discussion the nominal root of the verb and the direct object of the verb. For example, not any objects will afford the selection restrictions involved in *überdachen* imposed by the application relation. Basically, there are two cases to be distinguished. First, it may be the case that the nominal root of the verb fails to satisfy the selection restrictions imposed by the conceptual application relation as in (20).

(20) ?eine Terasse unterdachen
   a   terrace under.prfx.roof

While *unterdachen* as in (20) is superficially similar to *überdachen*, there is an important conceptual difference between the two. If a roof is conceptualized as being an object in the above region of the object which it protects, then the combination of *dach* with *über* is conceptually coherent. But for (20), this conceptualization runs into a problem: a roof cannot be conceptualized as being in the below region of the object with respect to which it is conceptualized as a roof. That is, although *unterdachen* is perfectly acceptable from a formal point of view, conceptualization rules out *unterdachen* as a possible word. The second case of selection restrictions applies to the conceptualization of *überdachen* with respect to the direct object *Terasse*. This conceptualization requires that the direct object can be conceptualized as an object which provides a bounded 'above-region' in order for the roof to be applied: a terrace fulfills these restrictions whereas a basement does not. *einen Keller überdachen* as in (21) is conceptually incoherent because a basement is usually not conceptualized as providing an above region in which another object can be placed, and thus selection restrictions rule out *Keller* as a suitable direct object of *überdachen*.

(21) *einen Keller   überdachen
   a   basement over.prfx.roof

The argument that we develop in the following pertains to the relation between the degree of selectivity on direct objects imposed by the conceptual relation involved in the reconstruction of a p-verb and characterization of the three different types of conceptual relations that we introduced with our examples: (a) a conceptual relation of support as in *abstützen*, (b) a conceptual relation of application as in *überdachen* and (c) a conceptual relation of location as in *einlagern*. When we reconsider the relation between the geometric truth-conditions, i.e. the spatial configurations expressed by each of these verbs and the conceptual relation involved, then it appears that each of the verbs exemplifies a different proportion between the role of conceptual and formal meaning. For the geometrical relation of location inside a region as in *einlagern*, conceptualization with LOC does not impose any additional constraints on direct objects which are not already conveyed in terms of geometrical constraints. What is important to *einlagern* is only that the direct object fits into the space provided by the store, not conceptual properties of the direct object. For *überdachen*, conceptual properties of the direct object are relevant: as we saw with *Keller*, the direct object must be associated with a concept that provides a bounded above region into which the roof can be applied. Consequently, selection restrictions play a role for *überdachen* in that only a certain class of objects will be accepted. Finally, the strongest conceptual contribution can be found with support relations as in *abstützen*. The conceptualization of support involves conceptual properties that allow for the computation of forces and as such involve additional knowledge about gravitation and physics. Consequently, support p-verbs are quite restrictive with respect to their possible direct objects: e.g. direct objects must not absorb gravitational forces on their own in order to be propped up. These observations on the divergence between geometry and concepts in p-verbs suggest a measure on the relation between formal and conceptual semantics as follows.

Any well-formed logical form has an interpretation but not any interpretation of a well-formed logical form is conceptually coherent. Logical forms (whatever their extension is, individuals or geometrical objects) employed in truth-conditional semantics are insensitive to conceptual coherence. What distinguishes formal and conceptual semantics in our approach is not the distinction between lexicon and sentence but their respective contribution to the meaning of a construction. That is, if selection restrictions (i.e. restrictions pertaining to content) are the contribution of conceptual semantics and truth-conditions (i.e. restrictions pertaining to structure) are the contributions of formal semantics, then the relation between formal and conceptual semantics shows up in the contribution of selection restrictions on the fillers of argument positions of a logical form: selection restrictions reflect the contribution of conceptual semantics in the instantiation of a logical form. Consequently, the stronger conceptual restrictions are imposed on the selection of fillers of argument slots of logical forms, the more emphasis is put on conceptual structures in the meaning of the logical form. This hypothesis has a direct reflection in our pervasive approach of semantics. Instead of a divide between conceptual meaning in the lexicon and truth-conditional meaning in sentences, in our approach there is a continuum of relations between truth-conditions and conceptual structure with verbs such as *einlagern* focusing formal semantics and structural constraints on the one and verbs such as *abstützen* focusing conceptual semantics and selection restrictions on the other end.

Given the argument of the last paragraph, we expect that if application, support and inclusion *are* different conceptual relations, this difference shows up in terms of different selectional preference strength. That is, we expect that there is a correlation between the conceptual relation involved in the reconstruction of word meaning and the selectional preference strength of the verb. Consequently, we can measure the relation between formal and conceptual semantics in considering the selectional strength of conceptual relations against the insensitivity of logical forms to conceptual coherence. In our examples, we predict that conceptual relations are ordered according to their selectional preference strength, from strong to weak: $SUPPORT > APPL > LOC$. We saw that LOC in *einlagern* does not involve conceptual restrictions which are not already captured by the truth-conditions of geometrical inclusion: for putting an object in a store, it does not matter which concept is associated with the object to be stored as long as the geometry of the stored object can be included in the geometry of the store. We also saw that $APPL$ in *überdachen* involves a relevant conceptual restriction on the objects standing in the application relation which is not captured by the truth-conditions of geometrical inclusion: the direct object must have an above region with distinct boundaries. Finally, $SUPPORT$ in *abstützen* does not only involve conceptual constraints on the objects which stand in the support relation but also requires to take into account the additional concept of force dynamics. *abstützen* requires appropriate direct objects to be possible subject to the laws of gravity and to provide a below region.

5   A statistical measure for selectivity

The point we want to make with our analysis is the following: in our framework, there is a *linguistic* measure for the relation between formal and conceptual semantics in terms of selection restrictions, which exemplify the relation between conceptual semantics sensitive to conceptual coherence and truth-conditions insensitive to conceptual coherence. According to our proposal, if conceptual relations manifest linguistically in the strength of selection restrictions and selectional association, conceptual predicates may be considered as a stepping stone towards the linguistic exploration of conceptual meaning. In our approach, conceptual meaning can be defined linguistically without reference to conceptual structures in the first instance. Instead, our notion of conceptual meaning paves the way to a classification of concepts based on empirical observations (for p-verbs see e.g. Rüd 2012, Springorum et al. 2012), where conceptual predicates are labels for degrees of selection preference strength. Empirically, our hypothesis can be tested with the help of the observation of the relative entropy of verbs and the conceptual class of their direct objects as proposed by Resnik (1996). Resnik (1996) approaches selection restrictions as the degree to which a pair of a verb and a syntactic relationship, here direct object, constraints possible conceptual classes of fillers of the argument slots of the syntactic relationship.

The intuition behind Resnik's selectional preference strength (SPS) is that a verb-relation pair that only allows for a limited range of direct objects will have a posterior distribution of conceptual classes of direct objects in which the verb is taken into account that strongly diverges from the prior distribution of conceptual classes of direct objects in which the verb is not taken into account. In order to quantify the degree of restrictions in a verb-relation pair, the overall probability distribution of noun classes is compared to the distribution of noun classes in the direct object position of the verb. Technically, this is achieved by calculating the relative entropy (the Leibler-Kullback divergence) D of two distributions, the prior distribution $P(c|r)$ and the posterior distribution $P(c|v,r)$. The parameters $P(c|r)$ and $P(c|v,r)$ can be estimated from the corpus frequencies of tuples (v,r,a) and the membership of nouns a in GermaNet classes c.

(22)
$$SPS(v,r) = D(P(c|v,r)||P(c|r)))$$
$$= \sum_{c \in C} P(c|v,r) \log \frac{P(c|v,r)}{P(c|r)}$$

Resnik's approach relies on Wordnet for the generalization from direct objects to conceptual classes, but it should be noted that selection restrictions can be induced without lexical resources by using e.g. co-occurence for the generalization step (Erk & Padó 2010).

Measuring out the relation between formal and conceptual semantics

6 Testing our predictions on Corpus Data

Verb	Concept	SPS(4)	SPS(7)
einlagern	IN	0.1	0.2
einsperren	IN	0.7	0.9
überbrücken	APPL	0.6	2.0
überdachen	APPL	0.8	4.1
abstützen	SUPP	1.3	8.0
aufbocken	SUPP	1.7	4.9

Table 1: Selectional Preference Strength SPS(n) for selected p-verbs with respect to mappings of direct objects to GermaNet Classes of level n, counting levels from the top-level concept.

To give the reader a first impression of how Resnik's Selectional Preference Strength relates to our predictions, we conducted a proof-of-concept study. First, we estimated the prior distribution of nouns occuring in the direct object position of verbs mapped to GermaNet Classes (Hamp & Feldweg 1997) from the first 200.000.000 sentences of SdeWac (Faaß & Eckart 2013). Second, we extracted pairs of p-verbs and their direct objects with accusative case from SdeWac, manually disambiguated the set of direct objects to those objects which do not imply a metaphorical or non-spatial usage of the verb and mapped the remaining direct objects to GermaNet Classes in order to calculate the posterior probability of a GermaNet Class to occur in the direct object position of a p-verb. Table 1 shows the results for some of the verbs for which we were able to acquire enough instances which were covered by GermaNet. The higher the SPS of a verb, the more restrictions it imposes on possible fillers of its direct object argument slot. Intuitively, the data in table 1 reproduces our predictions quite well. P-verbs such as *aufbahren* or *aufbocken* are quite restrictive with respect to the type of direct objects they accept. In fact, *aufbocken* selects for land vehicles and *abstützen* selects for physical objects such as buildings. *einlagern* and *einsperren* on the other hand select for a wide range of GermaNet classes of direct objects and thus receive a lower SPS number.

7 Summary

We introduced a pervasive approach to semantics which does not postulate a structural distinction between lexicon and sentence. We proposed that in our framework, the relation between formal and conceptual semantics can be measured out empirically in terms of selectional preference strength.

References

Adger, D. 2003. *Core syntax*. Oxford: Oxford University Press.

Alexiadou, A. 2001. *Functional structure in nominals. Nominalization and ergativity*. John Benjamins.

Asher, N. 2011. *Lexical meaning in context: A web of words*. Cambridge: Cambridge University Press.

Bierwisch, M. 2007. Semantic form as interface. In A. Späth (ed.). *Interfaces and interface conditions*. 1–32. de Gruyter.

Borer, H. 2005. *Structuring sense*. Vol. I & II. Oxford: Oxford University Press.

Chomsky, N. 1995. *The minimalist program*. Cambridge, MA: MIT Press.

Cooper, R. 1983. *Quantification and syntactic theory*. Dordrecht: Reidel.

Erk, K. & S. Padó. 2010. A flexible, corpus-driven model of regular and inverse selectional preferences. *Computational Linguistic* 36(4). 723–763.

Faaß, G. & K. Eckart. 2013. SdeWaC - a corpus of parsable sentences from the web. In I. Gurevych, C. Biemann & T. Zesch (eds.). *Language Processing and Knowledge in the Web*. Proceedings of the 25th International Conference, GSCL 2013. LNAI. Springer.

Fellbaum, C. 1998. *Wordnet: An electronic lexical database*. Bradford Books.

Fillmore, C. J. 1982. Frame semantics. In T. L. S of Korea (ed.). *Linguistics in the morning calm. Selected papers from SICOL-1981*. Seoul: Hanshin.

Hale, K. & S. J. Keyser. 1993. On argument structure and the lexical expression of syntactic relations. In K. Hale & S. J. Keyser (eds.). *The view from building 20: Essays in linguistics in honor of Sylvain Bromberger*. Cambridge, MA: MIT Press.

Hamm, F., H. Kamp & M. van Lambalgen. 2006. There is no opposition between formal and cognitive semantics.

Hamp, B. & H. Feldweg. 1997. GermaNet - a lexical-semantic net for German. In *Proceedings of the ACL workshop automatic information extraction and building of lexical semantic resources for NLP applications*. Madrid.

Harley, H. 2009. The morphology of nominalizations and the syntax of vP. In A. Giannakidou & Rathert M. (eds.). *Quantification, definiteness, and nominalization*. Oxford University Press.

Harley, H. 2011. A minimalist approach of argument structure. In C. Boeckx (ed.). *The Oxford handbook of linguistic minimalism*. Oxford University Press.

Kamp, H., J. van Genabith & U. Reyle. 2011. Discourse Representation Theory. In D. M. Gabbay & F. Guenthner (eds.). *Handbook of philosophical logic*. Vol. 15. 125 – 394. Springer 2nd edition.

Kaufmann, I. 1995. *Konzeptuelle Grundlagen semantischer Dekompositionsstrukturen. Die Kombinatorik lokaler Verben und prädikativer Komplemente*. Vol. 335. Tübingen: Niemeyer.

Kratzer, A. 1996. Severing the external argument from its verb. In J. Rooryck & L. A. Zaring (eds.). *Phrase structure and the lexicon*. 109–137. Dordrecht: Kluwer Academic Publishers.

Marantz, A. 1997. No escape from syntax: Don't try morphological analysis in the privacy of your own lexicon. *U. Penn Working Papers in Linguistics* 4.2.

Pustejovsky, J. 2001. Type construction and the logic of concepts. In F. Busa (ed.). *The language of word meaning*. 91–123. Cambridge: Cambridge University Press. http://dx.doi.org/10.1017/CBO9780511896316.009.

Rappaport Hovav, M. & B. Levin. 1998. Building verb meanings. In M. Butt & W. Geuder (eds.). *The projection of arguments: Lexical and compositional factors*. 97–134. Stanford: CSLI.

Resnik, P. 1996. Selectional constraints: an information-theoretic model and its computational realization. *Cognition* 61. 127–159.

Roßdeutscher, A. 2011. Particle verbs and prefix verbs in German: Linking theory versus word-syntax. *Leuvense Bijdragen* 97.

Roßdeutscher, A. 2012. Hidden quantification in prefix and particle verbs. In *Proceedings of Sinn und Bedeutung 16*. Vol. 2. 513–526. Utrecht: MIT WPL.

Roßdeutscher, A. 2013a. Denominal spatial prefix-verbs revisited. In A. Roßdeutscher (ed.). *Sub-Lexical Investigations: German particles, prefixes and prepositions*. Working Papers of the SFB 732 (SinSpec). Vol. 11. 58–88. University of Stuttgart.

Roßdeutscher, A. 2013b. A syntax-semantics interface for P-elements in german verbal constructions. In A. Roßdeutscher (ed.). *Sub-Lexical Investigations: German particles, prefixes and prepositions.* Working Papers of the SFB 732 (SinSpec). Vol. 11. 1–57. University of Stuttgart.

Roßdeutscher, A. & H. Kamp. 2010. Syntactic and semantic constraints in the formation and interpretation of ung-nouns. In *Nominalisations across languages and frameworks.* Berlin: Mouton de Gruyter.

Rüd, S. 2012. *Untersuchung der distributionellen Eigenschaften der Lesarten der Partikel 'auf' mittels Clustering-Methoden.* Unpublished master's Thesis. IMS, University of Stuttgart.

Springorum, S., S. Schulte im Walde & A. Roßdeutscher. 2012. Automatic classification of German *an* particle verbs. In *Proceedings of LREC-2012.* Istanbul.

Stiebels, B. 1998. Complex denominal verbs in German and the morphology-semantics interface. *Yearbook of Morphology.* 265–302.

Svenonius, P. 2003. Limits on p: *filling in holes* vs. *falling in holes. Nordlyd* 2. 431–445.

Travis, L. 1984. *Parameters and effects of word order variation.* Unpublished doctoral dissertation. MIT.

Wunderlich, D. 1991. How do prepositional phrases fit into compositional syntax and semantics. *Linguistics* 29. 591–621.

Wunderlich, D. 2012. Lexical decomposition in grammar. In M. Werning, W. Hinzen & E. Machery (eds.). *Oxford handbook of compositionality.* 307–327. Oxford University Press.

Zwarts, J. 1997. Vectors as relative positions: A compositional semantics of modified PPs. *Journal of Semantics* 14. 57–86.

Zwarts, J. 2005. Prepositional aspect and the algebra of paths. *Linguistics and Philosophy* 28. 739–779.

Zwarts, J. & Y. Winter. 2000. Vector space semantics: A model-theoretic analysis of locative prepositions. *Journal of Logic, Language, and Information* 9. 169–211.

A. Detailed Analyses

For the detailed representation of *überdachen* and *einlagern* in this section, we use an extension of a basic DRT language (Kamp et al. 2011) with presuppositions and a λ-calculus for variable stores (Cooper 1983). λ-conversion selects the leftmost variable from the store. The storing of variables instead of immediate existantialization allows for a greater flexibility in the derivational process when it is necessary to distinguish between the introduction of existentially quantified discourse referents and manipulations of variables for discourse referents. A Discourse Representation Structure (DRS) K with a presupposition P, λ-abstracted variables x, y and a store v, z is represented as in (23). For more details on the semantic formalism, see (Roßdeutscher 2013b).

(23) $\lambda x.\lambda y. \langle \{P\} \langle v, z\ K \rangle \rangle$

The composition of DRSs is governed by applying λ-conversion and consequent merge of DRSs at each node of the syntactic structure. For example, the composition at the bottom of (27) on page 147 consists of a DRS taking a predicate (represented with capital letters) as an argument.

(24) $\lambda P \langle x, \boxed{P(x)} \rangle$ + $\sqrt{}$dach $\rightarrow$ $\lambda x \boxed{roof(x)}$

Also, at each node in the composition it is checked whether presuppositions can be resolved by considering the new information made available. For example, when P' is merged with the DP introducing the direct object in (27), the presupposition $\{\boxed{z}\}$ introduced by the root $\sqrt{}$über is resolved to the discourse referent introduced with the direct object DP.

The introduction of discourse referents for states captures incorporation in that all conditions involving discourse referents predicated by the state are relocated into an inaccessible sub-DRS K representing the semantic content of the state. For example, when P and SpaceP are merged with the predication of a state in (27), all conditions and existentializations involving discourse referents affected by the conceptual predicate APPL are grouped together in a new sub-DRS, thus rendering the nominal root $\sqrt{}$dach inaccessible as a discourse referent:

(25) $\langle x, \boxed{roof(x)} \rangle + \lambda u.\lambda y. \boxed{\begin{array}{l} s \\ s : \boxed{APPL(y,u)} \end{array}} \rightarrow \lambda y. \boxed{\begin{array}{l} s \quad x \\ s : \boxed{\begin{array}{l} APPL(y,x) \\ roof(x) \end{array}} \end{array}}$

In example (28), we use a version of Kratzer (1996)'s event identification principle applied to prepositional phrases in order to chain together the internal 'Ground' argument of a preposition and its figure. The referential argument to be identified is a set of vectors v and the thematic role to be added is that of a Figure, see (26). Spatial refential arguments are existentialized at pP.

(26) $\lambda x.\lambda v. \boxed{figure(x,v)} + \lambda v. \boxed{\begin{array}{l} u \\ IN(u,v) \end{array}} \rightarrow \lambda x.\lambda v. \boxed{\begin{array}{l} u \\ IN(u,v) \\ figure(x,v) \end{array}}$

Measuring out the relation between formal and conceptual semantics

A.1. überdachen

(27) eine Terasse überdachen, full analysis

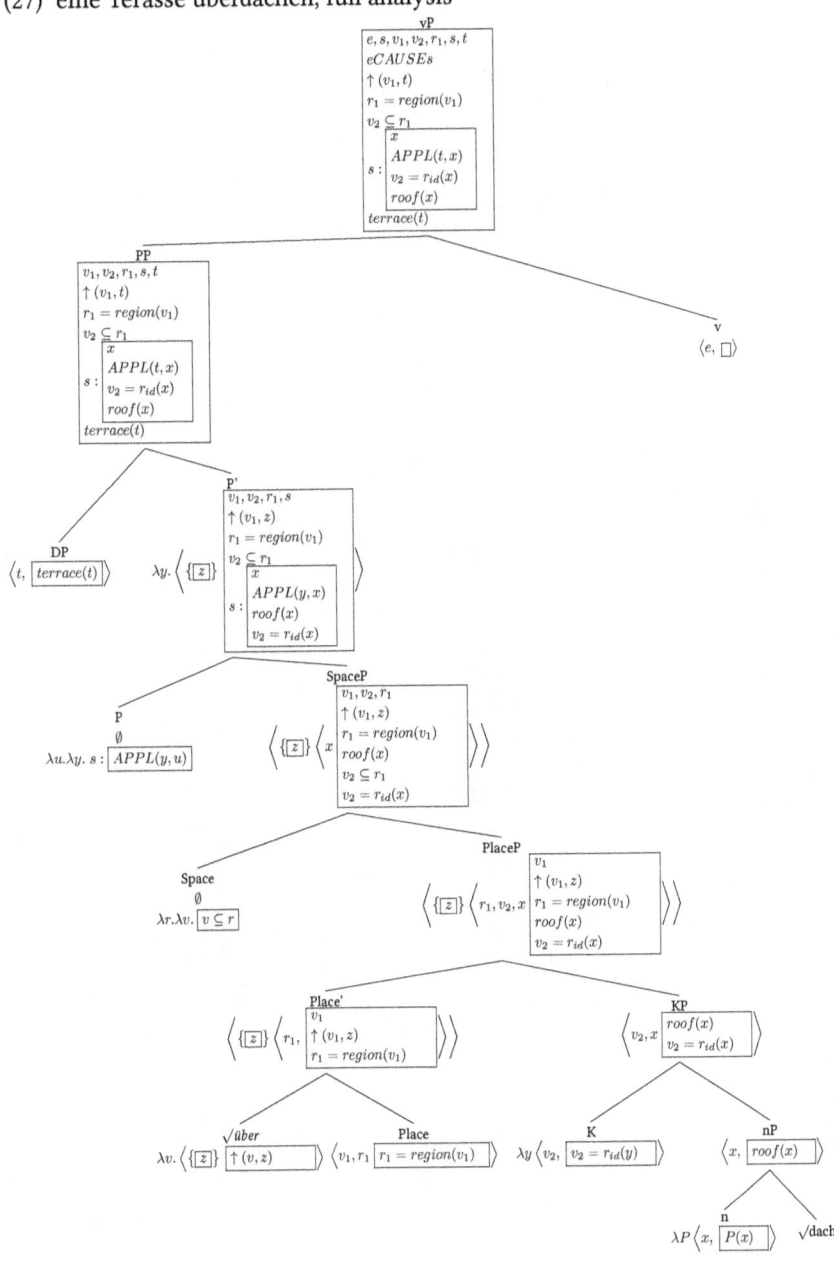

A.2. einlagern

(28) eine Flasche in den Keller ein(lagern), pP branch

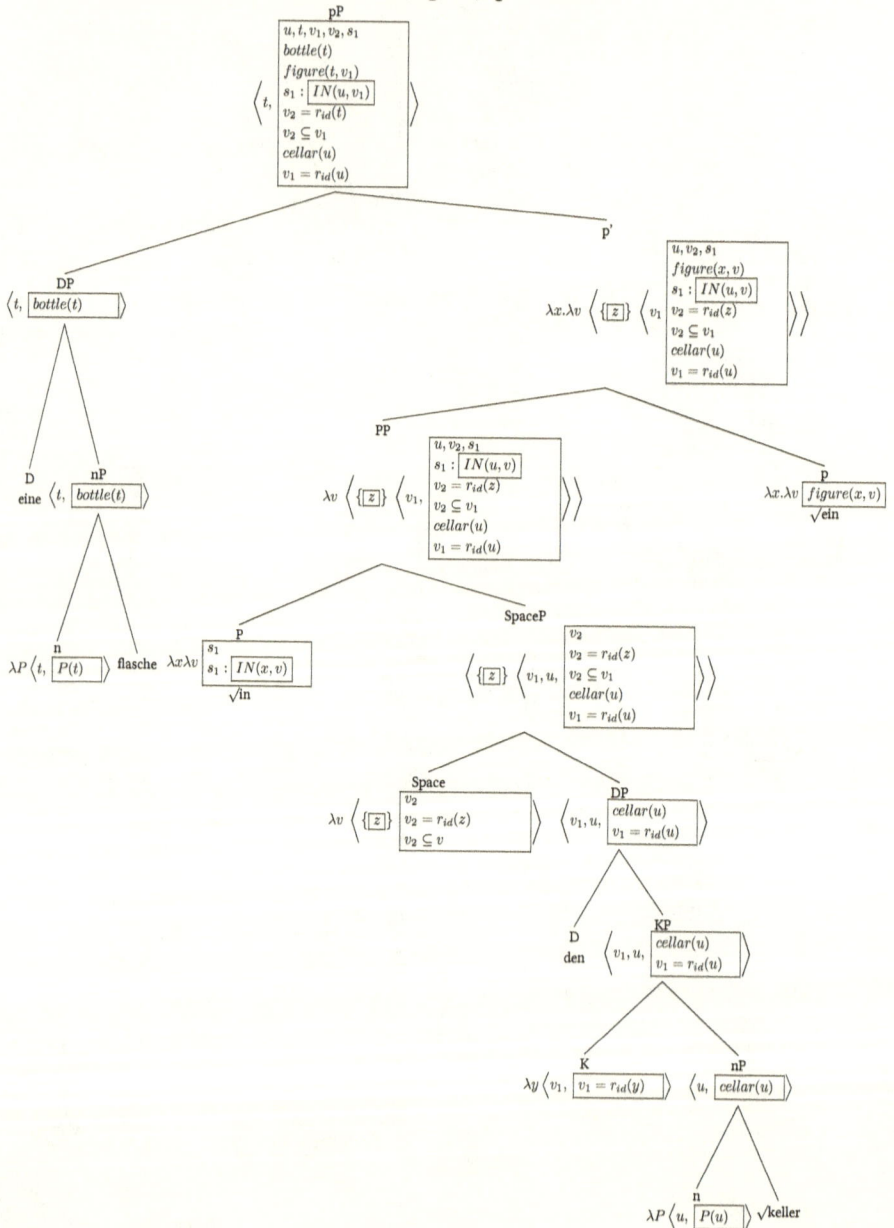

Measuring out the relation between formal and conceptual semantics

(29) (eine Flasche in den Keller ein)lagern, vP branch

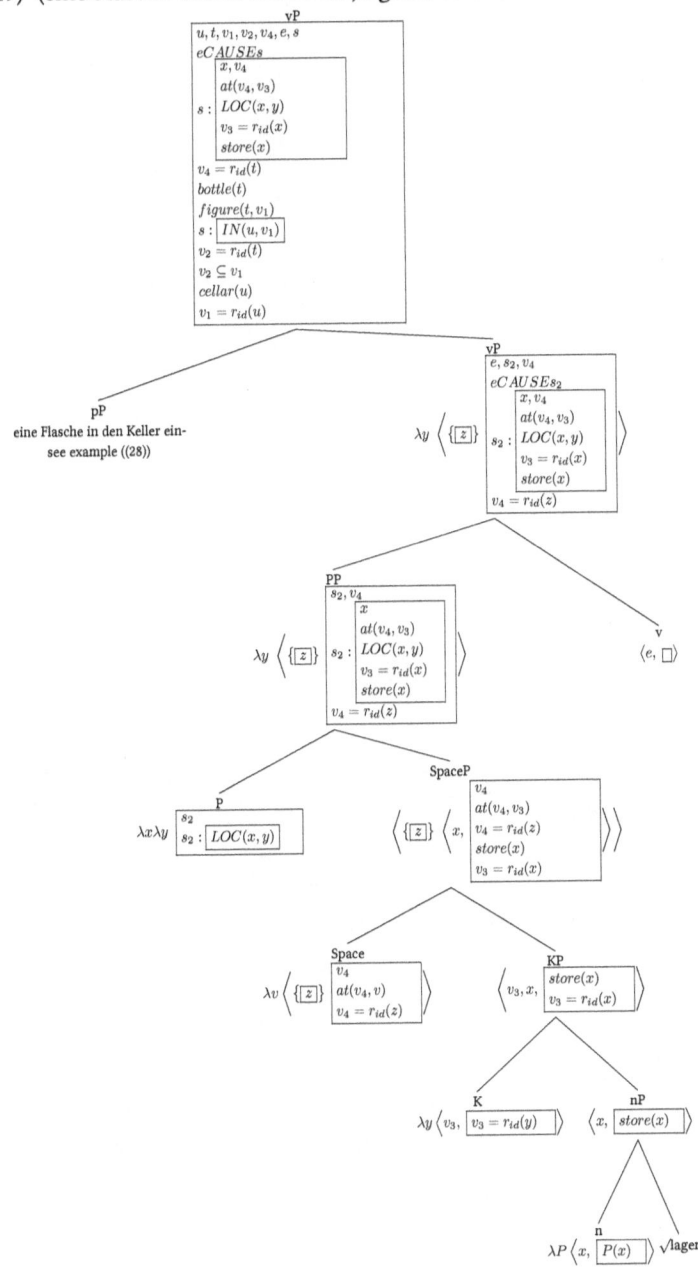

Authors

Tillmann Pross
IMS, Universität Stuttgart
tillmann.pross@ims.uni-stuttgart.de

Antje Roßdeutscher
IMS, Universität Stuttgart
antje@ims.uni-stuttgart.de

Representing the Lexicon: Identifying Meaning in Use via Overspecification

Henk Zeevat, Scott Grimm, Lotte Hogeweg, Sander Lestrade & E. Allyn Smith[*]

1 Lexical Specification and Meaning in Use: Traditional Views on the Lexicon

Traditionally, the lexicon is the list of words of a language or communication system. From a biological perspective, the lexica of human languages are special with respect to animal communication systems because they can be freely extended, both by the creation of new (lexical) forms and by the extension of the meaning of these words. Notwithstanding this extensibility, the construction of dictionaries as fixed lists of words with their meanings pays off for the purposes of language education, reliable communication and translation.

Computational models of language largely share this view, as it seems initially reasonable to think that such a lexicon could be part of what characterizes the human ability to code thoughts into linguistic expressions and to recover thoughts from such expressions. What is needed for conventional dictionaries—in the tradition started by such eminent scholars as Samuel Johnson and Jacob Grimm—is precision with respect to the characterization of the word senses described. Such a task would be

---

[*] We wish to express our thanks to audiences at Szklarska Poreba, the Workshop Bridging Formal and Conceptual Semantics, and Formal Semantics Meets Cognitive Semantics as well as to Katrin Erk, to Louise McNally and, especially, to an anonymous reviewer of these proceedings for many useful comments, more, in fact, than we could integrate into this preliminary report. In addition, Lotte Hogeweg and Sander Lestrade would like to thank the the Netherlands Organization for Scientific Research (NWO) for their financial support. All errors are our own. Authors after the first author are listed in alphabetical order.

difficult with an entailment-based semantics only, since many word senses include connotations that are usually but not always associated with an utterance of that word. However, abandoning formal semantic approaches ignores the fact that the senses distinguished by lexicographers do often reflect truth-conditional differences, e.g. *Anna went to the bank* would entail 'Anna was very near a flowing body of water' in one of the word *bank*'s senses but not another. We contend that a formal account would need to distinguish as many senses as traditional dictionaries do, and one goal of the present paper is to suggest some steps toward such an account.

The main challenge faced by lexicographers and semanticists alike with respect to characterizing word senses precisely is lexical disambiguation. Given the large number of senses that dictionaries distinguish for the same word, one needs a cognitively plausible account of the fact that listeners only rarely interpret the sense of a word in a way unintended by the speaker. Suppose that the list of word senses were simply a list and that lexicalisation meant just choosing a word for a concept. Now suppose further that all concepts linked to a word after lexicalisation were listed with it and that disambiguation occurred by making a random choice from the list of senses. In this case, the chance of speaker-hearer coordination would be very small, namely 1 divided by the number of word senses of the item in question.

Given that this is not what we find, a natural extension to such a simplistic model would be to include stochastic data with the senses. The first type of stochastic data to consider would be the relative frequency of the senses (such as the fact that 'financial institution' is perhaps more frequent than 'river bank' as the intended meaning of *bank* in industrialized societies), but this by itself would predict that the best choice would always be to select the most frequent sense, so the very existence of the other senses makes this option implausible. A second stochastic approach in line with recent proposals (Baroni et al. 2014, Erk 2014) also includes frequency data about the words that a given sense is likely to combine with (the "distributional semantics" of the sense). For example, the presence of words like *deposit* and *savings* around the word *bank* will bias the financial institution interpretation. The option of adding distributional semantics to senses needs further study. It is, however, our suspicion that this will only work properly in combination with a decompositional approach to senses because decomposition would be needed for estimates in the presence of data scarceness. These distributional approaches nevertheless aim to solve the same problem that we address in this paper, namely that of predicting the meaning of lexical items in use (i.e. in the speech contexts in which they appear), but they use a different representation of lexical knowledge than the one we advocate here.

The approach pursued in this paper tries to exploit semantic decomposition of word senses to arrive at a cognitive representation that is effective in selecting the meaning in use: one of a word's potentially many senses that should be listed in a full traditional dictionary. In some respects our approach is in line with other more linguistically-oriented approaches to lexical representations. For example, it shares the assumption of decomposability of word senses with cognitive approaches such as Jackendoff's Conceptual Semantics (e.g. Jackendoff 1996). It is similar to more formal theories like Pustejovsky's (1995) Generative Lexicon and Blutner's (2004) Lexical Pragmatics in its aim to systematically account for meaning alternations. Our approach differs from these approaches in that, in our proposal, words typically overspecify their meanings, and it is the combination with context that trims the overspecified meaning down to the meaning in use, i.e. the word sense that applies. The meaning in use may be determined by earlier language use, but it can also be computed for the first time.

After a discussion of semantic features in the following section, we examine previous accounts of overspecification of meaning upon which we build. We provide an analysis of lexical items in terms of stochastic sets of features in section 3, with an extended treatment of the verb *fall* in English, Dutch and German, which demonstrates how one overspecified representation can apply in different contexts resulting in different word senses. In section 5, we then discuss the issue of overgeneration and the subsequent need to put constraints on the production of words, in turn defining the lexicalization process. We conclude in section 6.

2 Semantic Features and Moderate Universalism

In this section, we want to defend the view that word senses are composed of a set of (moderately) universal semantic features combined with natural classifications of experience. By 'moderately universal,' which we return to below, we mean that any two languages will have a significant overlap in the features they use to construct word senses, but there may be unique features as well. To demonstrate what we mean by "a natural classification of experience", take the verb *walk*. The particular kind of locomotion that we achieve in walking is difficult to analyse further by people who can walk, and AI attempts at modelling it have revealed how little humans understand about how it functions.[1] But it is part of the human repertoire of activities and, as such, humans use it in planning their behaviour and in recognizing it in the behaviour of other humans and animals. This particular kind of locomotion is thus a "natural classification of experience".

The decomposability of word senses has been a controversial issue in the literature on the lexicon. On the one hand, there are proponents of a atomistic view of the lexicon such as Fodor (e.g. Fodor & Pylyshyn 1988, Fodor & McLaughlin 1991 and Fodor & Lepore 2002) and more recently Relevance Theorists, e.g. Carston (2010). On the other hand there are advocates of more complex lexical representations such as Pustejovsky (1995). A common argument against a decompositional view is the lack of necessary and sufficient features in defining word senses (e.g. If a tiger is defined as having four legs, does that make a three-legged tiger not a tiger?) Furthermore, one could argue that semantic features are cognitively meaningless if features can freely be invented and added to a representation. We argue that semantic features are needed for overspecification and for formalizing the selection of meaning in use. We contend that these features need to be moderately universal in order to account for the fact that knowing one language's lexicon helps in learning another language's lexicon and also to account for typological generalisations about the lexicon and morphology. But most importantly for our purposes, universal features are needed for methodological reasons to ensure that the decompositions of verbal meaning are cognitively meaningful. They should not be freely inventable (since there are things that are difficult or impossible for us to conceptualize) and, like optimality-theoretic constraints, they should preferably come with a demonstration that they are typologically valid.

For an example of typologically-valid semantic features, one can turn to agency, and more specifically to the proto-agent and proto-patient features set out by Dowty (1991), such as *sentience, volition, control* and *cause*. The typical agent of *walking toward the sunset* forms the intention of doing so within the situation she finds herself in, causes her movement to start, controls and monitors her progress and has a criterion for when it is finished. The notions of *agent, intending, controlling*, and *end of action* all belong to the realm of typologically-valid features.

---

[1] Introductory AI texts take as given that locomotion, grasping something with your hands, and seeing objects belong to the everyday behavioural repertoire of humans and that they turn out be much more difficult than the naive views of these activities would suggest. The use of natural language falls in the same category.

Grimm (2011) shows that these features are central to the typology of case systems, in the sense that they play a role in accounting for the variation between languages that one finds in the realisation of case systems. Typological research and monolingual investigation of central semantico-pragmatic themes such as case, tense, aspect, modality and definiteness provide a large number of ostensibly-valid semantic features.

It is further possible to give a foundation for semantic features using the semantic map method in typology (de Schepper & Zwarts 2010). In the semantic map approach, one studies the meaning of a word or a group of related words using comparison with other languages, by systematically looking at translatability. This provides a natural way of dividing words into their uses without appealing to semantic intuitions. If one uses translations into sufficiently many languages, one can map them onto a two-dimensional graph where the points are sets of translation equivalents. If two languages do not make a meaning distinction that is made in a third language, the first two are connected in the graph. For example, neither English nor French distinguishes direction and recipient in their prepositions, but German does, which would mean that English and French are connected in the graph for this semantic concept (Haspelmath 2003).

De Schepper and Zwarts (2010) show that such maps can be systematically represented by feature clusters, with each of two minimally distant points differing in precisely one feature. Ideally, the sets of features representing a map can be analyzed in terms of typologically well-studied semantic features. This analysis can also be taken as underpinning the view that meanings in use can be seen as sets of semantic features.

Our approach relates to the semantic map approach and other cognitively-oriented approaches such as Conceptual Semantics (e.g. Jackendoff 1996) in the assumption of cognitively realistic semantic features. It is still a task, however, to define how they combine into a logical expression that characterizes the truth-conditional contribution of the combined features in terms of the truth-conditional contribution of the individual features. For this purpose, it is useful to adopt the view of (Barsalou 1992) that meanings in use should be characterized as frames. Features typically set the value of attributes in a frame, unify attribute values, or indicate that certain attributes have a value and that composition can be modelled by unification. The truth-conditional interpretation of a set of attribute value structures is the claim that the class of complex entities that meet all the constraints is non-empty. In contradistinction to the semantics provided for feature structures modelling linguistic objects by, e.g., Johnson (1988), attributes for these semantic uses must be understood as operations in the external world.[2] The object (e.g. an event of falling) would be related to whatever falls by the attribute *theme*, interpreted as the operation that maps events to their themes. While in this particular case it is not unreasonable to think that the theme in some sense constitutes the event, the use of frames by itself does not commit one to this view.

In this respect, we see no distance between the current proposal and formal semantics. There would be one if formal semantics were interpreted as committed to the view that nothing could be said about the structure of meanings beyond their contribution to truth-conditions, which would make it irrelevant for language learning and cognition. The view defended here demands that basic features make sense from the perspective of classical truth-conditional semantics. We forego a discussion of the typical problems for a view of this kind: vagueness, taste predicates, information structural features, and emotional expression.

As mentioned above, the proposal introduced here adopts a moderate form of universalism towards linguistic lexical meanings, but it is the building blocks of lexical meanings and not the lexical meanings themselves that are universal. There is no assumption that any feature will play a role in all languages, nor that any language uses all features. New semantic features may be introduced for the description of a new lexicon if they correspond with a learnable classification. We opt for this moderation rather than for absolute universalism on the basis of evidence showing that speakers of one language are sensitive to semantic differences that speakers of other languages are not sensitive to. For example, Korean has two variants of the English preposition *in* depending upon whether the object is in a close-fitting container (like a SIM card in a cell phone) or in a non-close-fitting container (like a pear in a bowl). McDonough et al. (2003) use preferential looking tasks and a "which of these things is not like the others?" task to show that while Korean and English infants are both sensitive to differences in closeness of fit, as adults, only Korean speakers and not English speakers are sensitive to this difference. Thus, the distinction in close versus loose fit as articulated in the

---

[2] We here part company with those who like to maintain that semantics is merely in the brain. We take the line that a proper semantics should also explain logical inference relations between natural language utterances and thereby should have a model theory. This is the line also taken by Kamp in DRT (Kamp & Reyle 1993). We also feel that many aspects of Conceptual Semantics allow a model-theoretic treatment and that its proponents undersell their theory in this respect.

Korean choice between prepositions is not present in the adult English lexicon or in adult English cognition and should not be posited as an absolute universal. In fact, it would be a Korean-particular extra feature in our formalisation that has arisen through a grammaticalisation process under the influence of a forced choice between lexemes. Our moderate universalism leads to a decomposition in terms of universal features (where typology and cognition supply the foundation for the universal character) with a minimum number of additional idiosyncratic features. We now turn to discussing previous accounts of word meanings based on overspecification of meaning.

3 Overspecification of Meaning: The Hogeweg- Smolensky Account

In his response to the criticism of connectionism in Fodor & Pylyshyn (1988), (Smolensky 1991) offers an analysis in which the distributed representation of *coffee* can be derived by subtracting the representation of *cup with coffee* from the representation of *cup without coffee*. In Smolensky's analysis, the representation of a *cup with coffee* consists of a set of micro-features like 'upright container', 'hot liquid', 'porcelain curved surface', 'burnt odor', 'brown liquid contacting porcelain', 'finger sized handle' and 'brown liquid with curved sides at the bottom'. The representation of *cup without coffee* consists of the features 'upright container', 'porcelain curved surface' and 'finger-sized handle'. If the representation of *cup without coffee* is subtracted from the representation of *cup with coffee*, this yields a representation of *coffee*, consisting of the features 'hot liquid', 'burnt odor', and 'brown liquid contacting porcelain'. Crucially, however, this is a representation of *coffee* in a particular context. In another context, other features of coffee (like *shrub, red fruit, brown bean*) would be activated. The features of coffee that are activated in a particular context are therefore a subset of the much larger set of features potentially projected by *coffee*.

Following Zwarts's (2004) analysis of the preposition *(a)round*, (Hogeweg 2009) turns this approach into an account of computing the right set of semantic features in a context from a lexical (over-)specification using an OT grammar FIT > STRENGTH. FIT demands that the output is consistent with the context, and STRENGTH demands that the output set for the specification is maximal by ensuring that any set larger than the output does not meet FIT.

To illustrate the working of the two constraints, let us look briefly at Hogeweg's analysis of the interpretation of the Dutch discourse particle *wel*. Like most discourse particles, *wel* is highly polysemous. Hogeweg analyzes the different senses of *wel* as ranging in strength depending upon how much information a use presupposes. In Tableau 1, the possible interpretations are ordered according to their strength. The strongest meaning is illustrated by the following small conversation:

(1) a. Speaker A: *Amsterdam is niet de hoofdstad van Nederland* (Amsterdam is not the capital of the Netherlands).
b. Speaker B: *Amsterdam is wel de hoofdstad van Nederland* (Amsterdam is the capital of the Netherlands)

This discourse can be described as an instance of Speaker B's correcting Speaker A. An utterance containing *wel* expressing the proposition p requires that a statement expressing the proposition $\neg p$ was uttered. Implicit contrast, for example, is weaker since it does not require that the proposition $\neg p$ is expressed but just that it is inferrable from the context. For example, in a context where a husband is putting on his coat, his wife could utter: *Je moet wel de afwas nog doen*, 'You have WEL to do the dishes'. What is important here, however, is the interaction between the two constraints STRENGTH and FIT. STRENGTH requires that all meaning aspects are activated so that the word is interpreted with the strongest meaning, in this case, a correction. A candidate violates this constraint as many times as there are stronger interpretations available. FIT requires that the output is consistent with the context. If *wel p* is uttered in a context where a statement expressing $\neg p$ is not part of the common ground, interpreting *wel* as a correction violates FIT. If there is information in the common ground from which $\neg p$ could be inferred, implicit contrast does not violate FIT. Note that the requirements put on the context entail one another. (For example, if $\neg p$ is uttered, it can also be inferred.) That is why if an interpretation does not violate FIT, all the weaker interpretations also meet the requirements set by this constraint.

(2)

Context: Husband is putting on coat. *Je moet* **wel** *de afwas nog doen.* 'You still have to do the dishes.'	FIT	STRENGTH
Correction	*	
Contrast	*	*
⇒ Implicit contrast		**
Surprise		***
Modifier		****

The account is quite successful in the application that Hogeweg provides. It has also been successfully applied to other types of function words such as prepositions Zwarts (2004). Nor is it difficult to come up with further applications. Another advantage of the approach is that, while it was developed in OT, it does not require OT-specific mechanisms that would limit its generalizability.

For example, one can interpret FIT as the maximization of prior probability and STRENGTH as the maximization of the likelihood of the signal given the input. The more features associated with the word that show up in the input, the more likely the use of the word becomes, such that adding more features projected to an interpretation hypothesis increases the likelihood of the signal. The most probable interpretation is thus a set of features that is as large as possible and yet still consistent with the context. The OT system thus reduces to a decomposition into priors and likelihoods for finding the most probable interpretation.

Perhaps this is all that one needs to model functional lexemes.[3] For lexical words, however, it runs into problems. This stems from the fact that all features are treated as equal, whereas certain kinds of phenomena bode against such equality. These include absolute features, dependencies among features and forced choices between features, exemplified below. In the next section, we illustrate these properties of feature sets by an analysis of the verb *fall*. The verb *fall* in English, Dutch, French[4], Russian and modern German is non-volitional. This property survives in all of

---

[3] The use of *already* observed by (Fong 2001) as an expression of the perfect in *You eat already?* in Singapore English (British English informants also report this use in informal standard English) can be used as an argument against this view. Arguably, *already* expresses both surprise (at the early start of a state) and the fact that the state started. Surprise is removed when *already* expresses the perfect, but there are no uses where the perfect is removed. This makes the perfect an absolute feature and surprise, a default feature.

[4] French is not yet integrated into the formal representation of *fall* discussed below.

the derived meanings, which is what makes it an instance of an absolute feature. That there are dependencies between features can be seen for example in that a spatial source for a use of *fall* such as *fall to the ground* forces a spatial goal and a spatial dimension which are interconnected. *Fall* also forces a choice between dimensions, including the aforementioned spatial dimension as well as moral (*He resisted the temptation for a long time, but then he fell.*), fortune (*fall on hard times*), and grace (*fall from grace*), among others.

4 Lexical Entries as Stochastic Sets of Features

In the previous section we argued for a feature-based analysis of words senses. In contrast with the previous approaches, we argue that a word is not related to a set of features but to a stochastic set: a distribution over sets of features. Such distributions can be learnt from experience by counting how often the various feature combinations are expressed by a word. However, the distribution itself cannot be used for explaining the intersubjective status of these stochastic feature sets. The experience of the individual users will be different and therefore the distribution that they learn. While learning a distribution is what constitutes a speaker's competence with respect to the semantics of the word, it cannot be what the language or the language community associates with the word.

Intersubjective convergence can be modeled by considering equivalence classes of such distributions: the distributions that agree on 0, 1 and $<$. Two competent speakers will almost certainly have different frequencies and probabilities for the same feature bundle b in an interpretation of a word w. By using equivalence classes for $\leq$, 0 and 1, we define competence for w as the speakers always agreeing that bundle b is less probable than bundle c in an interpretation of w, or that bundle b is always, or never, occurs in such interpretations.

Let F be the set of all features. Since $p(\emptyset) = 1$ and $p(F) = 0$, p and q will give 0 and 1 to the same elements if they preserve $\leq$. So (3) is sufficient.

(3) $p \sim q$ iff $\forall b, c \ (p(b) \leq p(c)) \leftrightarrow (q(b) \leq q(c))$

While different language users build up different distributions, a small amount of data suffices to guarantee that language users have distributions in the same equivalence class. For specifying such equivalence classes, the following operations can be defined in (4). Speakers know the equivalence class by having learnt or

Representing the Lexicon: Identifying Meaning in Use via Overspecification

converging to a distribution that belongs to it by being exposed to utterances in language use. The equivalence class (and a particular distribution in it, almost certainly different from the distribution of any user) can be attributed to language use or to the language community producing language use.

(4) absolute features: $p(b) = 1$
 excluded features: $p(b) = 0$ (not normally considered)
 conditionally absolute features: $p(b|c) = 1$
 conditionally excluded features: $p(b|c) = 0$
 forced choice: $p(b_1 \vee \ldots \vee b_n) = 1$ and $p(b_i \wedge b_j) = 0$ for $i \neq j \leq n$
 default in a forced choice: $b_1 \ldots b_n$: a feature b_i such that $p(b_i) > p(b_j)$ for $j \neq i$ and $1 \leq j \leq n$

In the following, we will illustrate how such operations enable us to give a representation of the verb *fall*. We chose to exemplify this approach to the lexicon with *fall* not only because the central concept expressed facilitates cross-linguistic comparison, but also because *fall* and its cognates typically lend themselves to extended uses, i.e. a large number of word senses, as mentioned above. Apart from its most straightforward interpretation as a motion verb, *fall* is used with various other interpretations, including non-spatial ones such as a fallen soldier or a fallen woman. As such, it provides a sufficiently difficult modeling task to develop a representation from which all the different uses could be specified in a context.

In the project database based on data extraction efforts from dictionaries and the internet, we currently have 78 uses of "fall". This reduces to a smaller, but not much smaller number of uses for a particular language. Example (5) lists 18 of the 35 uses that seem acceptable in English and is meant to illustrate the variation.

(5) John fell out of the tree.
 The glass fell on the floor.
 John fell (down).
 The house fell.
 The corporal fell
 The rain fell.
 The evening falls.
 Christmas day falls on a Sunday this year.
 He fell asleep.

His eyes fell on the gem.
The cabinet falls.
The thaw fell over the fields.
The water fell.
Dark curls fell around her white neck.
It fell into oblivion.
The goblet fell to the bottom of the river.
The waves fell on the beach.
The curtains fall.
The path falls. (goes down)
Grief fell from our hearts.

Many of these examples can be seen as metaphorical extensions from a basic use. In canonical views on metaphors, space and in particular the up-down opposition is an important source for metaphorical extension. As Lakoff & Johnson (1980) argue, most of our fundamental concepts are organized in one or more spatialization metaphors. They provide many examples in which a more abstract concept is expressed in terms of the opposition between up and down, among which health and life (health and life are up, sickness and death are down), morality (virtue is up, depravity is down) and quantity (more is up, less is down), many of which are also applicable to *fall*. However, the aim in this paper is not to capture metaphor but to find meanings in use. Dead metaphors are dead and the language user is stuck with them even if the metaphorical extension could not have happened anymore. Our strategy stands in competition with an approach which would want to predict the metaphorical use from a more basic use. Maybe that is possible and would lead to similar predictions. A reason to be skeptical about that, however, is that what works in one language does not seem possible in another in many cases and that general accounts of metaphor, even if tied to notions like natural metaphor will fail to predict correctly when a particular metaphor is possible and when it is not. In our case, the starting point is what has happened already and is recorded in the lexicon. Interestingly, we then predict more possible interpretations than were found in the lexicon and standardly correct ones. This can be interpreted as metaphor formation, but so far nothing very much can be claimed for this method of finding new meanings in use. It certainly does not seem to end up (yet?) as a serious general theory of metaphor. The aim of our account should not be confused with the legitimate enterprise of explaining why certain metaphors are more natural and acceptable than others. The project may supply interesting input to such an enterprise since our data are suggestive of what is natural and not, but the enterprise itself will not make any contribution to this essentially psychological question.

The problem for specification is the problem of dealing with all 78 uses from one single representation. It follows from our moderate universalism that this should be possible and—surprisingly, since this is a strong claim—it seems that this is the case. As it turns out, again surprisingly, the language specific representations are not really simpler than the cross-linguistic one.

We now outline the different components of the representation. We use a frame formalism because it comes with a natural decomposition (unlike first order logic), has a properly defined semantics (Johnson 1988, Ait-Kaci & Podelski 1993) and has been claimed by many to be a natural format for the description of concepts. Barsalou (1992), Loebner (2014), Petersen & Werning (2007), and Sag et al. (2003) all give substantial empirical evidence for a frame-like structure of mental representations. For us, having a natural decomposition is the most important advantage and while we regard the current development as promising, we are no way committed to sticking to this particular formalism in future developments of this material.

Though it is too early for a detailed formal proposal, semantic features are interpreted as constraints on relationally restricted frame structures, giving both the structure of the events or states denoted and the concept of these events and states. Equivalence classes over distributions over these features are the lexical specifications.

The lexical specifications have maximal consistent sets of constraints over features allowed by the distribution. These determine classes of frames which in turn determine what kind of objects they can denote.

The following are examples of the different frame constraints on *fall*. Relations and sorts are written with lower case heads, variables appear in upper case.

(6) THEME := the frame has a path attribute with the variable THEME at its end

at(THEME,LOCATION) := THEME is at LOCATION

SOURCE:location(DIMENSION) := SOURCE has the sort of being one of the objects in DIMENSION

nocontrol(THEME) := THEME has the sort 'nocontrol', i.e. the theme does not control the continuation, path or speed of the movement denoted by the verb

A frame is thereby a statement about the external world: the external world should contain an object that is mapped by operations in the external world interpreting the attributes to other objects. The objects should stand in the external relations or have the external sorts that are imposed to them by the structure.

On top of this basic structure, there is information structure implemented by assigning or not assigning a property *new* to a feature. The interpretation is that features lacking this feature should be identified in the context (or accommodated), while new features give properly new information.

Furthermore, semantic features may be annotated for properties of the distribution. This is so already in the case of forced choices: a forced choice $x \in \{y_1, \ldots, y_n\}$ is just the features $x : y_1, \ldots, x : y_n$ but in a situation in which $x : y_i$ and $x : y_j$ are inconsistent for all different $i, j \leq n$. Much the same applies to implications. Other properties of that kind are *absolute* and *default*, which in this setting is understood as a feature that is part of some meanings in use, but can be omitted by conflicts with the context or in the case of competition between two or more incompatible features as the feature which is probabilistically dominant. Annotations with *new* and of this distributional kind are in small capitals. Below, we detail each one in turn.

First, there is a forced choice between the type of theme occurring with *fall* in any given instance (where the 'theme' is that which falls). The fact that this is a forced choice means that the verb obligatorily has a theme. In a given use, the theme will be resolved and represented as, e.g. THEME:light for an instance like *The light falls on the table*. 'Concrete' means that the theme is a concrete object such as a person.

(7) THEME ∈ { concrete, light, precipitation, task, date, judgment, proposal}

The next two statements make the theme a non-agent of a non-action:

(8) nocontrol(THEME)
    nocause(THEME)

Falling is strongly correlated with a lack of intentionality with respect to its direct cause, the movement and its path and for all contemporary languages considered, these are absolute features. These are also background features, as is the specification of the theme.

We next propose a *source* and a *position*, each of which is defined with respect to a *dimension*. The source can be understood as the point of departure for the falling, and the position as the theme's placement at the end of the falling act.

(9) SOURCE: location(DIMENSION)
POSITION: location(DIMENSION)
DIMENSION $\in$ {space, posture, life, health, moral, quantity, level, outcome(PROCESS)}

The inclusion of the dimension specification in our analysis is necessary to our account and is motivated by its further necessity in the analyses of the functions *direction* and *down*, among others (only *down* will be discussed in this particular paper). Dimensions are sets of positions ordered by a natural ordering relation. Here is what is meant by each of the types included above. *Space* is the set of spatial positions close to the earth ordered by the direction of gravity. *Posture* would be the set of body postures ordered by degree to which they are upright, and the same for postures of other things like walls, houses, poles, dogs, etc. It is a good idea to make posture a dependent sort (like *outcome(PROCESS)*), i.e. *posture(X)* where X should be filled in by the type of the theme. This assigns to each X a special set of postures. *Life* is a metaphorical transfer to the "postures" *alive* and *dead* where the first one corresponds with uprightness. *Health* includes healthiness and degrees of unhealthiness ordered from more to less healthy, *morality* is the set of moral states ordered from more to less moral, and *quantity* is the set of quantities ordered by the greater than relation. *Level* corresponds to the set of levels of something again ordered by 'greater than' on some numerical scale (see Lakoff & Johnson 1980 for suggestions about the origins of these metaphorical extensions).

There are a number of dimensions that have degraded into a set of down locations for an often not very clear source. Such cases are:

(10) The prize fell on Tim. (Tim won the prize.)
A cruel fate fell on those left behind. (Dutch: Those left behind suffered a cruel fate.)
Eating falls me difficult. (Dutch: I find it hard to eat.)
Christmas falls on Wednesday.
The task falls on me. (Dutch, German: This happens to be one of my tasks.)

Locations for prizes in races and lotteries are the winners, locations for fates the people whose fate they are, locations of holidays are days in the year assigned by the holiday definition (which may involve human decisions), tasks are one by virtue of one's office or of the moral order. Activities of somebody moreover assign a degree of difficulty or painfulness in the experience of that somebody. What these cases seem to have in common is a dimension that is just a set and a process or non-subjective procedure that assigns locations from the dimension to the theme.

Provisionally, we take these dimensions to be parametrically defined as *outcome(PROCESS)* where the identification of *PROCESS* is crucial for the identification of the set making up the dimension. For this last type, sources may be missing and be identified with the process itself.

One additional difficulty that arises with SOURCE pertains to cases such as *Her hair falls (perfectly)*, where the hair itself is not changing position, but rather, where two different parts of the hair are salient, and the ends of the hair 'fall' by comparison with the hair nearer to the crown of the head. In these cases, which also include falling paths, falling valleys, etc., we define the *split* relation where PART1 and PART2 are the higher and lower parts of the THEME, respectively:

(11) SOURCE=PART1
   split(PART1, PART2, THEME)

For meanings in use in which *split* is defined, the specification that SOURCE=PART1 is obligatory in the representation (i.e. it is an absolute feature).

The next component *at* relates two features such that $at(x, y)$ can be paraphrased as 'the x is in/on y'. For example, $at(John, lying\_down)$ indicates that John is lying down. *At* is a component that appears multiple times in each representation. One of its instances is given information, and one is new information. The one that is given is as follows, where *down* picks out the set of elements in the order given by the dimension that are lower than the one named by the source:

(12) at(POSITION, down(SOURCE,DIMENSION))

For example, $at(lying\_down, down(standing, posture))$ would mean that the lying down is 'down' (lower on the order for the posture dimension) from standing. Another way of saying this is that lying down is down from standing with respect to posture. The next instance of *at* is new information:

(13) at(THEME,POSITION)

This is like the example above, where $at(John, lying\_down)$ indicates that John is lying down. Taken in combination with the given/presupposed use of *at*, we can see that for an example like *John fell*, part of the given information is that lying down is a lower posture position than standing, but the new information includes the fact that John is in fact now in the lying down position. This is sometimes all that is specified as new information, but there are other cases where a movement event is also new information. These are the cases in which a source is either specified or implicit. Continuing this example, the source would be specified as 'standing' (on the posture dimension), and thus we would have new information that there was an event in which John moved from standing to lying down, following this specification:

(14) movement(THEME,SOURCE,POSITION)

In cases where *split* is defined, having the new information be $at(THEME, POSITION)$ would be problematic, since it is not the entirety of the theme that is in the lower-ordered position. Thus, in these cases, we have the following absolute feature, which is analogous to the other but with PART2 replacing THEME:

(15) at(PART2, POSITION)

(16) recapitulates the above with the universal level labels and the bar indicating the split between given and new. It also indicates that space is the default dimension and that *at(THEME,POSITION)* is the default for new information.

(16)
THEME ∈ {concrete,light,precipitation,task,date,judgment,proposal} ABSOLUTE
nocause(THEME)
nocontrol(THEME) ABSOLUTE
SOURCE: location(DIMENSION)
POSITION: location(DIMENSION)
DIMENSION ∈ { space:DEFAULT, posture, life, health, moral, quantity, level, outcome(PROCESS)} ABSOLUTE
SOURCE= PART1 **If** split ABSOLUTE
split(PART1, PART2, THEME)
at(POSITION, down(SOURCE,DIMENSION)) ABSOLUTE

at(THEME,POSITION) DEFAULT, NEW
at(PART2, POSITION) **If** split ABSOLUTE, NEW
movement(THEME,SOURCE) **If** at(THEME, SOURCE) ABSOLUTE NEW

We will now discuss our data with respect to this representation. First of all, there were not many differences between the languages we examined with respect to these representations. The full list is discussed here.

A. The dimension *outcome(PROCESS)* is prominent, especially in Dutch, as in (17).

(17) De prijs viel op mij.
 The prize fell on me.
 'I received the prize'.

B. Older German (Grimm 2011) includes an example where the person doing the falling was causing an action as in (18).

(18) Er fiel in die Sachsen.
 He fell into the Saxons
 'He wildly attacked the Saxons.'

This data point is the reason that $nocause(THEME)$ is not listed as an absolute feature above.

C. Finally, English allows a source without a destination/position ("Grief fell from his heart"), unlike the other languages considered. There is one further important type of difference among the languages, which will be discussed in Section 5 and force a major revision.

These three differences indicate that small adaptations must be made to obtain the specification for particular languages. Dutch overuse of *outcome(PROCESS)* and pre-modern German's causality with *fall* are two cases where one predicts failure of comprehension between languages. Beyond that, however, speakers of one language should be able to make sense of all the uses of the other languages. Languages that are less related than those under discussion may, however, differ more greatly, which is something that we are examining in our continued research.

If information from the context of the word is taken into account, the formal model proposed here makes sense of all the uses we collected on the basis of the language-independent specification and perhaps surprisingly lends itself to implementation. Particularly important is the type of the theme and of the source or location which restricts the choice of the dimension and, thereby, the sort of the unspecified source or location (if either of these is in fact unspecified). Finding this information is easy using prepositions and parsing. It is harder to use information that is not syntactically coded, but clearly often necessary: *he fell* can mean many things given the right context. While the specification is good at suggesting the right questions to ask the context, the answers cannot always be supplied by a simple heuristic method defined over the context. Despite this, trial implementations by Jonathan Mallinson and Jacob Verdegaal show that good results are possible when the necessary contextual information is given syntactically and lexically. It then works to the degree that the syntactic and lexical analysis is correct. This would be the same in cases where one cannot rely on lexical or syntactic information and identifications between variables in the lexical specification and elements in the interpreted linguistic context need to be inferred. The difference is that there are no good off-the-shelf systems for doing these inferences.

We now proceed through a set of examples taken from our collection of different uses of *fall* from Dutch, English, French, German, and Russian. The inferences are generally trivial, but this partly reflects the source of the examples, since dictionaries often give examples in which it is not necessary to use further context beyond the clause. The annotation NEW is replaced below by a double line: the new features are below the double line.

For the sentence given in (19), *The glass fell on the floor*, the space dimension is the default and the floor is a location in that dimension. The glass is obviously somewhere (on the table, in somebody's hands), which may be given in the linguistic context. Glass is moreover a concrete noun. Together, this selects the specification in (19).

(19) 'The glass fell on the floor.'

> THEME:glass
> glass:concrete
> nocontrol(glass)
> nocause(glass)
> SOURCE:location(space)
> at(floor,down(SOURCE,space))
> ———————————————
> at(glass,floor)
> movement(glass,SOURCE)

Continuing with the example used to explain the representations above, in (20), the context needs to put John in a "low" location (to prevent the spatial dimension) and a "high" posture, e.g. standing. Whether one assumes that John falls to the floor, in which case he is lying down at the end of the event, or falls into a chair, in which case he is sitting at the end of the event is a question of what the default value is for the individual hearer in the posture dimension below standing. Note that defaults of this kind are not indicated in the abstract specification above and should be inferred from the context.

(20) 'John fell'.

> THEME:John
> John:concrete
> nocontrol(John)
> nocause(John)
> SOURCE: standing
> POSITION: lying_down
> lying_down:location(posture)
> at(lying_down,down(standing,posture))
> ─────────────────────────────
> at(John,lying_down)
> movement(John,standing)

(21) involves a further specialization of posture applied to houses.

(21) 'The house fell.'

> THEME:house
> house:concrete
> nocontrol(house)
> nocause(house)
> SOURCE:erect
> POSITION:collapsed
> collapsed:location(posture)
> at(collapsed,down(erect,posture))
> ─────────────────────────────
> at(house,collapsed)
> movement(house,erect)

(22) presents another specialization of dimension restricted to military people and battles. This needs a special constraint in the specification of *fall* via the proposed 'life' dimension: If somebody military is the theme, the movement and its cause are part of a battle, then the dimension can be life.

(22) 'The corporal fell.'

> THEME:corporal
> corporal:concrete
> nocontrol(corporal)
> nocause(corporal)
> SOURCE:alive
> POSITION:dead
> dead:location(life)
> at(dead,down(alive,life))
> ═══════════════════════
> at(corporal,dead)
> movement(corporal,alive)

(23) would be derivable through the theme type *precipitation*, which entails the source to be the sky and the dimension to be *space*. Precipitation differs from people, stones and houses by not being a spatio-temporal continuant.

(23) 'The rain fell.'

> THEME:rain
> rain:precipitation
> nocontrol(rain)
> nocause(rain)
> SOURCE:sky
> POSITION:ground
> ground:location(space)
> at(ground,down(sky,space))
> ═══════════════════════
> at(rain,ground)
> movement(rain,sky)

Dates induce a stative use of *fall* and invoke the *outcome(process)* dimension on a process called *calendar*.

Representing the Lexicon: Identifying Meaning in Use via Overspecification

(24) 'Christmas day falls on a Sunday this year.'

    THEME:Christmas

    Christmas: date

    nocontrol(Christmas)

    nocause(Christmas)

    SOURCE: location(outcome(calendar))

    POSITION: Sunday

    at(Sunday,down(calendar,outcome(calendar)))
    ───
    at(Christmas, Sunday)

A number of Dutch uses involve other kinds of processes that lead something to be at some location. A Dutch use where the subject determines the process is given in (25).

(25) *De taak valt op mij.*
    the task fall on me
    'It is my task.'

    nocontrol(task)

    nocause(task)

    ME:location(outcome(taskassignment))

    at(ME,down(taskassignment,outcome(taskassignment)))
    ───
    at(task,ME)

This is not the place for overly long explanations of the formalism used above, but some discussion is necessary to make at least some connections with truth-conditional semantics. Dimensions would be modeled as ordered sets of various kinds. The hardest is here the default setting, normal space; yet, here are by now many formalisms to deal with space and a gravity based high-low ordering over locations (See Aiello et al. 2007). The other dimensions are very limited in comparison, they essentially are small finite partial orders: *life* and *health* have only two elements, while the complexity of the *outcome(process)* dimension is mainly in stating the range of possible outcome locations, e.g. different participants in a lottery, different people who can be burdened by some task, success, ease, hardship and failure for eating, etc.

175

Notions like *control, cause, theme* and *at* seem to be proper universal semantic features. The first two are amenable to a treatment of cause like e.g. the one pioneered by Pearl (2000) (*control* would be the ability to change the course of the event or change the state if whatever has control would want to). The theme would be a Dowty (1991)-style decomposition in similar semantic features. Finally, *at* would be the relation between between objects and where they are, in space or in a metaphorical extension.

These remarks are not meant as a truth-conditional treatment of the concepts we develop, but are meant to take away worries in that respect: this subject as been successfully addressed and there is no reason for thinking that a truth-conditional account cannot be given. In fact, such accounts will considerably help learning systems for the word-feature associations by providing a criterion of consistency for feature bundles.

In this section we provided an overspecified lexical representation for the verb *fall* which accounts for all occurrences we found in our data set. In the next section we discuss, however, that this analysis runs into problems when we look at the second verb we investigate in the project: *run*.

5 Observed Production Probabilities and Lexicalisation

The following problem emerges when we turn to *run*, the second verb in the project sample after *fall*. While there is no significant conceptual distinction between English *run* and Dutch and German *rennen* in their primary uses, there are nonetheless very significant divergences between the verbs in their special uses. In English, machines and noses run, while in German and Dutch these objects engage in *lopen*, for which the best English equivalent is *walking*. The logic for deriving meanings in use from the previous section, however, derives the English meaning in use for "De machine rent", "De neus rent", "Der Machine rennt", and "Die Nase rennt".

It is just a brute fact that, in these cases, the Dutch and German verbs do not have these meanings in use. The reason why is obvious: because another verb has won in these cases as the preferred means of expressing the meaning in use. And the formalism should be able to express this. It is, however, not easy to come up with a natural method extending the equivalence classes of distributions over features in which this can be directly stated.

Representing the Lexicon: Identifying Meaning in Use via Overspecification

It is an overgeneration problem: more meanings in use are predicted than are observed. Yet—at the same time—the logic and the over-determined lexical specifications seem on the right track.

The correct way to rule out unwanted meanings in use in a probabilistic setting is to add production constraints in interpretation. It seems a correct observation that Dutch and German speakers select *lopen* or *laufen* when confronted with the meaning in use given by English: "the machine runs" or "the nose runs". This section recasts the previous proposal to incorporate this dependency on production.

There should be a part of the production mechanism which assigns words to bundles of features with a certain probability: lexical selection. This process can be captured as a function f that maps pairs made up from a bundle of semantic features and a word to a probability. The function values will often be 0 for all words for a certain bundle: the bundle is not a sensible meaning in use or it is sensible but lexemes are missing. It will also very often be 0 for most words: those words were never used to express this bundle. The function can be read off directly from a corpus of word and meaning in use pairs as in (26). The function gives the frequency of the word for the bundle divided by the frequency of the bundle. Notice that the precise bundles of features count: a use of w to express a superset c of b does not count as a use of w for b. We assume here that the corpus is given as a set C of triples <index, bundle, word>.

(26) $f(b)(w) = \frac{|\{j: <j,b,w> \in C\}|}{|\{j: \exists w' <j,b,w'> \in C\}|}$

The function counts the number of indices at which w expresses b and divides that number by the number of indices at which b is expressed by any word whatsoever. The function therefore measures the strength with which a bundle of features keys a lexeme and can be seen as a component of what determines lexical choice. The rule could be to choose that w for b for which $f(b)(w)$ is maximal.

The function f—or the data from which it can be read off—can be equated with the mental lexicon. The mental lexicon cannot be equated with the set of distributions over semantic features keyed by specific lexical items as was assumed in the last section, since that does not give a handle on production, which we need to deal with our overgeneration problem, as will be shown below.

There are no problems with multi-word lexical items. In fact, it is natural to assume that certain sets of features would correspond to groups of lexemes. All that one would need to do is to consider a generalization of the function in which w ranges over bags of words. There would then no longer be any principled division between multi-word lexemes and groups of lexemes that jointly express the bundle, and this is as it should be. The difference would be in the possibility to regain the probability of the bag for the bundle from the probabilities of its components for parts of the bundle: do we get the same number or is the probability of the combination higher? In the last case, it has become or is becoming an idiom. While this definitely must be explored further, let's ignore composition for the time being and let w simply range over words. It would seem that the revision fares better as a data structure that can be learned and represented by the brain as an association and is better suited for multi-word expressions than the proposal from the last section to equate the mental lexicon with probability distributions $p_w(b)$ over the words w of the language. While we leave these issues open, it is still the case that the competition we define below, sometimes is between a word and a multi-word expression or between multi-word expressions.

This new account of the mental lexicon can help with the problem at hand. If a meaning in use is just expressed differently, it cannot be the meaning in use of the word for which it was hypothesized (cf. the use of *lopen* 'walk' rather than *rennen* 'run'). The earlier approach does not need to be given up, it merely needs an amendment in which it is checked for an interpretation b that the production probability $f(b)(w) \neq 0$ while for another word w' $f(b)(w') > 0$.

But then, what should be used for arriving at meanings in use? At first sight this seems problematic. The revision gives a criterion for having found the meaning in use. The new data structure gives the likelihood $p(w|b)$ of the word w for the meaning in use b. If a prior $p(b)$ for the set of features b is given, the most probable interpretation is $argmax_b p(b) f(b)(w)$, the feature bundle b for which the product of the prior probability $p(b)$ and the likelihood as given by f applied to b and w is maximal.[5] But how can it be guaranteed that that is indeed the maximal bundle that fits in the context? $p(b)$ will be bounded by $p(b')$ if $b' \subset b$. And the likelihood is learned from experience as f. It would seem that this does not give the prediction that larger bundles are preferred. A second problem is that it gives no results in case w has not been used for b before.

---

[5] That this is the most probable interpretation follows by Bayes' theorem. Models of interpretation in which the most probable interpretation is computed by finding a maximum for $p(b)p(w|b)$, the product of the prior and the likelihood of the interpretation are standard in signal processing and computer vision.

The solution is not to give up on the earlier proposal but to use it as a model of Bayesian interpretation. This can be done since f almost directly reconstructs the distribution p_w over semantic feature bundles keyed by a lexeme w. In (27), $p_w(b)$ is defined, where b is a semantic feature bundle. To do this correctly, we need to measure the frequency of b, $m(b)$, in the corpus as its frequency divided by the corpus size. F is the set of all features.

(27) $p_w(b) = \frac{\Sigma_{b \subseteq b' \subseteq F} m(b') f(b')(w)}{\Sigma_{b' \subseteq F} m(b') f(b')(w)}$

$p_w(b)$ measures how often w is used for b within all uses of w.

While humans learn f automatically, it seems that linguists like ourselves are better in discovering p_w directly from lexical and internet data, with semantic blocking occasionally offering a window on properties of f that cannot be recovered from the functions p_w.

Lexical interpretation is still computing $argmax_b p(b) p(w|b)$, but there will be more information in $p(w|b)$ than directly follows from f. Any semantic feature $s \in b$ associated with w helps to increase the likelihood of w: $p(w|b)$. But simultaneously $f(b)(w)$ is a filter on the result, blocking certain realisations, i.e. this can make $p(w|b) = 0$. If there are $f(b)(w')$ with a high value, b has lexical means of expression and using w for b will be unlikely if $f(b)(w) = 0$. So if $f(b)(w)$ has a high value while $f(b)(w') = 0$, b is not a proper interpretation of w'.[6] So the new "mental lexicon" can continue as the base for the solution in Section 4.

Let us recapitulate these observations in some definitions:

(28) **Lexical interpretation**: b is a lexical interpretation of w iff $f(b)(w) >> 0$.[7]

(29) **Standard lexical choice**: w is a lexical choice for b iff $f(b)(w) >> 0$.

(30) **Smolensky/Hogeweg interpretation**: An optimal interpretation can be defined by the following three constraints:

  1. All variables are bound from the context, all forced selections are executed, all absolute features projected, and the interpretation is closed under *modus ponens*
  2. It is consistent with the context
  3. It is maximal

---

[6] This gives a simple intuitive solution for the "cause to die"-problem of (McCawley 1968). "Black Bill caused the sheriff to die" cannot "mean" under this rule that he caused him to die in some normal way. "Cause-to-die" is blocked to mean that by the lexical expression "kill".

[7] We require a proper number of occurrences, beyond what could be attributed to error.

In terms of OT, (1) gives conditions on candidate interpretations and makes these conditions thereby absolute. (2) and (3) are identical with FIT and STRENGTH and can be defeated: a new statement may correct the context, non-absolute features can be dropped to gain consistency. (2) is entailed by prior maximisation in Bayesian interpretation. (3) is part of likelihood maximisation. So for practical purposes and within the enterprise of computing lexical meanings in use from abstract specifications, it seems reasonable to equate Bayesian interpretation and Smolensky/Hogeweg.

(31) **Proper lexical choice**: w is a proper lexical choice for b in c if w is a lexical choice for b and b is a proper interpretation of w in c

Many bs will not have a lexical choice: in that case w is a proper lexical choice for b in c iff b is a proper interpretation of w in c

(32) **Proper interpretation**: b is a proper interpretation of w in c iff b is computed by Smolensky/Hogeweg for w in c unless there exists $w' \neq w$ where w' is a lexical choice for b while w is not a lexical choice.

The situation in which the interpretation b found for w cannot be lexically expressed (no word has a non-zero observed probability for it) is interesting, because now it is reasonable to stick with the hypothesis found by Bayesian interpretation, i.e. FIT > STRENGTH that the meaning in use is b: a new meaning in use for the word w was found. This would be an extension of the use observed so far.

The information in f is typically partially reflecting ongoing learning. Every 0 may have the meaning that the use of w for b has not been observed so far. But there are situations where the 0 can be taken seriously. The first case would be for inconsistent bundles. The second case would be the case where the bundle b has been expressed often enough to be confident that w will not be used for the bundle. In all other cases, one can learn that w is used for b by encountering a use and inferring that b is its meaning in use. And one use is good enough.

Like (Hogeweg 2009), we assume that there is the beginning of an account of metaphorical use of lexical items in this setup. The information in f can block or select an hypothesis obtained by the reasoning that computes meanings in use from lexical specifications, the new version of FIT > MAX. It however does not block unobserved hypotheses and it should not. These are—or are from the perspective of the learning structure f—metaphorical extensions. Since learning f is also learning the distribution over semantic features p_w, it follows that new hypotheses can also be obtained by overriding zero's in that distribution. The latter are new metaphors.

Now it is not easy, but possible to come up with new metaphors for *fall*. For example, in the project we might perhaps say (speaking Dutch or Russian) that the word *rennen* falls to Lotte, meaning that it is her task to collect uses of *rennen*. The specification rules that out even for Dutch: words are not associated conventionally with a process that assigns them to humans. But as a project member, Lotte can be assigned tasks and in the project words are tasks: a new metaphor. It would seem that one can deal with cases like this by shifting from a definition by listing of process (necessary for Dutch: many processes work, but not all) to an intensional characterisation (task or reward assigning process). A more proper exploration of these limits and ways of overcoming them is for future work.

Accordingly, we find ourselves siding with Giambattista Vico in claiming that originally—at least in acquisition—language use is poetry in which everything is interpreted metaphorically (Pompa 2002). Learning from use slowly leads to prose, i.e. the semantic discipline brought by conventional means of expression emerging from experience.

6 Conclusion

We have argued that the traditional view on the lexicon does not offer a way of accounting for the selection of meanings in use, a task that humans seem to perform routinely with high degrees of success. The proposals of Smolensky and Hogeweg for dealing with selection by means of overspecification were then examined and found to be wanting for the meaning of lexical words. We argue that decomposition of word meanings and meanings in use in terms of moderately universal semantic features is possible and consistent with truth-conditional semantics and typology. But that more structure is needed over the features than just set membership.

The method can be made to work in a natural way, if rather than a set of semantic features one uses equivalence classes over distributions over bundles of semantic features expressed by the words. Such equivalence classes offer a natural inventory of operations over semantic features and we show that with these operations, one can arrive at a natural and effective representation for the verb *fall* that can be used to model the interaction with the context that performs selection.

The approach however overgenerates, since in many cases the interaction with the context will yield feature bundles that should be expressed differently in certain languages. In order to remedy that we propose that lexical representation takes the form of two functions: f that maps feature bundles and words to a probability and m that maps feature bundles to the probability that they will be expressed. It is now possible to define the necessary semantic blocking as the requirement that f should not give zero for the interpretation b and the word w, while giving a high value to b and w'. At the same time, the distributions p_w over semantic features can be recovered from f and m and offer—like the Smolensky/Hogeweg proposal does—the first steps of an account of new metaphors.

References

Aiello, Marco, Ian Pratt-Hartmann & Johan van Benthem (eds.). 2007. *Handbook of spatial logics.* Dordrecht: Springer.

Ait-Kaci, Hassan & Andreas Podelski. 1993. Towards a meaning of life. *The Journal of Logic Programming* 16(3). 195–234.

Baroni, Marco, Raffaella Bernardi & Roberto Zamparelli. 2014. Frege in space: A program for compositional distributional semantics. *Linguistic Issues in Language Technology* 9(6). 5–110.

Barsalou, Lawrence W. 1992. Frames, concepts, and conceptual fields. In E. Kittay & A. Lehrer (eds.). *Frames, fields, and contrasts: New essays in semantic and lexical organization.* 21–74. Hillsdale, NJ: Lawrence Erlbaum.

Blutner, Reinhard. 2004. Pragmatics and the lexicon. In L. R. Horn & G. Ward (eds.). *Handbook of pragmatics.* 488–514. Oxford: Blackwell.

Carston, Robyn. 2010. Explicit communication and 'free' pragmatic enrichment. In B. Soria & E. Romero (eds.). *Explicit communication: Robyn carston's pragmatics.* 217–285. Basingstoke: Palgrave Macmillan.

Dowty, David. 1991. Thematic proto-roles and argument selection. *Language* 67(3). 547–619.

Erk, Katrin. 2014. What do you know about an alligator when you know the company it keeps? Unpublished ms.

Fodor, Jerry & Ernest Lepore. 2002. *The compositionality papers.* Oxford: Clarendon Press.

Fodor, Jerry & Brian McLaughlin. 1991. Connectionism and the problem of systematicity: why Smolensky's solution doesn't work. In T. Horgan & J. Tienson (eds.). *Connectionism and the philosophy of mind*. 331–355. Cambridge: MIT Press/Bradford Books.

Fodor, Jerry & Zenon Pylyshyn. 1988. Connectionism and cognitive architecture: A critical analysis. *Cognition* 28(1-2). 3–71.

Fong, Vivienne. 2001. "Already" in Singapore English. Abstract, Aspect Conference. Utrecht, December 12-14, 2001.

Grimm, Scott. 2011. Semantics of case. *Morphology* 21(3-4). 515–544.

Haspelmath, Martin. 2003. The geometry of grammatical meaning: semantic maps and cross-linguistic comparison. In M. Tomasello (ed.). *The new psychology of language*. 211–243. Mahwah, N.J.: Lawrence Erlbaum.

Hogeweg, Lotte. 2009. *Word in process. on the interpretation, acquisition and production of words*: Radboud University Nijmegen dissertation.

Jackendoff, Ray. 1996. Conceptual semantics and cognitive semantics. *Cognitive Linguistics* 7. 93–129.

Johnson, Mark. 1988. *Attribute-value logic and the theory of grammar* CSLI Lecture Notes. Stanford, CA: Center for the Study of Language and Information.

Kamp, Hans & Uwe Reyle. 1993. *From discourse to logic*. Dordrecht: Kluwer.

Lakoff, George & Mark Johnson. 1980. *Metaphors we live by*. Chicago: University of Chicago Press.

Löbner, Sebastian. 2014. *Understanding semantics*. Routledge.

McCawley, James D. 1968. Lexical insertion in a transformational grammar without deep structure. In Bill Darden, Charles-James Bailey & Alice Davison (eds.). *Papers from the fourth regional meeting of the chicago linguistic society*. 71–80. Linguistics Department, University of Chicago.

McDonough, Laraine, Soonja Choi & Jean M Mandler. 2003. Understanding spatial relations: Flexible infants, lexical adults. *Cognitive psychology* 46(3). 229–259.

Pearl, Judea. 2000. *Causality: Models, reasoning, and inference*. Cambridge: Cambridge University Press.

Petersen, Wiebke & Markus Werning. 2007. Conceptual fingerprints: Lexical decomposition by means of frames - a neurocognitive model. In U. Priss, S. Polovina & R. Hill (eds.). *Conceptual structures: Knowledge architectures for smart applications: Proceedings of iccs 2007*. Lecture Notes in Computer Science. 415–428. Springer.

Pompa, Leon (ed.). 2002. *Scienza nuova (1725), the first new science*. Cambridge: Cambridge University Press.

Pustejovsky, James. 1995. *The generative lexicon*. Cambridge: MIT Press.

Sag, Ivan, Thomas Wasow & Emily M. Bender. 2003. *Syntactic theory: A formal introduction* CSLI Lecture Notes. Stanford, CA: Center for the Study of Language and Information.

de Schepper, Kees & Joost Zwarts. 2010. Modal geometry: Remarks on the structure of a modal map. In *Cross-linguistic semantics of tense, aspect, and modality*. 245–270. Amsterdam: John Benjamins.

Smolensky, Paul. 1991. Connectionism, constituency and the language of thought. In M. Loewer & G. Rey (eds.). *Meaning in mind: Fodor and his critics*. 201–227. Oxford: Blackwell.

Zwarts, Joost. 2004. Competition between word meanings: The polysemy of (a)round. In C. Meier & M. Weisgerber (eds.). *Proceedings of SuB8* University of Konstanz Linguistics Working Papers. 349–360. Konstanz.

Zwarts, Joost. 2006. Om en rond: Een semantische vergelijking. *Nederlandse Taalkunde* 11(2). 101–123.

Zwarts, Joost. 2008. Priorities in the production of prepositions. In A. Asbury, J. Dotlacil, B. Gehrke & R. Nouwen (eds.). *Syntax and semantics of spatial p.* 85–102. Amsterdam: John Benjamins.

Authors

Henk Zeevat
ILLC, University of Amsterdam
SfB991, University of Düsseldorf
H.W.Zeevat@uva.nl

Scott Grimm
University of Rochester
scott.grimm@rochester.edu

Lotte Hogeweg
University of Amsterdam
l.hogeweg@uva.nl

Representing the Lexicon: Identifying Meaning in Use via Overspecification

Sander Lestrade
Radboud Universitity Nijmegen
s.lestrade@let.ru.nl

E. Allyn Smith
Université du Québec à Montréal
smith.eallyn@uqam.ca

Russian predicates selecting remarkable clauses: Corpus-based approach and Gricean Perspective

Natalia Zevakhina & Alex Dainiak[*]

This paper reports upon the study of the lexico-grammatical distribution of Russian matrix predicates selecting *kakoj* remarkable clauses (or so-called 'embedded' exclamatives) in the Russian National Corpus, with some cross-linguistic parallels. It reveals that Russian matrix predicates belong to four conceptual classes: perceptual, mental, emotive, and speech. It shows that the phenomenon of 'embedded' exclamatives is irregular because: (1) matrix predicates seem to be lexically idiosyncratic and (2) the most frequent forms of matrix predicates (except for optatives) are on the way to be grammaticalized. The paper also suggests accounting for the observed distribution of predicates in terms of the Gricean maxims of conversation.

1 Introduction

To give an idea of the phenomenon under consideration, we present below some examples of 'embedded' exclamatives.

(1) Look what's happened to Rosemary's baby! (1975 TV movie)

(2) I'm amazed how tall John is! (Grimshaw 1979, p. 282)

---

[*] We sincerely appreciate the organization of the workshop Bridging Formal and Conceptual Semantics 2014 and the immensely valuable comments given by its audience and by an anonymous reviewer. All mistakes are solely ours. The article was prepared within the framework of the Academic Fund Program at the National Research University Higher School of Economics (HSE) in 2015—2016 (grant No. 15-01-0026) and supported within the framework of a subsidy granted to the HSE by the Government of the Russian Federation for the implementation of the Global Competitiveness Program.

(3) You won't believe who Ed has married! (Huddleston 1993, p. 175)

Two opposite approaches to whether the structures in (1)–(3) are embedded exclamatives or embedded interrogatives have been proposed, see (Elliott 1974, Grimshaw 1979, Zanuttini & Portner 2003) vs. (Huddleston 1993, Abels 2005) among many others. There has been offered a number of arguments for and against each of these two views. However, for the current purposes, this debate seems to be irrelevant: both approaches are compatible with the view that we adhere in this paper. In what follows, we refer to the constructions under consideration as subordinate clauses with remarkable interpretation, or *remarkable clauses*.

Our goal in this paper is two-fold. The descriptive part reveals the lexical and grammatical distribution of matrix predicates which select remarkable clauses in the largest corpus collection of Russian texts, which is the Russian National Corpus (RNC). In particular, we discuss the following questions: what predicates select remarkable clauses as their complements; which semantic classes these predicates belong to; what lexical and grammatical properties they expose. The explanatory part accounts for the corpus findings in terms of the Gricean maxims of conversation.

The paper is structured as follows. Section 2 goes back to formal semantics studies which establish the taxonomy of English matrix predicates that embed exclamatives (remarkable clauses in our terms) only, interrogatives only, both or none. Section 3 presents cross-linguistic evidence for four conceptual classes of matrix predicates selecting remarkable clauses and reveals some lexico-grammatical peculiarities of such predicates. Section 4 discusses the lexico-grammatical distribution of *kakoj* 'what' (e.g., *Kakoj krasivyj dom* 'What a beautiful house!') remarkable clauses in the RNC. Section 5 accounts for the collected data in terms of the Gricean maxims of conversation. Section 6 concludes.

2 Exclamative-selecting vs. interrogative-selecting predicates

Studying exclamatives has commenced from studying so-called 'embedded' exclamatives.[1] To the best of our knowledge, the first prominent papers that shed light upon this issue were (Elliott 1974) and (Grimshaw 1979). The research question at that time (and later in (Abels 2004a, 2004b) among others) concerned the semantic

---

[1] In this section, we follow the authors' terminology and call remarkable clauses *embedded exclamatives*.

difference between matrix predicates embedding interrogatives and matrix predicates embedding exclamatives. Grimshaw (1979) pointed out that matrix predicates are semantically specified in the lexicon for whether they take interrogatives, exclamatives, both or none as their complements. In particular, she distinguished between semantic E and Q features, corresponding to exclamations and questions[2]: each predicate has zero, one or two of these features. Table 1, summarizing the data from these four sources, gives evidence for the distribution of matrix predicates embedding interrogatives and exclamatives. As we see, predicates like *believe* select neither interrogatives nor exclamatives, whereas predicates like *ask* and *wonder* allow for interrogatives but not for exclamatives. Emotive predicates take only exclamatives as their complements. Finally, verbs like *know*, *find out* and *realize* select both sorts of embedded clauses.

Table 1: Distribution of interrogative-selecting and exclamative-selecting predicates

	Embedded interrogative	Embedded exclamative
believe	#John believed how tall Mary is.	#John believed how (very) tall Mary is.
ask, wonder	John asked how tall Mary is.	#John asked how (very) tall Mary is.
emotive predicates[3]	#John was amazed how tall Mary is.	John was amazed how (very) tall Mary is.
know, find out, realize	John knows how tall Mary is.	John knows how (very) tall Mary is.

The explanation for the distribution proposed in (Elliott 1974) and (Grimshaw 1979) was that only factive predicates (originally introduced in (Kiparsky & Kiparsky 1970)) take exclamatives as their complements. This accounts for the fact that exclamatives, being complements of factives, are presupposed. Indeed, the sentence *John was amazed how tall Mary is* presupposes that Mary is tall. Moreover, factive uses of non-factive predicates, like *believe* in the form of *I can't believe* exemplified in (4), also allow for exclamatives.

(4) I can't believe how stupidly he's behaving. (Grimshaw 1979, p. 319)

Another implication is that non-factive predicates which do not allow for a factive reading (e.g., *claim*) do not select exclamatives, cf. (5).

(5) # I claim how very tall Bill is. (Elliott 1974, p. 239)

---

[2] *Exclamations* and *questions* are utterances and typically (although not necessarily, at least in case of exclamations) correspond to *exclamatives* and *interrogatives*, which are clauses.

However, there are exceptions to this general rule. According to Grimshaw (1979) and Elliott (1974) not every factive predicate takes an exclamative as its complement. For instance, (6) illustrates infelicity of factive predicates *concede* and *admit* with embedded exclamatives. In (7), the two factive verbs are used with presupposed *that*-clause.

(6) # Bill will never concede/admit what a big salary he makes. (Grimshaw 1979, p. 323)

(7) Bill will never concede/admit that he makes a big salary. (ibid.)

Grimshaw (1979, pp. 323-324) adds other factive predicates to this list of exceptions: *be sufficient, make sense,* and *count*. As she points out, "it seems that while it is possible to predict the ill-formedness of exclamations with non-factives, the behavior of factives is to some extent idiosyncratic".[4]

Furthermore, according to Grimshaw (1979) and Elliott (1974), not every form of a factive exclamative-selecting predicate takes an exclamative as its complement. On the one hand, the context of negated 1st person mental predicates called *a context of the speaker's ignorance* and exemplified in (8) does not allow for an exclamative. Compare contexts of non-negated 1st person form in (9) and of 3rd person form in (10) that take an exclamative.

(8) # I don't know what a fool Bill is. (Grimshaw 1979, p. 283)

(9) I know what a fool Bill is. (ibid.)

(10) John doesn't know what a fool Bill is. (ibid.)

On the other hand, as Elliott (1974) pointed out, impersonal negated forms of emotive predicates illustrated in (11) do not select exclamatives either. See a corresponding non-negated example (12) for comparison.

(11) # It is not amazing how beautiful this place is. (Elliott 1974, 241)

(12) It is amazing how beautiful this place is. (Googled)

---

[4] Remarkably, literature sources show contradictory data with regard to some of the factive predicates. To illustrate, Zanuttini & Portner (2003, p. 46, ft. 11) points out that "*regret* does not allow wh-complements in general", whereas Elliott (1974, p. 237) presents the same predicate with a wh-complement, see (i).

(i) I regret how very much trouble I have caused you. (Elliott 1974, p. 237).

As an interim conclusion, factivity can explain only some of the data.

Abels (2004a, 2004b) argues against Grimshaw's semantic features E and Q and suggests that embedded exclamatives are of the same semantic type as interrogatives, that is of the type $\langle\langle s, t\rangle, t\rangle$. In doing so, he focused mostly on the distinction between emotive predicates embedding exclamatives (e.g., *be surprised*) and predicates embedding interrogatives (e.g., *wonder*).

There are three questions left after reading his papers. To begin with, among emotive exclamative-selecting predicates, only one of those (*be surprised*) is discussed throughout most of the paper, however, the conclusions are tentatively drawn for all emotive exclamative-selecting predicates, or *surprise*-predicates, by which the author meant all such predicates, see (Abels 2004b, p. 205), as well as for all their grammatical forms. To put it differently, exclamative-selecting predicates are treated indistinguishably; the same goes for their forms. However, as we show in Section 3, cross-linguistically, emotive predicates exhibit grammatical restrictions. To illustrate, (11) is infelicitous, whereas (12) is perfectly possible. Moreover, according to the Russian corpus data studied in Section 4, emotive predicates are diverse with respect to their lexico-grammatical distribution. Secondly, there is no discussion of non-emotive predicates like *know* and *find out*. Fortunately, we know from (Grimshaw 1979) among others that such predicates are specified for both interrogatives and exclamatives. Thirdly, *who*-exclamatives are mostly examined (with a few examples of *how*-exclamatives), however, the former are impossible in English main clause exclamatives: cf. (13).

(13) # Who Ed has married![5]

To summarize, Abels (2004a, 2004b) mainly discusses *surprise* as a representative of the emotive predicate class regardless of lexico-grammatical restrictions among the predicates within this class, regardless of non-emotive exclamative-selecting predicate classes and with a strong emphasis on only one type of exclamative, *who*-exclamatives.

To conclude this section, factivity can only partly explain which predicates select remarkable clauses since not all factive verbs and not all grammatical forms of them allow for such clauses.

---

[5] English allows only for the following exclamative constructions: *what a* + NP, *how (very)* + adjective or adverb and *how many/much* + NP. Except for one example of *how*-exclamative briefly mentioned in Section 1, the rest of the exclamative constructions are not discussed at all by Abels.

3 Classes of predicates selecting remarkable clauses: Cross-linguistic perspective

To the best of our knowledge, no comprehensive cross-linguistic study which would determine the limits of variation among conceptual classes of matrix predicates selecting remarkable clauses in natural languages has beem undertaken. Judging by the data found in the literature, we tentatively distinguish among four such classes: perceptual, emotive, mental, and speech. This suggests that the variety of predicates selecting remarkable clauses is limited to these classes. Indeed, Ono (2006) reports on emotive predicates (e.g., 'be surprised'[6] and 'be amazed'), mental (e.g., 'think') and speech (e.g., 'say') in Japanese; Lipták (2006) mentions Hungarian emotive predicates; Potsdam (2011) gives evidence for Malagasy emotive predicates; Visan (2000) discusses mental and perceptual predicates in Mandarin Chinese, and De Urbana & Hualde (2003) exemplifies the use of Basque emotive and perceptual predicates, cf. (14) and (15).

(14) Basque

Arrituko   zinake,   ezer-en   indarr-ik gabe   eta esku
be.surprised.PROSP 2SG.AUX.POT any-GEN force-PART without and hand
bat-ekin   zer   gauza-k egi-ten ditu-en!
one-COM what thing-PL do-IPF AUX.TR-COMPL

'You would be surprised what things he can do without any force and with the help of only one hand!' (De Urbana & Hualde 2003, p. 565-566)

(15) Basque

Beha za-zu   nola ari d-en!
look AUX.IMP-2SG.A how act AUX-COMPL

'Look at the way he plays!' (ibid.)

The emotive class seems to be the most frequently mentioned. According to Michaelis (2001), emotive predicates are one of the cross-linguistic features of exclamatives: they are witnessed, e.g., in Palestinian Arabic, Mandarin Chinese, Croatian, French, Italian, Malay, Setswana, Turkish.

---

[6] We give only English translations here and further.

However, for the time being, it is hard to infer whether all the four classes of predicates are necessarily present in a given language. It goes without saying that a thorough cross-linguistic investigation is needed.

Moreover, the classes of predicates exhibit lexical variation: not all predicates of a given class select remarkable clauses. To illustrate, Ono (2006) points out that Japanese distinguishes between mental predicates like 'think' and like 'know': the former are felicitous, whereas the latter are not, cf. (16) and (17).[7]

(16) Japanese

John wa Mary ga nante takusan no hon o yon-da no
John TOP Mary NOM what many GEN book ACC read-PST NML
da-roo ka to omotte-iru.
COP-PRSM Q COMP think-PROG

'John thinks how many books Mary has read.' (lit., Japanese corpus "Kotonoha")

(17) Japanese

#John wa Mary ga nante takusan no gakusee ni okotta no
John TOP Mary NOM what many GEN student DAT angry NML
da-roo koto to sitte-iru.
COP-PRSM NML COMP know-PROG

'John knows how very many students Mary got angry at.' (Ono 2006, p. 51)

Also, Japanese distinguishes between speech predicates like 'say' and like 'claim': again, the former are felicitous, in contrast to the latter.

Conceptual classes of predicates that select remarkable clauses are subject to not only lexical but also grammatical variation. For instance, Castroviejo (2006) points out that Catalan perceptual predicates are used only in the forms of imperatives, yes-no interrogatives and future tense declaratives, cf. (18)–(20) respectively.

(18) Catalan

Mira quin home tan graciós que surt per la tele!
look.IMP what man so funny COMP go.3SG PREP DF television

'Look, what a funny man is on TV!' (Castroviejo 2006, p. 16)

---

[7] Remarkably, in English, it is the other way round.

(19) Catalan

Has vist quin noi tan alt que van amb bici?
AUX.2SG see.PASS.PTCP what boy so tall COMP go.3SG PREP bicycle

'Have you seen what a tall boy is riding a bike?' (ibid.)

(20) Catalan

Ja veuràs que bé que ens ho passarem.
already see.FUT.2SG COMP good COMP REFL.1PL this.ACC spend.FUT.1PL

'You'll see what a great time we'll have.' (ibid.)

Visan (2000) points out that Mandarin Chinese perceptual predicates solely allow for imperatives.

To recapitulate, firstly, cross-linguistically, the semantic diversity of matrix predicates that select remarkable clauses seems to be limited to four conceptual classes: perceptual, emotive, mental, and speech. Secondly, the felicitousness of lexical items that belong to these four classes and their grammatical forms is subject to typological variation. In what follows, we regard frequency distributions of lexemes of the four predicate classes and their forms in the RNC and explain their behavior in terms of the Gricean maxims of conversation.

4 Russian predicates selecting remarkable clauses: Corpus perspective

Russian allows for the following wh-words in main clause exclamatives: *kakoj* 'what' + NP (in an attributive position) and *kakov* 'what' (in a predicative position), *kak* 'how', *skol'ko* 'how many/much', *kto* 'who', *čto* 'what' (in an argument position), *gde* 'where' (location), *kuda* 'where' (direction), *kogda* 'when' and *počemu* 'why'.[8] Amongst this diversity, we limited our research to *kakoj* remarkable clauses and leave the rest for future investigation.

We studied the predicates that select *kakoj* remarkable clauses in the Main corpus of the RNC. The RNC is an open and constantly updated internet resource that contains a considerable collection of written and oral Russian texts (http://www.ruscorpora.ru/en). The Main corpus consists of 230m tokens and

---

[8] The latter two are possible in main clause exclamatives if they are somehow contextually supported: e.g., with help of the particle *nado že*.

includes written prose texts of various genres and styles from the mid-18th century to the present.

The search query in the Main Corpus of the RNC was as follows. Since we did not know which predicates select *kakoj* remarkable clauses and our goal was to collect most, if not all, of them, we searched for a verb at a distance of 1 word before *kakoj* that was at a distance from 1 to 20 words before an exclamation mark (it has a special label "bexcl" in the RNC).

We found 1 213 contexts and browsed through all of them selecting manually relevant contexts with a remarkable interpretation of *kakoj*. Afterwards, we intended to examine other contexts of each found matrix verb; in that case, the search query was identical to the previous one, except that the matrix predicate had to be at a distance of 2–5 words to *kakoj*.

In both corpus search queries, we looked at the sentences with exclamation marks. Generally, remarkable clauses do not require the use of an exclamation mark *per se*.[9] Also, they do not require the use of a dot either. The examples of remarkable clauses in the literature do not follow the same pattern: some of them end with a dot, whereas the others contain an exclamation mark (e.g., (3) vs. (4) with quite similar forms of the same predicate in the very same language). The advantage of considering solely sentences with an exclamation mark is that it helped us narrow down the set of relevant constructions in the corpus. The study of only such contexts does not seem to skew the results. To illustrate, the search query with an exclamation mark revealed a relatively small number of emotives (unexpected for the general theory of exclamatives), with *udivitel'no* as the most frequent item. However, their behaviour does not considerably differ in case of a dot at the end of a sentence: again, *udivitel'no* was the the most frequently occurring item in the corpus search (cf. Figures 4 and 5 in the Appendix). In other words, contexts with an exclamation mark reveal general tendencies of item frequencies that become more salient in dot-contexts. This certainly does not exclude studying dot-contexts. We only predict that such a study will not reveal an entirely new picture of the lexico-grammatical distribution of predicates. A more general research goal is to reveal (prosodic) conditions of which punctuation mark to use.

Having supplemented our collection of relevant contexts, we calculated instances per million (IPMs) for each witnessed grammatical form of each matrix lexeme

---

[9] We thank an anonymous reviewer for this comment.

using the following formula:

$$\frac{\text{number of the item instances in the search}}{\text{number of tokens in the corpus}}$$

In what follows, we present the results of our corpus study. We successively discuss the lexico-grammatical distribution of the predicates which belong to the four conceptual classes: perceptual, mental, emotive, and speech.

4.1 Perceptual predicates

The data (IPM rates) for perceptuals exemplified in (21) and (22) selecting *kakoj*-remarkable clauses as their complements are in Figure 1 in Appendix.

(21) Russian

Smotrite,   kakie
look.IMP.2PL what.NOM.PL

u   menja   v etom   godu   tykvy   vymaxali!
PREP 1SG.GEN in this.DAT.SG year.DAT.SG pumpkin.NOM.PL grow.PST.PL

'Look what pumpkins grew in my garden!' (RNC)

(22) Russian

Vidiš,   kakuju   xorošuju   kvartiru   nam
see.PRS.2SG what.ACC.SG good.ACC.SG appartment.ACC.SG 1PL.DAT

Serjožen'ka   našol!
Serjožen'ka.NOM find.PST.SG

'Do you see what a good apartment Serjožen'ka has found us!' (RNC)

As can be seen from Figure 1, the most frequent grammatical forms of perceptual predicates are as follows: imperatives (*smotri* (IPF) / *posmotri* (PF) 'look!', *slušaj* (IPF) / *poslušaj* (PF) 'listen!'), optatives in the form of subjunctive mood (*esli by ty videl / videl by ty* 'if you had seen!'), 2nd person interrogative (*vidiš?* 'can you see?').[10]

The most frequent lexical items are verbs of vision and hearing, namely *smotret'* (IPF) / *posmotret'* (PF) 'look', *videt'* 'see' (but not its perfective counterpart). They are stylistically neutral and very frequent in everyday discourse.

---

[10] Here we give examples in singular forms. However, plural forms are also felicitous.

4.2 Mental predicates

Figure 2 in Appendix graphically displays IPM rates for mentals and *kakoj* remarkable clauses exemplified in (23)–(26).

(23) Russian

Vy   ne predstavljaete   sebe, kakoe   zrelišče
2PL.NOM NEG imagine.PRS.2PL self what.NOM.SG spectacle.NOM.SG
predstalo   pered nami!
appear.PST.SG in.front 1PL.INSTR

'You can't imagine what appeared in front of us!' (RNC)

(24) Russian

Predstavljaju,   kakie   budut   probki!
imagine.PRS.1SG what.NOM.PL be.FUT.PL traffic.jams.NOM.PL

'Imagine what the traffic will be like!' (Newspaper "Arguments and Facts", 2001)

(25) Russian

Znaeš,   kakaja   očered'   byla!
know.PRS.2SG what.NOM.SG queue.NOM.SG be.PST.SG

'Can you imagine what a queue there was!' (RNC)

(26) Russian

Esli by   vy   znali,   kakie my   s   nim
if   SUBJ 2PL.NOM know.PST.PL what 1PL.NOM with 3SG.INSTR
druz'ja!
friend.NOM.PL

'If only you knew what close friends we are!' (RNC)

As Figure 2 clearly shows, the most frequent grammatical forms are optatives (*esli by ty znal / znal by ty* 'if you knew!'), 1st person positive and negative declaratives (*predstavljaju* 'I can imagine', *ne predstavljaju* 'I can't imagine'), 2nd person negative declaratives (*ne predstavljaeš* 'you can't imagine'), 2nd person interrogatives (*znaeš?* 'do you know?', *ponimaeš?* 'do you realize?').[11]

---

[11] Here we give examples in singular forms. However, plural forms are also felicitous.

The most frequent lexical items are *predstavljat'* (IPF) / *predstavit'* (PF) 'imagine', *znat'* (IPF) 'know' (but not its perfective counterpart *uznat'* 'find out') and *podumat'* (PF) 'think' (but not its imperfective counterpart *dumat'* 'think').

Comparing perceptual and mental predicates, we can conclude that they behave differently: perceptuals primarily occur in imperatives, whilst mentals principally take the forms of optatives, 2nd person interrogatives and 2nd person or 1st person declaratives. Notably, the perceptual verb *videt'* 'see' semantically behaves like a mental predicate since it mostly occurs in optatives and 2nd person interrogatives. A possible explanation can be that this verb, denoting perception, implies information processing in the receiver's mind.

4.3 Emotive predicates

The next class is emotives illustrated in (27) and (28). The data (IPM rates) for them with *kakoj* remarkable clauses are given in Figures 3 and 4.

(27) Russian

Udivljajus',   s   kakoj   ostrotoj   i   kak polno
surprise.PRS.1SG with what.INSTR.SG sharpness.INSTR.SG and how fully
pronjos   čerez   žizn'   vsjo   bogatstvo   svoix
carry.PST.SG through life.ACC.SG all.ACC.SG richness.ACC.SG 3.GEN.PL
detskix   vpečatlenij!
child.GEN.PL experience.GEN.PL

'I am surprised of the sharpness and integrity that he carried his childhood experience through his whole life with.' (RNC)

(28) Russian

Udivitel'no, kakoe   u   nego   tončajšee
surprising   what.NOM.SG PREP 3SG.GEN subtle.NOM.SG
vosprijatie   intonacii,   vyraženija   lica,
perception.NOM.SG intonation.GEN.SG expression.GEN.SG face.GEN.SG
žestov!
gesture.GEN.PL

'It's surprising how fine his perception of intonation, mimic and gestures is.' (RNC)

Initially, we calculated IPM rates for emotives in exclamation mark contexts. The fact that they were relatively few was unexpected for the theory of exclamatives since it predicts that embedding under emotives is a characteristic of exclamatives (cf. Michaelis (2001), among others). Therefore, we calculated IPM rates for emotives in dot contexts. Interestingly, their frequencies did not considerably change and generally they are still lower than those of perceptuals and mentals. Moreover, both sorts of contexts (and Figures 3 and 4 demonstrate that) reveal the same pattern: the most frequent emotive embedding remarkable clauses is *udivitel'no* 'it's surprising'.[12]

4.4 Speech predicates

Finally, let us look at speech predicates embedding *kakoj* remarkable clauses illustrated in (29). It is important to note that remarkable clauses do not encode direct speech. Figure 5 presents IPM rates for each speech predicate.

(29) Russian

Nado   li govorit', v kakom   nastroenii   ja   pela
necessary Q say.INF in what.DAT.SG mood.DAT.SG 1SG.NOM sing.PST.SG
spektakl'   dal'še...?!
performance.ACC.SG further

'Do I need to say in what kind of mood I was singing in the rest of the performance...?!' (RNC)

Figure 5 shows that speech predicates occur in contexts of remarkable clauses, however, they are the least frequent items among all of the studied predicate classes.

4.5 Towards grammaticalization of predicates

As stated, the most frequent grammatical forms of predicates are as follows: imperatives *smotri* (IPF) / *posmotri* (PF) 'look!', *slušaj* (IPF) / *poslušaj* (PF) 'listen!', 2nd person declaratives *podumaeš* 'you think', 2nd person interrogatives *vidiš?* 'do you see?', *znaeš?* 'do you know?', *ponimaeš?* 'do you understand?', 1st person

---

[12] Morphologically, this predicate is an adjective (short form, neutral gender), like some other items from Figures 3 and 3 that have "it's" component in their English translations (e.g., *neverojatno* 'it's unbelievable', *porazitel'no* 'it's astonishing'). Therefore, for such predicates, the forms 1st and 2nd person are non-applicable.

positive and negative declaratives (*predstavljaju* 'I can imagine', *ne predstavljaju* 'I can't imagine'), 2nd person negative declaratives (*ne predstavljaeš* 'you can't imagine'), optatives *esli by ty znal/ znal by ty* 'if only you knew!', *esli by ty videl / videl by ty* 'if you had seen!', *udivitel'no* 'it's surprising'.

We assume that most of them (probably except for optatives) are on the way to be grammaticalized for 5 reasons. First, their grammatical variation seems to be limited to the listed forms (both singular and plural), except for *podumaeš*, which is grammaticalized to a higher degree than the rest (it allows only a singular form), and *udivitel'no*, which morphologically does not have a plural form. Second, their semantics is not transparent; e.g., the questions expressed by interrogatives can be answered neither positively nor negatively. Third, they are used without personal pronouns. Fourth, their position just before a remarkable clause seems to be the most natural (positions inside or after a clause are less felicitous).[13]

Cross-linguistically, a similar phenomenon is witnessed in Archi and Agul (< East-Caucasian). According to Kalinina (2011), in these languages, verbal predicates 'look' and 'see' function as discourse markers,[14] cf. Archi example (30) for 'look'. Notably, in contexts of remarkable clauses, 'look' always has the imperative form and 'see' always has the past (aorist) form.

(30) Archi

Wajo,   os   sa<r>k:e,   godo-w lo   χab-kul   uw-na
INTERJ once F.look.IMP this-M child fast-NML M-do-PF-CONV.IRR
heʕršur-t:u!
run.IPF-ATTR.M

'Oh, just look, the boy is running so fast!' (Kalinina 2011, p. 162)

5 Russian data through the prism of the Gricean maxims of conversation

This section describes the conceptual semantics and lexico-grammatical frequencies of Russian matrix predicates in terms of the Gricean maxims of conversation.

---

[13] On the contrary, optatives still seem to be semantically transparent; personal pronouns are obligatory in their case; they are used not only in the forms of the 2nd person (singular and plural) but also in the forms of the 3rd person, although the 2nd person forms are much more frequent than the 3rd person.

[14] Although (Kalinina 2011) describes this phenomenon differently, we still think it is quite similar to ours.

For both main clause exclamatives and their subordinate counterparts, we introduce a speaker-dependent pair of mappings (g_{expected}, g_{real}), each of which assigns a degree on a scale shared by these mappings. g_{expected} stands for the speaker's expectation of the degree of the gradable feature of object x, whereas g_{real} denotes the speaker's evaluation of the degree. The exclamative utterance meaning can be modelled by the relation $g_{\text{real}}(x) \gg g_{\text{expected}}(x)$.[15]

To illustrate, consider the sentence *What a tall man I saw yesterday!*. The real value of tallness of x (x is a member of some ontological category and this category implies particular norms of the expressed gradable feature – in the example, this is the particular man the speaker saw yesterday) is greater than the expected norm for this category.

By gradable feature we mean not merely a predicate that has to be gradable but also any implicit gradable aspect of a situation. For example, if a language allows for predicate-elliptical constructions like *What a man I saw yesterday!*, relying on the context of utterance, the hearer has to decode the particular feature of a person under consideration: cleverness, braveness, tallness, etc.

From the point of view of pragmatics, we employ the expressive illocutionary force operator introduced in (Rett 2008), (Rett 2011) which was originally defined in terms of gradable predicates and can be reformulated in our terms as follows:

(31) E-Force(p), for proposition p uttered by a speaker, is appropriate in a given context C if inequality $g_{\text{real}}(x) \gg g_{\text{expected}}(x)$ holds for the speaker's expected degree of a given gradable feature of x in C and the speaker's evaluation of the real degree of x's feature.

Furthermore, for remarkable clauses, the presence of the E-Force operator is a necessary condition. It means that speaker's surprise always holds, even when the grammatical subject of a given sentence with an embedded remarkable clause is 2nd or 3rd person. In other words, we might say that the speaker somehow assigns her belief to the hearer or to the person being talked about. To illustrate, whilst

---

[15] g_{expected} is not always what can be called a speaker's direct expectation, but rather a representation of common knowledge shared between the speaker and the hearer. E.g., in *Look how high John can jump!* we would say that g_{expected} can reflect speaker's direct expectation if the speaker is unaware of John's ability, but we cannot consider so if the speaker is John's close friend who has seen this kind of jumping many times before and only made his utterance to attract hearer's attention to the difference between John's ability and that of an ordinary man. In the latter case, expected in g's subscript actually refers to speaker's expectation of the hearer's state of knowledge.

uttering sentences *You won't believe what a tall man I saw yesterday!* or *She won't believe what a tall man I saw yesterday!*, the speaker is surprised at some degree and shares, or perhaps better to say, aligns her knowledge with the hearer's or with the 3rd person's.

Moreover, we might think of the Gricean maxims as regulators of the tendency of the predicate class use. In what follows, we only discuss the use of those grammatical forms which reflect (in)direct speaker-hearer interaction, namely the use of imperatives, optatives, 2nd person interrogatives and 2nd person negative declaratives. Hence, we do not account for the speaker's own beliefs expressed by virtue of 1st person declaratives and for speaker-hearer established mutual knowledge conveyed with help of positive 2nd person declaratives.

We argue that the frequency distribution of forms of mental and perceptual predicates depends on the possibility of witnessing in a given context. By the possibility of witnessing we mean that at the moment of the utterance the hearer can witness the degree of object's feature. E.g., in *Look how tall my house is!*, there is the presupposition of the hearer's possibility of seeing the house, whereas in *If you only knew how tall my house is!*, it is presupposed that the hearer cannot witness the height of the house at the moment of utterance.

The following analysis is based upon the assumption that the speaker's primary goal of using a remarkable clause is to change the hearer's mental state and upon the scheme "actions $\xrightarrow{cause}$ mental states" (that is, the speaker's belief that some hearer's actions imply a change in the hearer's mental state). Moreover, we assume that the probability that the hearer will change her mental state is higher if she witnesses the object herself.

As the Brevity submaxim (of the Manner maxim) states not to be verbose, it is sufficient for the speaker only to prompt the hearer's action (in a witnessing-possibility situation), and the most common way is to use imperative. To give an example, if the speaker exclaims *Look how funny she is!* or *Listen how beautifully she is singing!*, she induces the hearer to perceptually evaluate the given situation and, consequently, encourages the hearer to share her attitude towards that. This accounts for why there is a high frequency in the corpus for using imperatives in case of perceptual predicates. The exception is *videt'* 'see' that is used in the form of optatives and interrogatives rather than in the form of imperatives. This is partially explained by the fact that in the studied sentences, *videt'* functions as a mental rather than perceptual predicate ('see' ≈ 'understand').

In witnessing-impossibility situations, the speaker cannot provide a witness for her belief but, nonetheless, wishes the hearer to align her mental state with that of the speaker's, which correlates with using optatives. As a direct perceptual action in such a context is impossible, the use of perceptual predicates is ruled out. In this case, the scheme "actions $\xrightarrow{cause}$ mental states" lacks the first element and the most natural way of conveying mental states is using mental predicates. Consequently, we are left with mental predicates in optative forms. Mental predicates also exist in two other forms, which are 2nd person interrogatives and 2nd person negative declaratives; however, their total frequency rate is much lower than that of optatives.[16]

Emotive predicates[17] violate the Brevity submaxim (of the Manner maxim) since the speaker-hearer alignment of information involves duplicate communication of expressive content in the case of emotive predicates (i.e., main clause predicates). Hence, the use of emotive predicates seems to be redundant.

Finally, we hypothesize that main clause exclamatives do not necessarily imply the hearer (i.e., they can be uttered in case of the hearer's absence). However, subordinate remarkable clauses always involve the hearer, with whom the speaker wants to share her emotion. This can serve as a plausible explanation for why the 2nd person sentences in the forms of imperatives, optatives, declaratives, interrogatives are much more frequently employed than the 3rd person sentences (1st person sentences do occur but not as frequently as the 2nd person ones).

6 Conclusion

In this paper, firstly, we show that the existing formal semantic accounts can only partially explain the distribution of matrix predicates embedding remarkable clauses. Relying on cross-linguistic data, we tentatively suggest distinguishing among four conceptual classes of matrix predicates — perceptual, mental, emotive, and speech.

Secondly, on the basis of corpus data from the RNC, we study lexico-grammatical distribution of Russian matrix predicates selecting remarkable clauses. The most

---

[16] However, there is an exception to this general trend. It concerns the imperative *predstav'* 'imagine' that directly stimulates the hearer to obtain a particular mental state. This can be explained by the fact that almost anything can be imagined directly without any help from the senses. So imagining something can be thought of as a direct mental action.

[17] We do not account for speech predicates in this paper since their semantics is mostly idiosyncratic.

frequent grammatical forms (except for the optatives of *znat'* 'know' and *videt'* 'see') have started losing the status of matrix predicates and are on the way to be grammaticalized, with *podumaeš* being at the final stage of this process. Generally, the phenomenon of 'embedded' exclamatives is irregular (compared to, e.g., embedded interrogatives): matrix predicates that select exclamatives demonstrate lexical and grammatical idiosyncrasy and low corpus frequencies.

Thirdly, we argue that the conceptual semantics and lexico-grammatical peculiarities of matrix predicates can be accounted for in terms of the Gricean maxims of conversation.

Abbreviations

2 — 2nd person, 3 — 3rd person, A — Agent, ACC — Accusative case, ATTR — Attributive, AUX — auxiliary verb, COM — comitative affix, COMP — complementizer, COMPL — marker of subordinate clause, CONV — Converb, COP — copula, DAT — Dative case, DF — Definite, FUT — Futurum, GEN — Genitive case, IMP — Imperative mood, INF — Infinitive, INSTR — Instrumentalis, INTERJ — Interjection, IPF — Imperfective, IRR — Irrealis, M — Masculine gender, NEG — Negation, NML — Nominalizer, NOM — Nominative case, PASS.PTCP — Passive Participle, PF — Perfective, PL — Plural, POT — Potential mood, PREP — Preposition, PROG — Progressive aspect, PROSP — Prospective tense, PRS — Praesens, PRSM — Presumptive, PST — Past, REFL — reflexive marker, SG — Singular, SUBJ — Subjunctive, TOP — Topicalizer, TR — Transitive marker.

References

Abels, K. 2004a. Deriving selectional properties of "exclamative" predicates. In I. Comorovsky & M. Krifka (eds.). *Proceedings of the Workshop on the Syntax, Semantics, and Pragmatics of Questions (16th European Summer School in Logic, Language, and Information).* 63–69.

Abels, K. 2004b. Why surprise-predicates do not embed polar interrogatives. *Linguistische Arbeitsberichte* 81. 203–221.

Abels, K. 2005. Remarks on Grimshaw's clausal typology. In E. Maier, C. Bary & J. Huitink (eds.). *Proceedings of Sinn und Bedeutung 9.* 1–15.

Castroviejo, E. 2006. *Wh-exclamatives in catalan*: Universitat de Barcelona dissertation.
De Urbana, J. & J. Hualde. 2003. *A grammar of Basque*. Berlin/New York: Mouton de Gruyter.
Elliott, D. 1974. Toward a grammar of exclamations. *Foundations of Language* 11. 231–246.
Grimshaw, J. 1979. Complement selection and the lexicon. *Linguistic Inquiry* 10. 279–326.
Huddleston, R. 1993. Remarks on the construction you won't believe who Ed has married. *Lingua* 91. 175–184.
Kalinina, E. 2011. Exclamative clauses in the languages of the North Caucasus and the problem of finiteness. In G. Authier & T. Maisak (eds.). *Tense, aspect, modality and finiteness in East-Caucasian languages*. 161–201.
Kiparsky, P. & C. Kiparsky. 1970. Fact. In *Progress in Linguistics*. 143–173.
Lipták, A. 2006. Word order in Hungarian exclamatives. *Acta Linguistica Hungarica* 53. 343–39.
Michaelis, L. 2001. Exclamative constructions. In M. Haspelmath, E. Koenig, W. Oesterreicher & W. Raible (eds.). *Language typology and language universals. An international handbook (vol. 2)*. Berlin/New York: Walter de Gruyter.
Ono, H. 2006. *An investigation of exclamatives in English and Japanese: syntax and sentence processing*. University of Maryland dissertation.
Potsdam, E. 2011. Expressing exclamatives in Malagasy. In F. Yap, K. Grunow-Hersta & J. Wrona (eds.). *Nominalizations in Asian languages: diachronic and typological perspectives*. 659–683. Amsterdam/Philadelphia: John Benjamins.
Rett, J. 2008. A degree account of exclamatives. In *Proceedings of SALT XVIII*. 601–618. CLC publications.
Rett, J. 2011. Exclamatives, degrees and speech acts. *Linguistics and Philosophy* 34. 411–442.
Visan, F. 2000. *The nature and the status of exclamatives in Chinese*. University of Bucharest.
Zanuttini, R. & P. Portner. 2003. Exclamative clauses: at the syntax-semantics interface. *Language* 79(1). 39–81.

Appendix

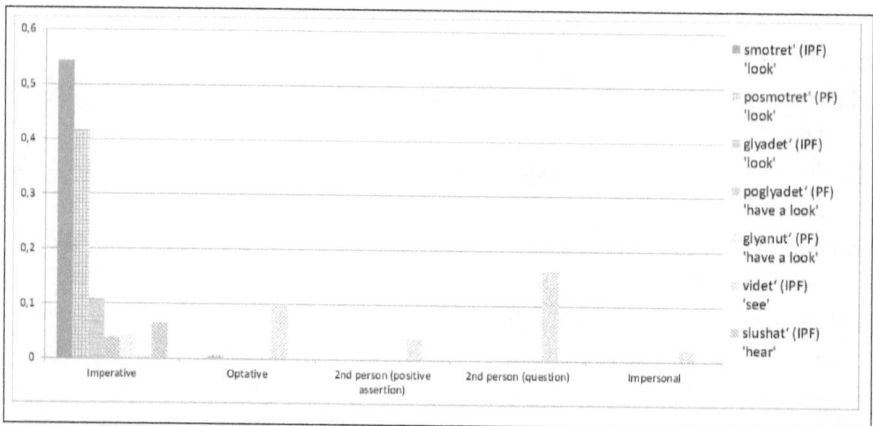

Figure 1: *kakoj* remarkable clauses with perceptual predicates (sentences ending with exclamation mark)

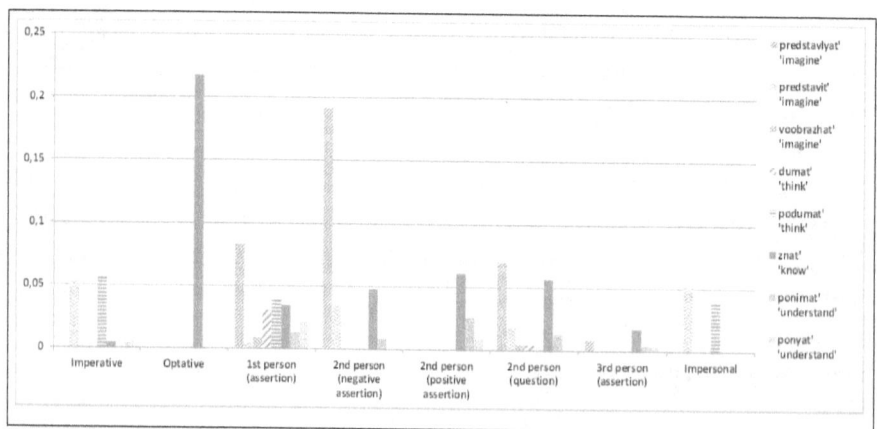

Figure 2: *kakoj* remarkable clauses with mental predicates (sentences ending with exclamation mark)

Russian predicates selecting remarkable clauses

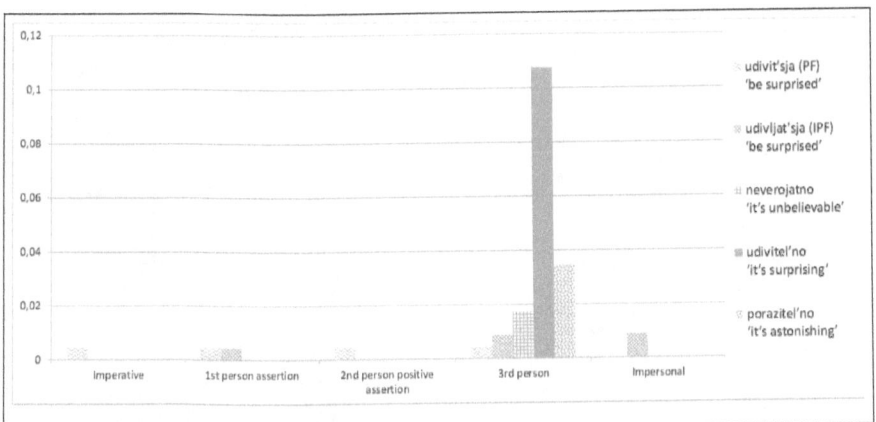

Figure 3: *kakoj* remarkable clauses with emotive predicates (sentences ending with exclamation mark)

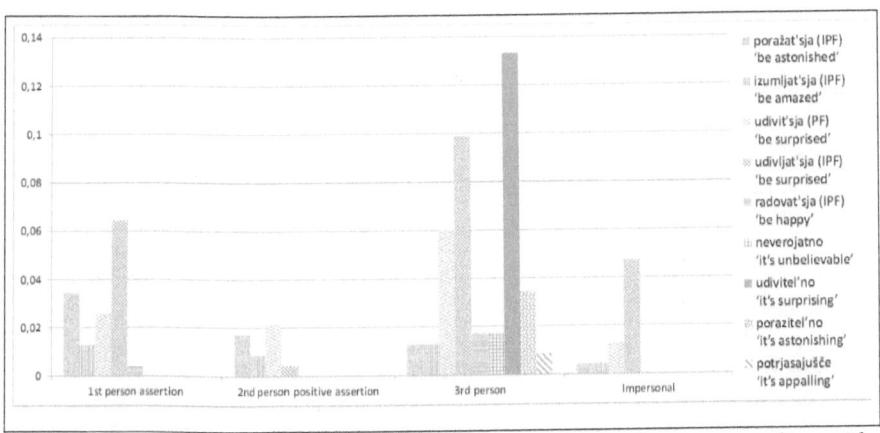

Figure 4: *kakoj* remarkable clauses with emotive predicates (sentences ending with dot)

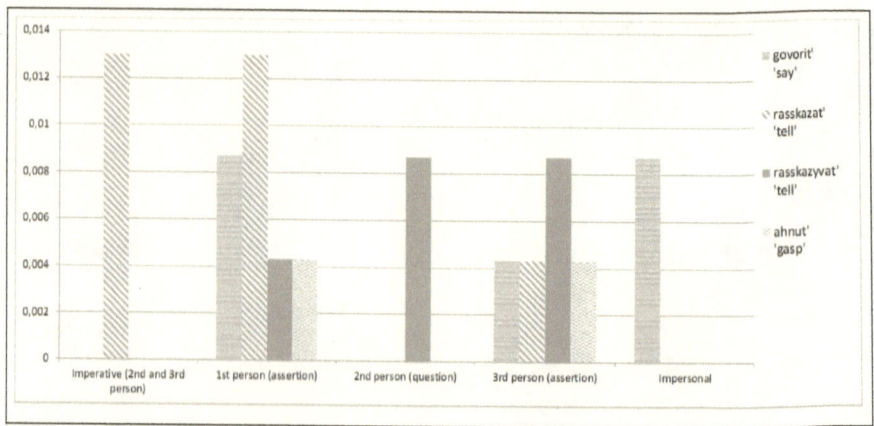

Figure 5: *kakoj* remarkable clauses with speech predicates (sentences ending with exclamation mark)

Authors

Natalia Zevakhina
National Research University Higher School of Economics
Moscow
nzevakhina@hse.ru

Alex Dainiak
Moscow Institute of Physics and Technology
dainiak@phystech.edu